EDDY MERCKX
THE CANNIBAL

DANIEL FRIEBE

EBURY
PRESS

This edition published 2012
First published in 2012 by Ebury Press, an imprint of Ebury Publishing
A Random House Group company

The Random House Group Limited Reg. No. 954009

Addresses for companies within the Random House Group can be found at
www.randomhouse.co.uk

A CIP catalogue record for this book is available from the British Library

ISBN 9780091943165

To buy books by your favourite authors and register for offers visit
www.randomhouse.co.uk
Penguin Random House is committed to a sustainable future for
our business, our readers and our planet. This book is made from
Forest Stewardship Council® certified paper.

MIX
Paper from
responsible sources
FSC® C018179

Printed and bound in Great Britain by Clays Ltd, Elcograf S.p.A.

To Mum, Dad, and everyone who got eaten

contents

prologue

Through the gloom a blink of white, suspended between the twin strobes of a car's headlights. Seconds pass, the murk recedes. The scene sharpens. The picture acquires light, but also urgency, movement, violence. Two eyes blaze, two shoulders sway, two lips purse. Two thighs thump, pound and pummel.

A hundred metres closer to us – no 90, no 80, no 70 – another figure advances on his bicycle. Here, somewhere in the dwindling airspace between them – 50 metres, now 40 – the similarities end. They are as different as tiger and a tabby cat, a flail and a combine harvester. Not in stature but menace. Both gazes are fixed on the road, but the quarry's legs and heart now beat as though to the rhythm of death's chime.

Twenty, fifteen, ten metres…

A raindrop topples off the hunter's nose. He doesn't twitch. He kicks and breathes harder. The prey wipes sweat from his forehead, then lowers and tilts his head to face the triangle of daylight between bicep and ribcage.

He watches, waits and listens.

One second, two. Two metres, one…

Eddy Merckx's old teammate, Vittorio Adorni, used to say there was a key difference between Merckx and Jacques Anquetil, the cyclist he usurped as the world's greatest. Anquetil appeared without warning, as silent and deadly as a dagger in the back. His pedal stroke was 'soft', 'velvety'. He arrived with a murmur. He was gone with a whoosh.

Here was the difference between 'Master Jacques' and Merckx, said Adorni. You *heard* Merckx. Felt him. Not necessarily sounds but signs, a sense. The feeling of something brewing, stirring at your back. A creeping intuition. Not the normal whirring of pedals and wheels but a thudding through the atmosphere. 'A different way of pedalling from the rest of us,' as Dino Zandegù, the 1967 Tour of Flanders champion, put it. A trouble. The rustling wrath of the 'one-man forest fire' that Italian rider Giancarlo Ferretti said came upon professional cycling in the late 1960s – and destroyed everything in its wake for nearly a decade.

You still know when Eddy Merckx is close by today but for different reasons. On a chilly April morning in Merckx's 66th year, his movements can be traced by the bulges and constrictions of a vast crowd in Bruges's Grote Markt, like an egg passing through a snake's abdomen. This is the most important day in the most important sport in Belgium. Yet it seems the tens of thousands here for the start of the Tour of Flanders only have eyes for Merckx. A good 15, maybe 20 kilos plumper than in his racing days, but slimmer than a decade ago, he has the air, the attire and the practised smile of a dignitary. An urban legend goes that, in the late '60s and '70s, his one-time hunting partner the King of Belgium would occasionally put on street clothes and head out for a drive in his Mercedes. No one would recognise him. The yarn continues, though, that Merckx 'was better known than the king'. He would 'cause a riot' if he ever tried the same trick.

A Flemish journalist observes the scene, his arms folded in admiration. Arms that 15 years ago, when he prepared to interview his boyhood idol for the first time, were prickly with upright hairs. 'He grabbed my wrist and said, "Talk!",' the hack recalls. When it comes to writing about or talking to Eddy Merckx, one of his colleagues tuts, Belgian journalists sometimes stop being journalists.

Everyone who is anyone who rode a bike in the '60s and '70s remembers the moment they first met Merckx. But they also remember their first 'Merckx moment'. Usually it involves that noise, a jangle in the bones, and a glance over the shoulder. A silhouette appears, the wind seems to flinch, the features reveal themselves then recognition kicks in. And with it panic.

At the 1967 Tour of Flanders, Barry Hoban heard the engines before he heard Merckx. 'I thought, what's going on? Then I looked back at these cars arriving through the rain – it was a rotten day – and in front of them saw *him*, Merckx. Then I thought, "Uh oh."'

A couple of months later, the Italian Italo Zilioli had a similar experience. Alone off the front, within a few hundred metres of the summit of the Blockhaus climb and the finish line of Stage 12 of the Giro d'Italia, Zilioli sensed an imminent commotion. His instinct told him to turn. 'You couldn't say he really loomed, because it was two separate images,' Zilioli recalls. 'He was maybe a hundred metres behind me and then he was in front. Immediately. A few seconds must have elapsed in between, but not in my mind... My feeling at that moment was, well, it was like being struck by lightning.'

Merckx's peers all have stories like this. In the 1990s, the advent of the new wonder-drug EPO caused what those not in the first wave of abusers described as a sudden and vicious jolt. 'The speed suddenly went up by five kilometres an hour,' they complained. Worse still, they didn't know why. But as word of the drug's potency spread, the mystery disappeared; EPO-enhanced blood could deliver 10 or 20 per cent more oxygen to the muscles in some cases. It stood to reason that performances should also soar.

The former French rider Raymond Riotte recalls a similar phenomenon in the sixties. But that wasn't drugs, or at least not new ones that weren't available to and taken by the bulk of the peloton. 'It was Merckx,' Riotte says. 'I rode the Tour that Roger Pingeon won in 1967, and Jan Janssen's in 1968, and I swear that everything felt ten kilometres quicker when Merckx arrived in 1969. The difference was, it was…*c'était terrible.*'

Riotte's voice still tremors with aftershocks 42 years later. What, indeed, was going on? Who was this prodigy, this phenomenon? This, this brute. Football had Pelé, golf had discovered Nicklaus, but weren't they just an upgrade on everything their sport had seen before, mere offspring of evolution? Higher, faster, stronger, said the Olympic ideal, its three pillars the very synthesis of sporting advancement – but nowhere did it mention *difference*. For when, as early as 1968, newspapers started saying that Merckx was 'in another league' and 'racing against himself', they weren't only saying that he was much better than the rest. 'No, at times it was *actually* like a different sport,' observes former opponent Johny Schleck. Different from the past, from the sport Anquetil had dominated before Merckx, and the Italian Fausto Coppi before him. Different from the one practised now by his contemporaries.

Bicycle racing is a strange game. Such are its vagaries that even the strongest cyclist will lose far more often than he wins. One rider, the Italian Marzio Bruseghin, once declared that his chosen profession boiled down to 'two hundred idiots trying to cross a white line', and you could sort of see what he meant. Some riders will go through an entire career without winning a race yet still be admired. Ace climbers flounder in sprints, the best sprinters hate having to climb. Even the most successful and prolific rider will start perhaps 60 per cent of his races in any given season knowing full well that he has zero chance and zero ambition of breaking the tape. If you don't think you can win, don't bother taking part, goes one of sport's oldest clichés. Well, if a professional peloton heeded this advice, that number of idiots would be down to double, and in some cases single, figures.

Merckx's brilliance and difference revealed themselves in this context over several months in the mid and late 1960s. Silly as it sounds, history and logic indicated that the biggest idiot in that period was the one who arrived at every race thinking that he could win. Except that Merckx was no fool, and win often he did. Over 500 times by the end of his career in 1978. Still, though, the concept that one could and should race to win on every outing – and that anyone was capable of attempting it – seemed utterly alien. Where was the catch? Why didn't everyone ride like this? Perhaps those vagaries were just excuses. Ah, but you see, sceptics consoled themselves, Merckx would soon burn out. The newspapers said it, commentators echoed them, his rivals too, and even Merckx made mutterings to the same effect. But on he rolled, confounding everyone and every precedent. 'Often we thought he was crazy – but in the end he was the one who ended up making us look like fools,' admits Giancarlo Ferretti.

Merckx's French biographer Philippe Brunel is right when he says that it wasn't just how he approached his sport, but also his life. 'He had a different way of attacking life from the rest of us,' Brunel says. Again, that word: 'different'. In a sport that glorifies suffering, sacrifice and endurance, Merckx turned them from a kind of martyrdom into forms of private elation and personal compulsion. The hunger for victories that prompted a teammate's daughter to christen him

'The Cannibal' – and the world to adopt that moniker – was really a craving for what he found only at the outer limits of his physical and mental capabilities. 'The whole point of a race is to find a winner. How can you take part without trying to win? How can you be criticised for doing what is the object of your chosen work?' he pleaded almost *ad nauseam*.

A simple sport for a complicated mind – that was cycling as seen by Merckx. 'I'm only truly happy when I'm on my bike,' he admitted in 1970. Thus, one man's search for simplicity found its outlet in perfectionism. Or perhaps absolutism was a better word. For when Merckx said 'when I'm on my bike', what he really meant was 'winning on his bike'. And that meant battling not only his adversaries but also himself. Especially himself. To the point where he suffered nightmares, nerves that tied knots in his stomach, and endless, labyrinthine self-doubt.

All of which gave us two Merckxes: the pedalling despot, blunt and guileless, and the Sphinx who stepped off his bike and on to race podiums. Joy would flicker briefly across otherwise inscrutable features, relief would exhale from his lungs, but the overriding impression was one of impatience or at least restlessness. The opposition may have been far behind – sometimes, literally, still racing on the road – but Merckx's ears already thumped to a familiar beat. This was the noise drumming at *his* back. Where was his bike? – the same question he asked wife Claudine within moments of returning home after the crash that nearly killed him in Blois in 1969. Where was his next race? When, if ever, would his appetite be sated?

For all that has been written about Merckx, so much of his persona remains unexplained. Flemish journalist Walter Pauli said that continual losses and humiliation harboured one consolation for his rivals and a curse for their perpetrator: 'In one sense, they saw more of life than him. They became more real. They realised that losing was a fact of life, not just sport. For Merckx, on the other hand, losing always meant that something had gone wrong.' In other words, as a group of boys became men, Merckx remained cocooned in a child's illusion of omnipotence, imprisoned by the very regime he had imposed. 'In order to be human, Eddy Merckx would have had to be superhuman,' is Pauli's wry conclusion.

So who really knew Merckx? His teammates? Not according to Roger Swerts, one of the best and longest-serving, who said he was still none the wiser after 25 years in the Merckx orbit, during and after their careers. Misty-eyed former comrades describe the Faema and Molteni teams which grew around him as 'a band of friends'. The more clear-sighted among them, though, also speak of a latent, inescapable, asphyxiating tension. At the dinner table, the captain's mood dictated that of his lieutenants. There was nothing unusual about that, but it became troublesome when not even they could tell exactly what he was thinking. It was maybe no coincidence that, for many years, Merckx's best friend in cycling was the painfully sensitive Italo Zilioli – a man in the grip of his own torments. More straightforward characters like Martin Van Den Bossche grew weary of the aura that came to resemble a fortress. 'If he ordered a Trappist beer, everyone ordered a Trappist beer. As an individual, you might as well have been dead when you were next to Merckx,' Van Den Bossche told Rik Vanwalleghem in the 1993 book, *Eddy Merckx – De Mens achter de Kannibaal*.

It seems clear, then, that a lot remains to be deciphered. As well as Merckx himself, there is the peer group he eclipsed, practically effaced, but which formed as bright a constellation as cycling has ever seen. The swashbuckling Ocaña, the mercurial Fuente. The pride of Van Looy and the De Vlaeminck brothers. Gimondi's tenacity,

Maertens's audacity. These were rich, textured, vulnerable personalities. As rich and textured, no doubt, as Merckx, but with the freedom of expression which only fallibility affords.

It was an age, too, when humanity itself was in flux. While Merckx was making his first grand tour appearance in the 1967 Giro d'Italia, 100,000 hippies were preparing to converge on San Francisco for their 'Summer of Love'. The following year, he rampaged through the Giro as students and workers tore through cities across the world and American troops through Vietnam. In July 1969, Neil Armstrong walked on the moon within hours of Merckx going where no one had been before in the Tour de France – to a 17-minute winning margin in his very first Grande Boucle. A month later, across one long weekend, Merckx won criteriums at Londerzeel, Saussignac and Moorslede on the days that half a million people watched Janis Joplin, Jimi Hendrix and Crosby, Stills, Nash and Young make musical magic at Woodstock.

Nine months of interviews and meetings with these individuals form the basis of this portrait of Eddy Merckx. In amongst it all there are characters to decrypt, relationships to unpick, with friends, family members, teammates, enemies and observers. Merckx himself declined my request for an interview, as did his wife Claudine. In an email they informed me that they are contractually tied to their own, official project. But instead of proving a handicap, this turned into a blessing. In researching this book, painstakingly poring over dozens of volumes written about and with him, and hundreds if not thousands of interviews, I was struck by something curious: whatever he says and attempts to explain, the *essence* of Merckx, what they called 'Merckxisme', somehow remains elusive. A mutual friend, the *Het Nieuwsblad* journalist Hugo Coorevits put it like this: 'He was born as Eddy Merckx, he lives his life as Eddy Merckx, but he still some-how doesn't know what it's like to be Eddy Merckx in the eyes of other people.' Precisely: at the risk of stating the obvious, Merckx can't quite understand the fuss because his life is the only one he has ever known.

The public has a tendency to want to demystify, normalise, pare down the great and the good until we understand them on our own terms, as ordinary folk with the same humdrum habits and tastes as the rest of us, but also a single remarkable talent. This, patently, is how Eddy Merckx perceives himself. And because of that, his past musings may help us to understand certain actions and reactions, but they will never assist us in understanding a bigger, important part of Merckx – the essence and aura that will outlive him and his records.

Yes, time has passed and will eventually run out even for Eddy Merckx, and herein lay my final motivation: I never saw Merckx race and neither, in not too long, will anyone have witnessed him in action. Merckx's generation is getting older, dare we even say, old. In the hours I spent talking to them, they mentioned ailments and operations quite different from the ones that might once have kept them out of a Tour de France or cost them seconds in a time trial. The truths they never told, the memories they never shared, are near-ing expiry. As this happens, a new and less gilded recollection of their era begins to take hold, and open creaks a window of both opportu-nity and responsibility: those who grew up watching Greg LeMond and Bernard Hinault, Lance Armstrong and Jan Ullrich, as I did, must now decide how Merckx will be consigned to that dim, distant, two-dimensional place in history where some vibrancy is lost but a different kind of lustre can be gained.

1
folgorazione

'You see that kid over there. That's Eddy Merckx.
He's going to be a champion.' EMILE DAEMS

An electrocution. '*Una folgorazione*' – literally, in Italian, what happens when two pairs of eyes meet, the air sizzles with electricity, the spine tingles and the heart gulps.

It had happened in the spring of 1967. Not to Claudine Acou, a 21-year-old language student from Brussels who married Eddy Merckx on 5 December 1967. No, their romance had begun four off-seasons earlier in the room above her father Lucien's café, near the abattoirs in Cureghem. Eddy would come to the café, greet Lucien, the Belgian national amateur team selector, then they would both head upstairs to talk bikes, while Claudine pottered about, pretending not to listen. Soon Eddy's visits were becoming suspiciously frequent. Claudine was right to sense an ulterior motive. Which was fine by her; she liked his eyes, his smile. Which was fine by him; he liked her grace, her poise.

The real electrocution in 1967, though, was the one which had befallen Nino Defilippis in the third week of April, a month before the Giro d'Italia. It was a kind of blind date: Vincenzo Giacotto, the matchmaker, had called Defilippis, his former star rider from the

Carpano team, and invited him to Cervinia, the resort on the Italian side of the Matterhorn. Giacotto said that he had someone for Defilippis to meet. Truthfully, he wanted Defilippis's advice; there was a new Italian team in the offing, Giacotto had been lined up as its manager, and he now needed a headline act, preferably one to take the fight to Felice Gimondi in major stage races. Giacotto had seen Merckx win Milan–San Remo in 1966, excel in Paris–Nice the following spring, then retain his Milan–San Remo title, and now he wondered whether the kid couldn't be turned into more than just a flat-track bully. Giacotto thought he might be on to something, but he couldn't be sure, not 100 per cent. That was why he had called his old friend Nino.

Whether Merckx knew it or not, it was a kind of blind date, but also a sort of trial. The climb to Cervinia begins in Breuil and rises for 28 kilometres at an average gradient of 5.1 per cent. It is, Defilippis recalled in the book he wrote in 2004, six years before his death, 'a climb of a certain difficulty'. Giacotto and Defilippis wanted to see how Merckx would fare. Until that point, he had never raced in the high mountains.

They cleared the car seats and dashboard, sunk into their seats, and peered expectantly through the windscreen. It was then, moments after the engine started, as the road lurched towards the Matterhorn, Merckx shifted forward in his saddle and began devouring the slope, that Defilippis was 'electrocuted'.

'The power, the way he attacked the curves, the way he pedalled, I was bowled over,' Defilippis recalled. 'I can remember him getting off the bike at the end and asking me how Cervinia measured up to other Alpine climbs. Almost as if to say that he still felt fresh, and was this not a bit too easy?'

There was a third privileged witness to Merckx's marvellous ascent. Teofilo Sanson, an ice-cream maker from Turin, had sponsored a team managed by Giacotto in 1965. Surely the best excuse he'd ever have to return to professional cycling was now staring him in the face. That, at least, was Defilippis's view. 'I remember that I took Sanson and Giacotto to one side and asked them whether they didn't have a pen, a scrap of paper, something. Why? To get the kid to somehow sign a lifetime contract, money no object. He could put down whatever he wanted, because this was a real prodigy. And in fact Giacotto didn't let him get away, unlike Sanson.'

Giacotto's new backer would be Faema, the Milan-based coffee-machine maker. Formerly the title sponsor of the team where the last great Belgian, Rik Van Looy, had spent his best years, but absent from the peloton since 1963, Faema now prepared to make its grand re-entrance.

Its leader, the man Giacotto thought could win Tours and Giros if only he learned to 'think and race Italian', was a 22-year-old from Brussels who, before the spring of 1967, had barely if ever ridden up a proper mountain. Its leader would be Eddy Merckx.

Even with 45 years of hindsight, contemporaries of Eddy Merckx dispute the idea of an 'electrocution', some kind of juddering epiphany, when the full magnitude of what was about to strike professional cycling suddenly revealed itself.

In that respect Nino Defilippis was unusual. But it made sense: the Italian had retired from racing in 1964 and had kept his distance from professional cycling ever since. He had not seen Merckx in 1966 or the spring of 1967. He had probably paid scant attention to the way the defending champion had grabbed the peloton by the scruff of the neck at Milan–San Remo in March '67, like some uncouth ruffian, then dragged them at record speed along the Ligurian Riviera. To Defilippis, the uniqueness, the difference of Merckx, the way the bike became a threshing machine between his thighs, was surely striking. Giacotto had talked him up as Anquetil's potential successor; to Defilippis, who competed for years against the Frenchman, they must have seemed as equally brilliant yet as different as Mozart and the Rolling Stones.

For those who had been around since Merckx turned pro in 1965, the revelation, or the end of self-delusion, was much more gradual. The boat had been rocking for some time, the ripples near the surface were becoming ever more ominous, yet most continued to ignore the evidence. 'We knew he was a good rider, but he was one of several in Belgium and even more in the world. It was a kind of golden generation,' says Walter Godefroot, the man who up until the summer of 1967 had staked at least as strong a claim as Merckx to be Belgian's next world-beater.

Patrick Sercu endorses the view that 'we would still never have imagined at that point what he would go on to be'. Primarily a track rider, Sercu had swept on to the scene in the Belgian talent tsunami that included Merckx, Godefroot, Willy Planckaert, Roger Swerts, Joseph Spruyt and the two Hermans, Van Loo and Van Springel. In one sense, Sercu was the most precocious of the lot, having amassed Olympic, European, national and world titles on the track by the age of 23. He had won three of his national titles with Merckx in the Madison. Nonetheless, Merckx remained 'just a guy who had won a lot of races as an amateur, like a lot of others who had done the same, then totally disappeared,' Sercu says.

Years later, in an early glimpse of the anxieties that could gnaw at Merckx, he would reveal that this had been his own greatest fear on winning the world amateur road race title in Sallanches in 1964: he would turn pro and then sink without a trace. He feared the different speed, the longer distances of pro races, their reputation for violent and unexpected changes of pace, so unlike the cruising speed of most amateur competitions. Claudine, whom he had begun to woo within weeks of that 1964 Worlds win, watched apprehension threaten to overwhelm him.

The truth was that Merckx's problems in his first professional year would come mainly off the road. They began when he signed for Rik Van Looy's Solo-Superia team. This had been his manager, Jean Van Buggenhout's idea. An accomplished track rider in the 1930s, 'Van Bug' had reinvented himself as the burly, bespectacled big kahuna of Belgian cycling, some said its most powerful man. He was part agent, part promoter and, says Patrick Sercu, 'part dictator – absolutely terrifying'. He was also undeniably passionate about his sport, and had been immediately struck by the same quality in Merckx when they became acquainted in a brasserie opposite the Palais des Sports in Brussels in 1963. The previous day, Merckx had claimed victory in his first ever stage race, the amateur Tour de Limbourg. 'The way you talked to me about the race that day won me over. You sounded like a young man full of fervour,' Van Bug told Merckx years later. Needless to say, when Merckx became amateur champion in Sallanches, it was Van Buggenhout who acted as his agent, and who went on to fulfil that role for the next ten years.

On the face of it, Solo seemed the ideal place for Merckx. He was, after all, already being tipped as the new Van Looy. But therein lay the problem: as far as Van Looy was concerned, there would never be another Rik Van Looy, let alone a younger and potentially even better version in the same team. The Belgian cycling journalist and Merckx expert Walter Pauli says that this is because one word summed up, and still sums up, Van Looy: 'Pride'. It came from his modest upbringing in Herentals, in the far north-east of Belgium, a region of which Walter Godefroot remarks with a smirk 'the people are the most intelligent in Belgium…they say so themselves'. It came also, though, from Van Looy's uncompromising character, which had been sculpted like his extraordinary calf muscles as he hauled newspapers around Herentals as a teenager. Van Looy's early successes as a cyclist, including back-to-back Belgian national amateur titles, had then hardened his conviction that the very zenith of professional cycling was where he belonged. The condescending nickname 'Rik II' – and the inference that Rik Van Steenbergen remained the original and best of Belgium's post-war cycling superstars – merely reinforced that belief still further. His other moniker, the Emperor of Herentals, would soon more accurately reflect a palmarès bejewelled with every one of cycling's one-day Classics, and sit snugly alongside its owner's reptilian smile.

Van Looy's jealousy was, then, the brew resulting from many more or less organic ingredients. As is often the case with sportsmen, his pride and passion had also inspired the same fervency in his followers, which in turn fed Van Looy's own vainglory. Says journalist Walter Pauli, 'If you were Van Looy, you never left Van Looy, even when Merckx arrived. My grandmother, for example, was a die-hard Van Looy fan. He was mythical, he was strong…but he was also a very bad character.'

'Bad' or understandably frustrated, having warred for years with Van Steenbergen, finally outlasted him, then seen the nouvelle vague of Belgian riders threaten to engulf him. Moreover, early in 1965, Van Looy was still blissfully unaware that he was about to embark on his final season as the finest one-day rider in Belgium and probably the world. Supported by his now legendary 'Rode Garde', the 'Red Guard' which had first formed in his Faema days and which some still describe as cycling's first true sprint train, Van Looy was in no mood to make way for or groom possible heirs. The closest he came to endorsing a young rider was faint praise for Godefroot – who happened to be riding for another team, Wiel's-Groene Leeuw. Today, Godefroot is emphatic about why Van Looy and the Rode Garde didn't welcome Merckx. 'It's very simple,' he says. 'If I'd been a footballer, I'd have been a midfielder: I'd have been in the middle of the park, controlling the game. But Merckx is the guy putting it in the net. Van Looy too. As a super-champion, you're not a good teammate. You're a bit selfish, a bit individualistic. It's not your fault; it's the reality…'

He continues, 'Van Looy is the king, the "Emperor" as we say, and Merckx is the king in waiting. So of course there's a battle. And two clans form: the Van Looy clan and the Merckx clan. Some people in Van Looy's team are even in the Merckx clan. And you see it in races, even in the fight for bonus sprints. It lasts three or four years. And the public loves it, because it's war between Merckx and Van Looy and war between their fans.'

For all that, to some, it could seem there was much to dislike about Rik Van Looy in his twilight years, no one doubted either the bike racer he had been or the cunning old lizard he remained. While others cocooned themselves in denial, were blinkered by their own youthful ambition, or simply weren't paying attention, Van Looy had one beady eye permanently trained on the surrounding seas. It can't have been long before he noticed a stirring in the waves.

'Bikers are bikers, pros are pros,' says Walter Pauli. 'Van Looy could see what was coming, he could smell it. I'm sure of it…'

If that was true, the 'Emperor' appeared determined to revel in his own equivalent of the last days of Rome, winning his third Paris–Roubaix in 1965 even before Merckx had officially joined the Solo-Superia ranks. The amateur world champion would make his professional debut on 29 April 1965, in the Flèche Wallonne or

'Walloon Arrow'. The first half of the Ardennes double-header climaxing with Liège–Bastogne–Liège, Flèche is now known primarily for a mazy route through the wooded hills of southern Belgium and especially its grandstand finale atop the brutally steep Mur de Huy. 'Back then it was a very different race,' notes one of Britain's best riders in the 1960s and '70s, Barry Hoban. 'It was renowned more for the cobbles and tramlines in the town centres than for its hills. It was all about the rough roads.'

Given Merckx's reputation as a fast-finishing, bulldozer of a rider, there could have been no more hospitable venue for his professional premiere. But as Hoban points out, 'In Britain, we put amateurs on a pedestal. In Belgium an amateur is just that. It doesn't matter if you were a world champion. Their attitude is, "You've not done anything yet".'

Nonetheless, everyone in the peloton had heard of Merckx, most had seen him win his amateur World Champion in Sallanches the previous year, and many a neck was craned to catch a first glimpse of the new *wunderkind*. Many, though, would also be underwhelmed. In one quiet moment early in the race, the Belgian Emile Daems rode alongside his Peugeot teammate, the Italian Marino Vigna.

'You see that kid over there,' Daems said, nodding towards an eager-looking, raven-haired figure in a scarlet Solo jersey. 'That's Eddy Merckx. He's going to be a champion.'

Vigna was, naturally, intrigued.

'I kept an eye on him after that, and I saw him struggling, going backwards in the peloton whenever the road climbed,' remembers the Italian, who three years later would become Merckx's directeur sportif. 'He looked too big, too muscular to be good going uphill.'

Merckx would argue that there were other reasons for his huffing and puffing, and for his abandonment well before Roberto

Poggiali beat his compatriot Felice Gimondi in a sprint to the line. Merckx had punctured early and, he claimed, lost too much energy in his futile chase to rejoin the leaders, or indeed to compete in Liège–Bastogne–Liège two days later. The Classic known as *La Doyenne* was promptly scratched from his race programme.

Merckx was present in the Rocourt velodrome for the Liège finale – but as a spectator. He saw the sallow, sunken cheeks of the 34 riders who managed to finish and told himself he'd been better off on the sidelines. Nine days later that decision was vindicated: in Vilvoorde in the northern suburbs of Brussels, Merckx prevailed over his old training partner Emile Daems, the man who had pointed him out to Marino Vigna in Flèche Wallonne two weeks earlier.

It was Merckx's first professional race win. The first of 525.

If Rik Van Looy's internal sonar system had been humming before, it's fair to assume that it was now bleeping with some urgency. Vilvoorde would also be the venue for the 1965 Belgian national championship road race, to be contested on 1 August. Van Looy had worn the black, red and yellow jersey awarded to the winner of two previous occasions. This year the Emperor had a further incentive: it would be his first major race with, or rather, against Merckx.

Technically speaking, of course, the pair were riding for the same Solo-Superia team. When Godefroot attacked in a dangerous group almost from the gun, however, Van Looy seemed either impervious to or quietly amused by Merckx's growing state of alarm. 'I identified more with Godefroot than Merckx, who got too easily wound up,' Van Looy would admit years later. Sure enough, on this day, he ensured that Merckx got very agitated indeed by abandoning mid-race, without warning or explanation. It was left to Merckx to almost single-handedly bridge the gap and in doing so ride headlong into the trap laid by Godefroot and his Groene Leeuw teammate and future brother-in-law Arthur Decabooter. Decabooter jumped, Merckx pursued him, and Godefroot tootled in his wheel. Godefroot, a faster sprinter on almost any day or finishing straight, duly had too much zip for Merckx when Decabooter was caught. It was a sting that Godefroot would try to reprise on many occasions over the course of his career, always to Merckx's immense frustration when it came off.

And so Merckx's difficult initiation continued. Since the spring, Merckx claimed later, Van Looy had been showing his indecorous true colours as he led the Red Guard not only on the road but in their taunts. They had christened Merckx 'Jack Palance', after the Hollywood star who had played Attila the Hun in the movie *Sign of the Pagan*. It sounded innocuous, but Merckx later admitted that the constant mockery was 'really hurting', despite his best efforts to 'make it look as though it was all washing over me'. Van Looy's speciality, on a par with his sprinting, was his sarcasm. Whether it was Merckx's fondness for rice pudding or his meek ripostes to the put-downs, everything he did was ripe for ridicule. 'Van Looy knows exactly how to tease someone…for Merckx it must have been really humiliating,' Jos Huysmans, one of the mainstays of what later became Merckx's own inner circle, told the journalist Rik Vanwalleghem.

On the bike, too, Van Looy sometimes appeared to relish the role of the cruel cartoon villain. 'The Tour of Flanders used to start in front of Gent's Sint-Pieters station, and it would be mayhem,' says Barry Hoban. 'You'd be going at thirty miles an hour through the neutralised zone, then Van Looy would get the Red Guard on the front and go vroooooom on the Gent ring road and for ten kilometres until the first cycle path. Then Rik would swing over and have a good laugh. The French didn't even know the race had started.'

As the '65 season wore on, though, privately, Van Looy perhaps feared that Merckx had the strength if not the repartee to expose his waning potency, and so responded with even more venom. In August, they competed in their first stage-race together, the four-day Paris–Luxembourg, and Merckx outrode him. The younger man was third in one stage and second in another, while Van Looy and the Red Guard were notable by their absence at the front of the race. At the dinner table in the evening, the roles reversed as Merckx did his best to remain inconspicuous and indifferent to the sneers coming from the other end of the room. Again, that is what Merckx claimed; how much of it was good-natured raillery, and how much genuine unpleasantness, Van Looy has never truly cleared up. Either way, it was during one of these meals that Merckx made up his mind: he would tell Van Bug to find him another team for the 1966 season. Van Looy and his cronies 'would never be my friends', Merckx reflected in the 1974 autobiography *Eddy Merckx, Coureur Cycliste, Un Homme et Son Métier*. At the time he said that Solo felt to him like 'Van Looy's family business'. After just one season, it was therefore time to focus solely on beating, rather than joining, the man who had lorded it over cycling in Belgium for ten years.

After one stage in Paris–Luxembourg, the president of the Belgian Cycling Federation Arnold Standaert had taken Merckx to one side and asked him to promise that, if selected for the Belgian world championship team in San Sebastian, he would do nothing to sabotage Van Looy's chances. Merckx was bemused, but reassured Standaert. In the race won by the Englishman Tom Simpson, Van Looy went on to abandon, Roger Swerts to claim a bronze medal for Belgium and Merckx to finish his first world championship in 29th place.

A few days later, at a circuit race in Zingem, the men who had made up the Belgian squad in San Sebastian were bundled together for a belated team photograph. The resulting image, of eight riders spread across the start line, is both a neat bookend to Merckx's year with Solo-Superia and a tantalising snapshot of Belgium's national sport on the eve of its revolution. At either end of the frame, two at least nominal servants of the Red Guard, Bernard Van De Kerckhove and Ward Sels, stand upright and unsmiling, the Solo-Superia logo on their torsos thrust forward; dead centre is the fair-haired Walter Godefroot in his Belgian national champion's jersey, cool and unflustered as a riverboat rambler; to Godefroot's left, we see a frowning Jos Huysmans, a grinning Roger Swerts, then the 20-year-old Merckx, more boy than man, but with both hands clamped firmly on the handlebars and eyes, brow and shoulders squared to the camera. To Godefroot's right, Van Looy perches on his bike's top tube, facing Merckx and the others with his body and fixing something or someone to the left of the camera with his glare. If Van Looy exudes confidence, Merckx's hunger burns through the lens.

Van Looy had ended the season with 37 victories, Merckx with nine. While others like Godefroot admit now that they were in awe of Van Looy, so much so that Godefroot initially addressed him as 'Sir', Merckx had never been his fanatical supporter. Yes, the first *real* professional cycling jersey he had ever owned had been a Faema kit from Van Looy's time with the Italian team, but that had been a gift from the former rider Guillaume Michiels, a family friend who was also now Merckx's 'soigneur' – Francophile cycling speak for a personal assistant. Merckx may not have idolised Van Looy, but that didn't dilute his bitterness at how their year of cohabitation had turned out. While nine wins was a good first return, neither, it has to be said, had the 1965 season persuaded too many people that Eddy Merckx was a new king, or for that matter the new emperor in waiting.

*

Having already spent most of 1965 under the rule of one of the pro peloton's crowned heads, Merckx almost found himself in the same invidious position the following year. At the Worlds in San Sebastian, the volatile 'Grand Fusil' or 'Big Gun' of French cycling, Raphaël Géminiani, had approached him with an offer to join him and five-time Tour de France winner Jacques Anquetil at the Ford-Hutchinson team. Fearing his manager, the volcanic Van Buggenhout's reaction to not being consulted, Merckx had agreed in principle but stopped short of signing on the pretext that he was still nine months short of his 21st birthday and needed his father Jules's approval. Soon Van Bug had learned of Géminiani's overtures and was furious. He stormed into Merckx's room. 'You ugly monkey, you've gone and signed for Gem, haven't you?' he raged. It took minutes to convince him otherwise, and for Van Bug to calm down. Needless to say, on their return to Belgium, the idea of Merckx pairing up with Anquetil had become no more palatable, and a deal was duly signed with Peugeot and its manager Gaston Plaud in the autumn of 1965.

The choice seemed a good one when Merckx rode brilliantly at Paris–Nice in March '66 to win one stage and finish fourth overall. If Solo-Superia adopted the same, all-for-one ethos that Van Looy had imported from Italy and Faema, Peugeot under the fine-dining Gaston Plaud was a much more ad hoc affair. In Tom Simpson and Roger Pingeon, they had two of the most coveted riders on the international scene – but neither came with the same entourage or ego as Van Looy. Had, indeed, that been the case, it's highly unlikely that Merckx would have been allowed to shoot out of the peloton just after Capo Berta in Milan–San Remo, then win an 11-man sprint on the Via Roma to take his first major victory.

While Gianpaolo Ormezzano of *Tuttosport*, the journalist who had tipped Merckx after Paris–Nice, rubbed his hands, others in the press-box began a frantic forage for biographical nuggets, anything beyond the amateur world title in Sallanches two years earlier. 'He knows Latin – so says a Flemish colleague,' was the best *La Stampa*'s Gigi Boccacini could come up with. Naturally he didn't check with Merckx, who would have told him that his Latin translations were in fact so ropey that he'd had to retake his exams in his penultimate year at school before giving up altogether a few months later.

What Merckx did admit was that his victory had surprised him as much as anyone. 'I didn't consider myself one of the favourites because I had no idea how well I could do,' he said. 'I didn't know my rivals, but I'd have played my cards in a sprint anyway. I tried and it turned out well. I'm as happy today as when I pulled on the rainbow jersey in Sallanches. No, actually, I'm even happier.'

It wasn't only the journalists who now began monitoring rather than just noticing Merckx. Fellow riders gathered information, quizzed Belgian colleagues, scrutinised Merckx in the bunch. On 9 April, he took to the start line for his first Tour of Flanders, already a marked man.

It wasn't long before he had made a lasting impression. On the rutted, cobbled road heading out of Berchem towards Kluisbergen and on to the first *berg* or climb of the race, the Kwaremont, a filthy scrap for position ensued.

'The cobbles there led on to a cinder cycle path, and there was always a huge fight to be near the front,' recalls the Yorkshireman Barry Hoban, at the time a member of the French Mercier team. 'I was in a good position when suddenly I felt something hit my back wheel. I stayed upright and kept going but then it happened again. I looked around and saw that it was Merckx. "*Passen!*" I said – pay attention. No sooner had I turned around than he'd hit me again and we all came down. He'd caused one of the major crashes in the Tour of Flanders that year.

'You could see he was this enthusiastic young lad, but he was a bit impetuous,' Hoban continues. 'You wanted to pull him aside and say, "Look, lad, you're an apprentice. Learn your trade!"'

Merckx had paid for his overzealousness with a smorgasbord of cuts and grazes and an abandonment in his first Tour of Flanders or *Ronde*. Those three weeks straddling San-Remo and Flanders would set the tone for his 1966 season: by the end of the year there were 20 wins, mainly in minor races in Belgium, moments of inspiration but also many a time when, in Merckx's own words 'my inexperience or ignorance was mercilessly exposed'.

At the second major Classic of the Belgian spring season, Liège–Bastogne–Liège on 2 May, Anquetil had underlined just how far Merckx needed to progress with a consummate performance, almost desultory in its power and grace. Usually uninterested in the Classics, 'Master Jacques' had allowed himself to be goaded by his team manager Géminiani and a remark about Felice Gimondi's capacity to win not just the Tour de France but also Paris–Bruxelles and Paris–Roubaix. As much as Merckx would never quite understand how Anquetil seemed to pick and choose his objectives like canapés at a dinner party, it was clear later that the Frenchman's procession in the '66 Liège had left its mark on him. 'I'm sure that Anquetil could have won Paris–Roubaix, the Tour of Lombardy or a world championship, with the class he had,' he told Marc Jeuniau in the 1971 book *Face à face avec Eddy Merckx*. 'He only needed to get annoyed one day to win Liège–Bastogne–Liège. But [winning everything] didn't interest him. He'd decided to organise his career differently.'

At the Grand Prix des Nations time trial at the end of 1966 Anquetil would highlight another facet of Merckx's riding, besides his temperament, that needed work by inflicting a three-minute defeat. Although undeniably powerful, Merckx's pedalling style looked too untidy to be effective against the clock and the pacing of his efforts too ragged. Not that his performance in the Nations wasn't rich with promise; third behind Anquetil and Gimondi but ahead of Poulidor and Pingeon was no disgrace. Jacques Augendre later wrote in *Miroir du Cyclisme* that, 'A lot of observers noted, not without astonishment, that Merckx was good against the clock as well as in sprints.'

Some seemed to think during his first 14 months at Peugeot that there were other areas of the Merckx skillset that required more urgent attention. At the Giro di Sardegna, his first stage-race of the 1967 season, more than Merckx's two stage wins, the Italian Giancarlo Ferretti remembers his crash on an unchallenging descent. 'People had been talking him up in the press, but it was the first time I'd got a good look at him in the flesh,' Ferretti recalls. 'We were going down and I saw him coming, this flash of his black and white jersey, and he just went straight off the road. I thought to myself that he couldn't be that good if he was crashing there.'

Ferretti wasn't the only one who noticed Merckx's vulnerability on descents. Marino Vigna, who had seen Merckx struggle whenever the road climbed in his first ever pro race, the 1965 Flèche Wallonne, now made the same observation as Ferretti when Merckx went downhill. 'He was a bit stiff, rigid,' Vigna confirms. Merckx certainly hadn't been flattered by the comparison with Tom Simpson's feline efforts while descending at the 1967 Paris–Nice. He would later admit to learning a lot just from watching his Peugeot teammate sway and slide effortlessly through the hairpins.

Italo Zilioli, who would later strike up a bond with Merckx after their brief encounter near the summit of the Blockhaus in the 1967 Giro, disputes that Merckx was ever a poor descender, but concedes that this was one area where his head could rule his legs. 'He wasn't the instinctive descender that, for instance, I was. When he had to descend fast, Eddy could, whereas I would get carried away in the moment and do things that perhaps weren't very sensible.'

So, on that evidence, bike-handling posed Merckx no problem. What could bother him was the same anxiety which often caused him to throw up before races in his junior and amateur days, and which early in his pro career manifested itself in assorted forms of psychosomatic pain. 'Around the age of twenty, I suffered with terrible pain in my kidney for several months,' he revealed years later. 'The doctors I went to see couldn't find any cause…and it turned out to be a nervous thing. I was in the pit of despair, having put all of my eggs in the same basket and gambled everything on cycling. It was one of the blackest moments of my career.'

Fortunately for Merckx, his own prodigious physical gift was becoming irresistible to even the minor weaknesses he did possess. A susceptibility to cramps at the end of long races had also been rectified. When the familiar aches scuppered his hopes of a first professional world champion's rainbow jersey at the Nürburgring in September 1966, Merckx had been so distraught that it took all of Jean Van Buggenhout's powers of persuasion to coax him on to the set of *Lundi-Sports* for a live television debrief the following evening. It turned out to be a wise decision, as within hours of the programme airing, an 85-year-old viewer had called to recommend a miracle pomade that would cure his cramps forever. With it, another obstacle to perfection suddenly vanished.

For the most part, though, Merckx was creating his own luck, and was the architect of his own inexorable advance on the Felice Gimondis, the Gianni Mottas, the Walter Godefroots and the Roger Pingeons who had mistaken themselves for the next anointed ones. In an age when the first significant racing in a season took place in March, and many riders barely started training before February,

Merckx was hardly off his bike, competing and winning on the track throughout the winter. His Belgian teammate at Peugeot Ferdinand Bracke was flabbergasted by his work ethic. 'It's extraordinary – he trains with the same intensity in November as in January,' Bracke told *Miroir du Cyclisme*. 'People come up with all sorts of statistics about Eddy, but I'd be curious to know how many hours he's spent on his bike between races and training. I'm not far off thinking that he spends more time in the saddle than he does in his bed. This man is made of a metal tougher than steel.'

No one, though, was suggesting that all a rider needed to do was train longer and further than the rest to be the best, if indeed that's what Merckx did. The 125 kilometres he rode on average per day, 365 days per year, were remarkable, mind-boggling. But he wasn't the only rider covering that kind of distance. Gimondi, for one, knew and could follow the recipe of hard graft at least as well as Merckx.

No, there would have to be something else, something even beside his dauntingly powerful, God-given engine. Because even on that score, and even allowing for the fact that he was still growing in 1967, Merckx was outstanding, but not to the extent where major tour and Classics victories could be considered an inevitability. His lung capacity was at a good but not exceptional 5.9 litres, as compared with the Italian rider Marino Basso's 6.7 litres. His resting heart-rate was in the high 30s, but everyone knew that constituted no gauge of athletic potential. His VO2 Max, a measurement of the body's capacity to transport and use oxygen during exercise, today considered the ultimate gauge of athletic potential, was inferior to that of the best cross-country skiers. One of his most valuable endowments may in fact have been what looked like a morphological imperfection, his disproportionately long femur bones. According to Roger Bastide in his *Eddy Merckx, Cet Inconnu*, published in 1972, 'this creates a longer lever, and the rider gains power, as the angle of the pedal-stroke is less open'.

Bastide, though, followed this potentially crucial information with a disclaimer: the French rider Jean-Pierre Parenteau also had long thighs and short calves, but nothing like the success of Merckx.

There was, in truth, already something very different, unique about Merckx as the 1966 season ended and 1967 began, but it remained easier to discern than define. 'Hunger' partially covered it, but only partially. For all his pragmatism, his champagne-quaffing and alleged philandering, Anquetil was also ravenously ambitious – but in a way that couldn't have been more starkly juxtaposed with Merckx. Born poor, the Frenchman hoped to get rich, and realised that he could do so thanks to his one extraordinary talent: riding bicycles. 'I was inestimably lucky,' he said once. 'I didn't have to fight my way up because I became a star very quickly, but if I hadn't succeeded, I'd have really scrapped and I'd have become a star anyway.'

At this stage still relatively little was known about Merckx's upbringing in Woluwe-Saint-Pierre, the Brussels suburb where his parents owned and ran a grocery store. Enough, though, had filtered into the public domain for most to realise that the Merckxes were now solidly middle-class, and there was no way Eddy's motivation was an escape from poverty. Neither, it was quite clear, did money and fame occupy a prominent place in his hierarchy of needs. An old Merckx family maxim, 'Whatever you do, do it well', echoed permanently in his consciousness, and Merckx knew that the limelight was one place in which he could never excel. 'I'll admit that I'm a lot more at ease on my bike than in a lounge,' he told Marc Jeuniau. 'I don't have a commercial smile. My mother already used to say that when I helped my parents at the grocery store.'

Patrick Sercu could vouch for the comfortable surroundings in which Merckx was raised. He first teamed up with Merckx in track races when they were both teenagers. Sercu then became a regular visitor at the Merckx household when he was stationed in military barracks near Brussels during his national service in 1963. He remembers Merckx's 'very lovely mother' Jenny, her delicious cooking, Eddy's 'very disciplined father who didn't speak much' and thinking that they had 'maybe a bit more money than normal people, but had to work very, very hard for it'.

Sercu didn't need these glimpses of domestic serenity to convince him that his friend had a lust for cycling and for winning that went beyond the usual zest and bravado of youth. It was a fire burning deep, deep within. 'To tell the truth, Eddy has a very big advantage over all of us: he has remained a true amateur,' Sercu declared at the time.

Sercu meant that his Madison partner's was a pure, unfettered, unquestioned passion for cycling – one of an amateur in the word's original sense, 'lover'. People would later marvel at his professionalism, when really it was Merckx's amateurism that was unique. The lady who would become his wife at the end of 1967 knew it well. 'The problem with Eddy is that he was vaccinated with a bicycle spoke,' Claudine would joke. So viscerally did his love of racing translate into aggression that Claudine admitted to being frightened when she watched her husband hammering away on the front of a peloton.

Over subsequent years, those who knew the couple would describe their marriage as the final piece in the Merckx jigsaw, the solid ground from which he could plot the final ascent of cycling's Everest. Merckx once said that his days consisted of three things – 'cycling, recovering and sleeping'. It was not a complaint, more the honest admission of a person to whom life had given one immense blessing: not a talent but a calling. Anquetil had utilised one to cultivate the other; with Merckx, it was the vocation that came first. His talent was the flower that grew from that stem.

In his compelling study of how excellence develops, *The Talent Code*, Daniel Coyle cites several examples to illustrate how outstanding motivation underlies all outstanding progress and achievement. One of Coyle's most striking case studies involved 157 children as they prepared to start learning a musical instrument. Before their first lesson, the children were asked how long they envisaged playing the instrument – a year or under, to the end of primary school, to the end of high school or for the rest of their lives. The musicians' abilities were then plotted against their hours of weekly practice after nine months. The man who conducted the study, Gary McPherson, said the results were 'staggering': 'With the same amount of practice, the long-term commitment group outperformed the short-term commitment group by four hundred per cent. The long-term-commitment group, with a mere twenty minutes of weekly practice, progressed faster than the short-terms who practised for an hour and a half.'

McPherson's conclusion was this: 'It's all about their perception of self. At some point very early on they had a crystallising experience that brings the idea to the fore, that says *I am a musician*. That idea is like a snowball rolling downhill.'

Or, in Coyle's words, 'What ignited the progress wasn't any skill or gene. It was a small, ephemeral, yet powerful idea: a vision of their ideal future selves, a vision that oriented, energised and accelerated progress, and that originated in the outside world.'

Early in 1967, it was perhaps premature to speculate about what had 'ignited' Eddy Merckx, but the match under his natural ability, that searing desire which terrified Claudine, was there for all to see and envy. No wonder Nino Defilippis, witnessing it for the first time, spoke of an 'electrocution'.

Merckx himself still didn't know how far it would all take him, and neither, at this point, did rivals with their own designs on world domination. Merckx's 1966 season had been an improvement on 1965, with 20 wins including that first and to date only true pearl, Milan–San Remo, but most, including Merckx, would wait somewhat longer than Defilippis for their eureka moment.

And, yet, even a fortnight before lightning shook the Matterhorn, it had struck for the second time in two years 300 kilomtres to the south on the Ligurian coast.

2
something in the water

'We were too immersed in our own careers to see what was
going on. To an extent, we only realised what had happened
when it was too late...' WALTER GODEFROOT

San Remo's Via Roma is one of those places in sport where real
mystery and imagined mystique intertwine almost to the point where
they become one and the same thing. Augusta National's 12th tee
has its swirling wind, Lord's its slope, and the Via Roma its own
matrix of wiles. Real or imagined, they confuse and beguile. Failing
that, they provide explanations for the otherwise inexplicable, excuses
for the otherwise inexcusable.

It's the strange camber, say some. No, argue others, it's the
imperceptible rise in those final 400 metres. Another popular yet
preposterous theory is that this otherwise unremarkable shopping
street threading east–west through San Remo is beholden to its own
micro-climate. The breeze doesn't so much blow off the Mediterranean, just two streets to the south, it doesn't so much swirl as cast
a spell. Tonight there is talk of black magic. How else can the Italians account for their 14th consecutive Milan–San Remo without a
home winner, after 42 wins in the first 50 editions? Or, for that
matter, the second victory by a young Belgian in a Peugeot jersey
in two years?

When Eddy Merckx came thrashing, bobbing, brutalising across the line, Italian heads dropped as though from a guillotine. On the road, three of them – Gianni Motta, Franco Bitossi and Felice Gimondi. Then, tens of thousands more behind the barriers on either side, and a hundred or so among the journalists waiting behind the line. All except *Tuttosport*'s Gianpaolo Ormezzano. Ormezzano had gone out on a limb at Paris–Nice the previous year to report that a young Belgian named Merckx was riding strongly in France and was an outsider for victory at San Remo. When Merckx vindicated his judgement a few days later, Ormezzano began to regard the 21-year-old as his own project, his protégé. In March 1967, for the second year in succession, the journalist studied the delighted figure in the black-and-white Peugeot colours as they muscled him towards the podium. If Merckx was handsome, Ormezzano thought to himself, it was in a very un-Italian way. Baldassare Castiglione had spoken for all Italians then and now in his sixteenth-century *Il Cortegiano* – the *Book of the Courtier* – when he decreed that a man must not only look good and speak well but also and above all possess a *sprezzatura*, a certain nonchalance. 'He conceals art, and presents what is done and said as if it was done without effort and virtually without thought.' For all his precocity and talents, *sprezzatura* was not a quality displayed by Merckx. His facial features, like his riding style, brought to mind industry, not artistry.

If there was a modern-day expression of the Castiglione proto-type, a current 'King of Cool', it was the film star Steve McQueen, and Gianni Motta happened to be his spitting image. Right now, though, there was nothing cool about Motta's reaction to defeat. In two years' time, just up the coast in Savona, Merckx would curl up on a hotel bed, sobbing uncontrollably and vowing never to race again. That was Motta this evening. One by one, like mourners at a funeral, his Molteni teammates filed into his room to offer their support. Up the road in a different hotel, Motta's sworn enemy Felice Gimondi also stewed.

The night would bring counsel, plus some perspective. Rather than by Merckx, the great Italian triumvirate of Gimondi, Motta and Bitossi had been undone by the Via Roma. That and a universal sporting truth: there are certain horses that excel on certain courses. And also such a thing as a one-trick pony.

Merckx's sprint victory in the Gent Wevelgem semi-classic 11 days later would do little to change their mind; that picture of the finish line at San Remo, with three children of a golden generation fanned across the Via Roma, and Merckx just ahead of them, said unequivocally that the future looked sun-kissed for Italian cycling.

'I mean, how were we supposed to know?' asks Felice Gimondi today, almost pleading for understanding, compassion, maybe even forgiveness. 'I had won the Tour de France in my first year as a pro, I was about to win another Giro. Everything was going well…Who knows how many more Giri d'Italia I'd have won if *he* hadn't come along. But he did come along. And we didn't realise for months, years.'

'O sole mio
sta 'nfronte a te!
'O sole, 'o sole mio,
sta 'nfronte a te!

It's my own sun
that's upon your face!
The sun, my own sun,
It's upon your face!

Dino Zandegù says the urge to sing came spontaneously, the words just flowed. Well, not exactly: a large and vocal group of Italian migrants stationed close to the prize podium had watched him cross the line, his right arm thrust towards the angry skies, his face and hands black as theirs after a day in the mines of Charleroi and Marcinelle, and broken into their own chorus.

First an ironic, '*O sole mio!*', then an invocation to join them: '*Canta, Dino, canta!*': 'Sing, Dino, sing!' And so Dino had sung, to the delight of his countrymen and the tickled disbelief of cameramen and journalists from all over Europe.

A few paces away, making his way through the mêlée, Zandegù's Salvarani teammate Felice Gimondi also smirked. He had watched 'Il Dinosauro' win from 200 metres back down the finishing straight in Gent. Thirteen seconds later, Gimondi had followed Eddy Merckx across the line. As the blubs flashed and Merckx lunged, Gimondi harked the anguished cry of a beaten man.

If Zandegù's performance on the cobbled hills, the *bergs* of the Tour of Flanders on the second day of April was a revelation, his singing was not, at least not for the Italian public. Ever since his Giro d'Italia début three years earlier, the baker's son from Padova had enlivened many an uneventful race with his impromptu balladry, often accompanying an impressive baritone with exuberant arm-waving. If a birthday needed celebrating, all eyes would be on Zandegù in the middle of the peloton: his mouth and an eyebrow would rise mischievously at one side, he might disappear for a minute or twenty, then reappear balancing a birthday cake in the palm of his right hand and conducting the chorus with his left. '*Buon compleanno a te!* Happy birthday to you…'

'Typical', says Zandegù today: those three or four bars of '*O sole mio!*' became more famous than the victory they were meant to celebrate. More famous even than him beating Eddy Merckx on the Belgian's own patch.

It was to be the story of Zandegù's career. No, of his life. He was a talented cyclist but a better showman. And an utterly brilliant raconteur. These attributes now earn him an annual invitation to the Giro d'Italia from state broadcaster RAI. In their daily, pre-stage eyesore, exhibiting all the naffness that makes Italian television a national embarrassment, Zandegù is the performing seal in a circus commanded by the mustachioed ringmaster Marino Bartoletti. In 45 years, not much has changed; what Zandegù used to do within the bosom of the peloton, he now accomplishes in a makeshift studio in the Giro's hospitality village. At Bartoletti's unctuous behest, Dino sings, Dino dances, Dino jokes, Dino laughs.

Above all, Dino tells stories. On air and off it – to him it's the same. No sooner have the credits rolled than 'Il Dinosauro' is shuffling off, his fingers are clasped like five thick salamis around a new listener's, and he's away. His tales are breathless, hysterical, crescendoing monologues delivered through a north-east Italian accent as gravelly as the unpaved *sterrato* roads which are often their setting. What's more, says Zandegù, 'ninety-five per cent of them are true'. Unless, that is, it's the afternoon. Then, by Dino's own admission, 'the percentage falls to ninety'.

Dino, Dino, tell us about growing up…

'Well, we didn't have a lot but at least we weren't hungry because we owned a bakery. You just about scraped by. The first batch of bread that Dad used to bake at 6.30, we kept to one side just in case the oven broke and we were left with nothing. There were 18 of us in the family: eight brothers, six sisters, Mum, Dad, Gran and Granddad. We all used to get together at four every afternoon to boil up the dry, stale bread, the *pan biscotto*, and put it into a kind of *panzanella*, a bread salad. It was *buonissima*! Better than what my wife makes now! Anyway, when I won races as an amateur, I'd come home, tell my mum and sisters, and my reward would be a cup of *caffè latte* and a corner of bread straight out of the oven. If I didn't win, my mum pretended that she'd forgotten to cook and there was nothing you could do! Even my sisters were annoyed with me! Then if I got a bit friendly with a girl, they didn't like that either! They'd tell me that I had to go and explain to her that I had to race my bike and mustn't have any distractions. Thanks to them, I was practically a virgin at 26!'

Practically? Eh? Never mind…What about that Tour of Flanders in 1967? Beating Merckx, that must have been something…

'Ah, yes, well my teammate Gimondi and I attacked with Merckx and came across to Barry Hoban, Noel Foré and Willy Monty, who had been in the break earlier on. After the Mur de Grammont climb, I attacked with Foré and Merckx was stuck, because Gimondi wasn't going to help him. Foré was too tired after his earlier break to pose any threat in the sprint. I won easily. Then Merckx came over like this big, roaring lion, absolutely furious. I didn't pay him too much attention. The Italian fans were shouting to me to sing, and it just came naturally. *"O sole mio…!"*.'

Dino, Dino, seriously now, should you all have known in 1967? Should you, could you not have seen what was coming?

'We were all intimidated. We were. This kid just arrived, this big, handsome Belgian kid with high cheekbones – the face of an immense athlete – and pretty quickly we all realised that on the bike he was a brute. I say quickly but it wasn't straight away. It took a while, a couple of years. We, we didn't know, we didn't…'

For once even Dino Zandegù is lost for words.

*

If March had belonged to Merckx, victories for Zandegù in Flanders and the Dutchman Jan Janssen in Paris–Roubaix forestalled hype around the new star that may have followed what, after all, had been only two inspired performances in the space of eleven days in Milan–San Remo and Gent–Wevelgem. Yes, Merckx had won again at Flèche Wallonne at the end of April, this time with a vicious solo attack, but again there was an explanation: the magic sparkle dust named 'form', which could come over a rider for a month or six weeks and transform him from good to great, inconspicuous to irresistible. No one was disputing that now Merckx, at 21, had a glittering future; not many either, though, were getting carried away, partly because the last, the hardest and maybe most prestigious of the Classics had opened clear daylight between the two main young pretenders to 'Emperor' Rik Van Looy's throne. Walter Godefroot first, Eddy Merckx second; the line of succession had been determined by the finish line at Liège–Bastogne–Liège.

Van Looy, it has to be said, had always preferred Godefroot. First and foremost, he was a true Flandrian, like Van Looy. Godefroot's parents had worked in the textile factories which provided work and bare subsistence for thousands of families in and around Gent. When Godefroot was 13, they scraped together the last Belgian francs that Social Security Services and the Catholic Church wouldn't cover for Walter to go on holiday to Switzerland. 'That way, you'll at least get to go that far once in your life. We never will…' Godefroot's mother told him.

A few years later, in 1964, cycling would take him to Tokyo for the Olympics, where he won a bronze medal, which at the time he felt could have been gold with a little more help from Merckx, and in the three years since he had travelled and won all over Europe. His Liège win had now confirmed him as the best young Classics rider anywhere in the world. Or so Godefroot thought. He glanced at one

Flemish daily's sports pages the following day and flinched. 'Merckx undone' said the headline, and beneath it, in smaller writing: 'Godefroot wins Liège–Bastogne–Liège'. The author went on to espouse Merckx's view that he had been outsprinted only because he wasn't familiar with the cinder track at Rocourt in Liège, which had hosted a soggy finish. Godefroot cursed as he read. He had done all the chasing behind Merckx's Peugeot teammate Ferdinand Bracke, he had repelled every Merckx attack when Bracke was caught, and he had led Merckx into the velodrome. What else did he have to do? Maybe if he lived in the same city as clueless journalists and their newspapers, Brussels, like Merckx...

But at least Godefroot had bagged a big one. Merckx's victory two days earlier at Flèche Wallonne now paled. Even Merckx's Peugeot team manager, the debonair, dickie-bowed Gaston Plaud, seemed to think so. When Merckx told Plaud that he would consider renewing his contract on the condition that Plaud signed two or three Belgian domestiques to help him in the 1968 Classics, the Peugeot chief's expression glazed over. As usual, Plaud's mind seemed to be on other things. Food, wine, who he was meeting for dinner. If it didn't serve up such rich material for mockery, the sound of Plaud's voice on arriving at the team hotel every night would have driven his riders to distraction. '*Bonsoir, Madame. Qu'est-ce que vous avez comme spécialité de la maison?*'

The truth was that Plaud had his reasons for not trying harder to hold on to Merckx, plus two brilliant and highly marketable leaders: Tom Simpson and Roger Pingeon. Why would he kowtow to Merckx, a Belgian, at the risk of alienating that pair, respectively among the best one-day and stage-race riders in the world?

No, if Vincenzo Giacotto, another of professional cycling's *bon viveurs*, wanted Merckx, he could have him for his new Faema team in 1968. Before Plaud packed him off to Italy for good, he would send him to Treviglio, near Milan, for the beginning of his first major tour, the 1967 Giro d'Italia...

One Wednesday afternoon in October 2011, Walter Godefroot sits forward in his chair and shakes his head, probably much like he did when it dawned in April 1967 that some members of the Belgian press believed the real story from Liège–Bastogne–Liège was another stellar performance from Eddy Merckx.

'We were too immersed in our own careers to see what was going on,' he murmurs by way of an apology. 'To an extent, we only realised that had happened when it was too late...'

As the 1967 season wore on, it was coming to resemble a series of auditions, on a bigger scale and with higher stakes than Merckx's in front of a judging panel of Nino Defilippis, Vincenzo Giacotto and Teofilo Sanson at Cervinia in April. Most sports thrive on duality, rivalry, and cycling was no different, but there was also something inherent in what racing represented that compelled its followers to look for one superior being, a clear champion, and which somehow made them most comfortable in one's presence. Thus, the periods most clearly defined in the collective memory were those which were also synonymous with just one rider: in France, the Louison Bobet or Anquetil eras; or in Italy, those associated with Costante Girardengo, Alfredo Binda and Fausto Coppi, for all that Coppi's battles with Gino Bartali had promoted Coppi's deification. By contrast, times of transition, as one regime petered out and another readied itself to elect a leader, often gave rise to the most exciting racing but also a sense of general unease. In the early 1960s, there had been two rulers, Jacques Anquetil in major tours and Rik Van Looy in the Classics. By 1967 that pair was going but not yet gone – and wouldn't until someone truly stood up and stood out from the crowd.

Merckx was one pretender among many, although no one really believed that he could compete with the best in the mountains of Italy. That taster session at Cervinia led him and those watching to believe that his horizons may yet be broader than just the Classics, but three Italians he had beaten at Milan–San Remo, just for instance, had far greater pedigree on climbs much harder than what he had faced that day.

Had he needed it, a fourth Italian, Italo Zilioli, could also have told Merckx all about the fickle plight of the great white hope. Barely ten days in, it had already been a miserable Giro in an annus horribilis for Zilioli. Having burst on to the scene with a series of prestigious wins in 1963 Zilioli's career had been stuttering ever since. Now attacking through the sleet two kilometres from the top of the Block-haus climb, he thought he had saved his Giro and was homing in on a prestigious stage win. Then had come a noise, *that* noise, a glimpse of Merckx bearing down, a frantic and fudged attempt to change gear, a look up, and the final realisation that his predator had come and gone. Merckx's ability to hold off a chasing peloton on the flat had caught Zilioli's eye three months earlier at Paris–Nice. Never, though, did the Italian think him capable of the same thing 2,000 metres above sea level. Once, Zilioli's team manager had asked him why he always brought the same book, *Letters of Condemned Italian Resistance Fighters*, with him to races. Zilioli had replied, 'Because in moments when I feel desperate, when I feel the unluckiest person alive, I read a few pages and it helps me to understand what desperation really feels like.'

Zilioli can't remember what he read that night, but will never forget the headline in the following day's *Gazzetta dello Sport*: 'Italian disappointment: Belgian sprinter wins in the mountains'. As insults went, for a climber like Zilioli, it was a cracker.

'No wonder I looked miserable as sin when a photographer asked me to pose with Eddy just after I'd seen that,' Zilioli says now. He goes on, 'Of course Eddy won again two days later. With hindsight, that should have been another penny dropping...'

Only with hindsight?

As the man, Zilioli, said, Merckx won again two days after his maiden grand tour stage win on the Blockhaus, this time in a bunch sprint in Lido degli Estensi. The boy, it seemed, could do everything – within reason; after a farcical stage to the Tre Cime di Lavaredo, won by Gimondi but declared null and void because too many of the riders had been pushed up the final climb, the cream rose to the top on the final mountain stage to Tirano. Either that or, if the rumours were to be believed, a '*santa alleanza degli italiani*' or holy Italian alliance allowed Gimondi to attack the race leader Jacques Anquetil after the Passo del Tonale and easily set up overall victory. Any Italian 'in' on the deal was said to have pocketed a tidy sum in return for declining to help Anquetil's chase.

While Gimondi was heading for his second major tour title and a first Giro d'Italia to add to the Tour de France he had won on his début in 1965, Merckx, alas, had capitulated on the Passo del Tonale. At least he was in good company; Franco Bitossi had started the Giro with big ambitions, won the first mountain stage on Mount Etna, but was now in freefall down the general classification.

'Crazy Heart', they called Bitossi. His family had been the very incarnation of the Tuscan idyll, before mass tourism and before 'Chiantishire', with their farmhouse in Camaioni on the banks of the River Arno, 15 kilometres upstream from Florence and a short boat crossing from the nearest road. One day, though, Franco couldn't recall exactly what age he was, he had run out of the house to find his mother shrieking at the water's edge. His younger brother Al was missing and, when he heard his mum scream, little Franco was certain that he had drowned in the Arno. As his mind raced, his heart pounded at double, treble its normal speed. Al was fine, and found within minutes, but the drumming under Franco's ribcage continued. It would abate soon enough, but also return with distressing regularity once Franco had decided to pursue a career in cycling. Crazy Heart's first two seasons in the professional peloton had been hellish, yielding zero victories and innumerable variations on the same, tragicomic scene: a flash of heels, a blur of jet black hair, Bitossi clear of the field and then, moments later, stationary at the side of the road, hunched over his handlebars. Gradually, though, after numerous threats to give up, and races like the 1966 Coppa Agostoni where he had ridden rings around Merckx and Gimondi, been forced by palpitations to stop ten times, yet still nearly beaten them, he had reconciled himself to the problem and by doing so eased its symptoms. A barnstorming start to the 1967 season even had some wondering whether he might be the next '*campionissimo*', but the Giro and in particular the Dolomites and Alps had cut Bitossi down to size, just as they had Merckx.

As they struggled on together up the Tonale, flanked also by Merckx's teammate Ferdinand Bracke, Merckx coughed, wheezed and cursed the journalists who had kept him answering questions in the freezing cold after the previous day's stage to Trento. Whenever the gradient became steeper, Bitossi looked across at him and jotted mental notes.

Four days later, the Giro had finished with Gimondi the winner and Merckx in ninth position. Bitossi opened *La Gazzetta dello Sport* and read attentively. One of the godfathers of Italian sports journalism, Bruno Raschi, had reviewed the previous three weeks' action and judged each of the main protagonists individually. Bitossi looked for Merckx's name. 'He has shown his limitations in the mountains. The young Belgian will never win a major stage race,' it said.

Bitossi shook his head. Raschi might be a good journalist, but he knew nothing about cycling...

'I couldn't believe it when I read that, what Raschi said about him not winning the Tour. I mean, based on what I'd seen, it was obvious what the kid could do...'

While others dozed or dithered in denial, Crazy Heart Bitossi, at least, had not missed a beat.

By the end of July 1967, international cycling's crowded constellation had abruptly found itself with one star fewer. What a way, though, for its glimmer to go out; the recent winner of Paris–Nice, Tom Simpson, had collapsed and died on Mont Ventoux at the Tour de France.

Simpson had perished midway through a race in which his Peugeot teammate Roger Pingeon's talents had shone brighter than ever before. The pair had ridden in different colours at the Tour, race director Félix Lévitan having taken the controversial decision to revert to the old formula of national teams, but that hadn't lessened their Peugeot manager Gaston Plaud's delight at Pingeon's excellent start to the Tour and his horror at Simpson's death. Plaud made an easy target for ridicule but the man had virtues beyond his ability to pick the right suit and tie or bottle of Beaujoulais nouveau. He had a heart.

If only he'd been in charge on the Ventoux, or had convinced Tommy to quit the Tour the previous evening. He had tried, lord knows he had tried. Even on the Ventoux, when Simpson's cheeks had appeared even more wan and sunken than the night before, Plaud had ordered Tommy to call it quits. He didn't know about the five amphetamine pills that Simpson had supposedly been balancing on his tongue in the morning, and boastfully showing the other riders, or exactly what he'd drunk during an emergency stop in Bédoin at the foot of the Ventoux.

The fact remained that Plaud's dynamic dichotomy – the happy-go-lucky yet immensely driven Englishman, and the talented French dilettante – had been cut in two, leaving just Pingeon. Peugeot's third man had been Merckx, and Plaud suspected that he had already signed with the Italian start-up Faema during the Giro. Merckx learned of his friend and mentor Simpson's death back home in Belgium, when it flashed on to the evening news. He was distraught. Ever since he had joined Peugeot the previous year, Simpson's friend-liness and willingness to dispense advice had been in marked contrast to the antipathy of his previous team leader, Rik Van Looy. Merckx immediately made up his mind to travel to Simpson's funeral in Harworth in England a few days later. He would be the only rider from the continent to attend the burial.

Ninety-one summers young, in his home in Tours on the banks of the Loire, Gaston Plaud can still reel off names of the cyclists he helped guide to superstardom – Simpson, Pingeon, Charly Gaul, Ferdinand Bracke, Merckx and more. Plaud and his memory only show their age when he's asked how, *why*, for heaven's sake, he allowed a gem like Eddy Merckx to escape through his fingers at the end of 1967.

'But, but, Pingeon was a good rider. He had won the Tour…' Plaud starts to stammer.

But, but it's not good enough.

*

There was more one big opportunity to stake a claim, as well as the rainbow jersey of the World Champion to win. The rendezvous was at Herleen, a grimy mining town in the south of Holland, on 3 September 1967. The sandy-haired, smooth-talking, short-sighted Jan Janssen had won the Vuelta a España in the spring. He would be the home fans' talisman and one of the favourites. So too would Eddy Merckx and Gianni Motta.

Contrary to what had been written at the time, San Remo in March had not been Motta's 'funeral'. It was true that the left leg run over by a car at the 1965 Tour of Romandy had been hampering his form and his morale since the start of the year, but there was no doubt that he was taking his shot at redemption in Holland very seriously indeed. Since around the time of the Giro, he had been working closely with a Milanese doctor, a 38-year-old surgeon and biochemist by the name of Gianni Aldo de Donato. From what little was known of him, de Donato seemed an extraordinary character. In 1959 at the age of 30, he had reportedly discovered the world's first antiviral medicine. That had earned him a full-page homage in the *New York Times*. Since then, he had gone back to more mundane matters, and was carrying out one of his routine visits in May 1967 when he noticed 'a strange agitation' in one of his patients. Further investigation revealed the cause of the man's ills: he couldn't fathom why Gianni Motta wasn't riding better at the Giro d'Italia. Suddenly curious, de Donato had reached for a pen and paper and written a long letter. Motta had replied courteously, and quickly, because before the end of the Giro de Donato was filling another envelope with a handful of yellow capsules and a note about suggested dosage. The pills were perfectly legal, de Donato maintained. Sold under the commercial name LILLY, they contained 'a catalyst of the 13 biochemical reactions which take place in the muscle'. De Donato was certain that, had Motta taken them throughout the Giro, and had Gimondi not been able to count on the '*santa alleanza degli italiani*', Motta would have won the Giro. Not only that, but he reckoned that 24-year-old Motta had the body of a 21-year-old. He would 'explode' over the coming seasons.

'He's a squirrel, Mother Nature's been good to Gianni,' was the doctor's bizarre assessment. It got weirder: 'Put a squirrel and a mole at the bottom of a tree and the squirrel will climb up, while the mole will stay down below. He's a squirrel, he's been lucky. He can succeed in everything, he has to succeed in everything.'

Their collaboration had continued and intensified over the summer, to the point where de Donato was now commonly depicted as some kind of mystical shaman who had Motta 'in his thrall'. Everywhere the doctor went, suspicion stalked him. In the Italian team camp in Valkenberg near Herleen, that had then turned to outright hostility when Motta insisted on both training and eating apart from the other Italian team members, with only de Donato for company. The details of those training sessions defied conventional wisdom about how to prepare for a world championships as well as belief; on both the Wednesday and Friday before Sunday's World Championship race, Motta had covered 290 kilometres at 40 kilometres per hour. Wild speculation about exactly what de Donato was giving or doing to him spread through the foreign riders and press. Some claimed that de Donato was a 'neuropsychiatrist'. Others reported that, in the run-up to Herleen, Motta had followed the regimen of a NASA cosmonaut. Elsewhere, there were clear inferences that de Donato was feeding Motta much more sinister substances than the meat and vegetable milkshakes which had become his main sustenance.

'I've realised that drugs rule cycling. Doping is the riders' daily bread. The riders love it because it reduces their suffering. But in my opinion it has put the brakes on the technical development of this sport,' de Donato tried to argue, clearly to little avail.

The misgivings turned to astonishment on the day of the race when the start-gun sounded and Motta shot out of the bunch. Only de Donato nodded his approval; Gianni was sticking to their plan. In the confusion, five riders had jumped across with him: the Englishman Robert Addy, the Spaniard Ramon Saez, Janssen's compatriot Jos van der Vleuten and Eddy Merckx. Nineteen laps and over 250 kilometres remained.

The laps ticked by, the gap grew. At the end of each one, Motta scanned the huge crowds for his guru. De Donato responded with a 'Forza, Gianni!' or a clenched fist. Merckx, meanwhile, looked for the brown, shoulder-length hair of his mother, Jenny. Once or twice he took a can of Coca-Cola from her outstretched hand.

Back in the peloton, the local boy Janssen's worry and frustration grew. To use one of Janssen's favourite French expressions, he '*pédalait dans le beurre*' – literally, he was pedalling through butter. In other words, it was effortless. After eight laps, he could wait no longer. Towards the top of the only real hill on the course, Janssen accelerated and gained 50 metres. Two laps later, at the midway point of the race, he joined Merckx, Motta, Saez and van der Vleuten.

With two laps to go, Janssen drew close to Merckx. The pair of them had shared a ride the previous year when Merckx's car had broken down on the way to a race. Merckx now turned to him. 'So, between you and me, who wins? We need to be careful of the Spaniard Saez, because he's fast in a sprint, that guy. And Motta will be quick as well...'

'If we get to the finish all together, I'm going to ask van der Vleuten to lead out the sprint from a long way, a kilometre out. That OK?' Janssen replied.

'Yeah, yeah, yeah, yeah,' Merckx agreed.

Janssen knew that, in his eagerness, Merckx would want to squeeze between the two Dutchmen and come under the kilometre-to-go flag on van der Vleuten's wheel. The latter would fade 400 metres from the line, whereupon Merckx would launch his sprint and himself begin to slow in the last 100 metres. Janssen's superior speed, as a three-time former winner of the Tour de France's green jersey, would then guarantee him victory.

That was the theory, but not quite how it turned out: when the quintet reached the final bend, 500 metres out, van der Vleuten had still not kicked. By the time that he did, then jagged to the right at the 200-metre banner, Merckx was closing in on victory and Janssen had lost vital speed as he swung left to avoid his teammate. Janssen was clearly quicker but Merckx held on…by 30 centimetres. Exhausted by his last-ditch attack on the final lap, Gianni Motta came home in fourth place and collapsed into Doctor de Donato's arms.

The aftermath was dominated by recriminations – Janssen's aimed at van der Vleuten for not respecting orders in the final kilometre, Motta's at the entire Italian team for not marking Janssen, and theirs at him for attacking so early. Amid the brouhaha, the most important outcome was the one that too many still seemed determined to over-look: at age 22, Eddy Merckx would end the 1967 season as the champion, nay the king of the cycling world.

'We hadn't seen anything special,' protests Jan Janssen. 'He was like anyone else. We never thought for a second he'd be a really great rider. He was like Willy Planckaert, Godefroot and lots of others.'

He says this then pauses – a long, dramatic, meaningful pause. 'The first time I saw him do something really remarkable,' Janssen goes on, 'was at Heerlen. There I realised that, to beat that guy, you had to put your foot to the floor and then some.'

'I was the strongest that day, Eddy knew I was the strongest, but, yeah, I'll admit it, you could see at the end of '67 that Eddy was something else,' says Gianni Motta. 'Pingeon had won the Tour but, with Pingeon, you knew an hour earlier when he was going to attack. Merckx, by comparison to Pingeon and the rest of us, was Superman.'

Maybe, finally, someone was opening their eyes.

3
fire and ice

'I can still see Eddy on the climbs before the
Tre Cime di Lavaredo, in the snow...He can't contain himself.
He has magic in his legs.' MARINO VIGNA

In the hours leading up to what would be Eddy Merckx's second Giro and only his second major tour, he had fizzed with nervous energy in Faema's pre-race HQ in Gavirate. Eighteen months earlier, the same callow exuberance had led to a falling out with the Italian Vittorio Adorni in the sprint to the line at the 1966 Tour of Lombardy, won by Adorni's then Salvarani teammate Gimondi. Now, by some coincidence or serendipity, Adorni was lying on a twin bed in Merckx's hotel room, *their* hotel room, observing his young team-mate through half-amused, half-admonishing eyes.

Adorni had arrived in Gavirate, dragged his suitcase through reception, up the staircase and through the door a couple of days earlier and found Merckx already fussing and fretting. 'What are they?' were Adorni's first words, index finger outstretched accusingly towards the three large bags encumbering the space. 'No, you don't,' he'd said without waiting for an answer. 'Where do you think you're going? On holiday? No, you're not doing that. If we're sharing the same space, it's one suitcase each...'

Soon, it wouldn't be luggage but an item of clothing that was bothering Adorni: the hallowed *maglia rosa*, the pink jersey awarded to the Giro leader. Two kilometres from the finish line of what should have been a non-eventful first, true stage of the 1968 Giro to Novara across the plains of Piedmont, Merckx had catapulted out from behind teammate Martin Van Den Bossche's rear wheel and into the slipstream of a television motorbike. He had dwelled for a second, suspended mesmerically in front of the main peloton, before kicking again to finally cross the line six seconds ahead of the rest. He had then matter-of-factly made his way to the podium to exchange his world champion's rainbow-striped jersey for the pale pink of the *maglia rosa*, the same pink jersey that was now draped over a chair in his and Adorni's hotel room.

Before the lights went out that evening, thoughts and the conversation turned to the tactic they should now adopt over the next week, until what was predicted to be the first decisive stage of the race to Brescia.

'*Non ti preoccupare*' – don't worry, Adorni told his young companion. 'We'll give the jersey to someone else and let their team control the race for a few days. That way you can be *tranquillo...*'

Adorni waited for an answer. Silence. He looked across to see Merckx's lips pursed in defiance, his head shaking.

'No no no no no.'

'What do you mean, "No no no"?'

'Why would we lose the jersey? The race finishes in Napoli, right? Right, well, I want to keep it until Napoli.'

A long-standing member of the International Cycling Union's management committee, even now in his 70s, Vittorio Adorni is a frequent visitor to cycling's major races. More often than not a sweater is draped over his high, broad shoulders and the creases ironed in his slacks are the only things sharper than his observations.

'Eddy was adamant: he was going to lead the Giro from start to finish,' he remembers with a smile. 'I kept telling him, *tranquillo. Calmo*! But at first he wouldn't have any of it. Then, eventually, he saw sense. He learned more in that Giro than most people learn in a career.'

For all that he would raise his voice to Merckx more than once during the '68 Giro, Adorni was not generally known for his authoritarian style of leadership. 'Diplomatic', 'gentlemanly' or even 'ambassadorial' were more common descriptions. This, primarily, was why Vincenzo Giacotto had signed him a few months earlier. Giacotto wanted to 'Italianicise' Merckx and his racing, and Adorni had both the experience and the tact to impart a rigour that seemed to elude the Italians in everyday life, but for some reason imbued their approach to cycling. A former and possible future Giro winner in his own right, Adorni boasted another key selling point: he had spent three years in the same team as Gimondi and knew his every secret. He would therefore act not only as Merckx's mentor, his chaperon and his domestique de luxe, but also as his informant.

Adorni was certainly under no illusions about Merckx's potential. The previous year's world championship road race at Herleen was, he agrees, 'the moment when the penny dropped and we started to think "Oh dear"'. Fortunately by that time he already knew that he would be riding with and not against Merckx in 1968. After Nino Defilippis's 'electrocution', Vincenzo Giacotto's final meetings with Faema about budgets, and Merckx's committal to a three-year deal worth 400,000 Belgian francs a year, Adorni had been identified and recruited as Faema's in-race *éminence grise*. He was now 30 years old; it was time to think less about personal glory than putting '*fieno in cascina*' – literally putting hay in the barn. Saving. Thinking about his future. Adorni's father had been a bricklayer; Vittorio could scarcely have aspired to anything more glamorous before the day, aged 18, he and some mates rode from their homes in Parma out into the Apennines. A few hours and one ascent of the 1,041-metre Passo della Cisa later, he had been hooked.

He had been a pro for over seven years, but never had he seen anything quite like Merckx. At Faema's first get together of the winter in Reggio Calabria, Merckx had astonished his new teammates first with his efforts to learn Italian, then with his attitude to training sessions. A spot of good-natured jousting wasn't and indeed still isn't unusual between teammates in this setting, and normally Adorni would relish the impromptu races which often crackled into life on the climbs. But not here. Not with Merckx. 'He just wanted to race all the time,' the Italian says, still sounding exasperated. Whenever the road angled skywards, Adorni would hear that deadly whirr at his back, then within seconds, Merckx would appear and vanish in the same flourish of flesh and metal. 'There would be riders all over the road, absolute carnage,' Adorni remembers. And the worst – or best – of it: 'In spite of all the energy he seemed to be wasting on silly races in training, the kid was never, ever tired.'

There were still rough edges to smooth – but then that was why Giacotto had recruited Adorni. He and Marino Vigna, the former Peugeot rider who had been plucked straight out the peloton to become Faema's Italian directeur sportif, had set immediately to work. The first weakness that needed addressing was Merckx's tendency to stiffen up going downhill. Adorni had come up with a novel solution: he would ride directly in front of or behind Merckx calling out instructions, like a primitive GPS robot. 'Brake now!' 'Stay wide!' 'Accelerate!' Whereas, a year earlier, Merckx's screeching tyres provided the sound effects, within weeks, Adorni's voice was the only audible accompaniment to poetry in motion.

Having failed to impress Giancarlo Ferretti with his bike-handling at the 1967 Giro di Sardegna, now Merckx and his new troupe offered a masterclass at the same race in February 1968. Merckx didn't even wait to cross over the Med and into Sardinia, winning the first stage on the Italian mainland by over six minutes to make overall victory a formality.

That had been his first stage-race win of his pro career, to be followed by an equally emphatic one in the Tour of Romandy in Switzerland in April. Adorni says that Faema were becoming a 'super-team, everyone could see it'. In Adorni and the Belgians Roger Swerts, Vic Van Schil, Martin Van Den Bossche and Joseph Spruyt, Merckx suddenly had a Red Guard of his own, arguably even stronger and more versatile than Rik Van Looy's equivalent in the Faema team's previous incarnation.

At the Giro, though, Merckx and Adorni both knew that they were about to face their biggest test. It hadn't even been a year since Bruno Raschi's affirmation on the pages of Italy's most authoritative sports newspaper, *La Gazzetta dello Sport*, that Merckx would never win a major stage race. Franco Bitossi had laughed, but there were others who still harboured the same, serious doubts. For all that Merckx was the reigning world champion and had finished the 1967 season with 26 wins, so far these had all been in one-day or track races. Some even speculated that the victory in Novara on Stage 1 was proof that Merckx had come to Italy only to target stage wins. Adorni was his team's real captain, they maintained. They were half right, in the sense that the plan discussed and agreed upon in Gavirate had been for the road to anoint the Faema leader. If that was true, however, Stage 1 had cast an overwhelming vote in favour of Merckx.

A day later, Gianni Motta added his voice to the mounting consensus and building evidence that Merckx was the stronger of the

Faema pair. 'Merckx looks the strongest rider in the race. Faema should count on him,' the Italian declared, having survived the first major climb of the race, the Col de Joux, before beating Merckx in a two-man sprint in Saint Vincent. In the final four kilometres, Motta had looked like a man outriding not only the peloton but also a now omnipresent, taunting spectre – the pain in his left leg. His winning attack with Merckx had disguised desperation as liberation; poor Gianni's chances in the Giro and indeed his best days as a rider would soon be over. A positive drugs test announced at the end of the Giro – not to menton the unseemly end to his collaboration with Gianni Aldo de Donato when the doctor illegally fled to Argentina with his estranged daughter the previous autumn – were symptomatic of the way that Merckx's star had waxed while Motta's waned.

Midway through the first week of the Giro, Motta hadn't been the only rider in the Giro *gruppo* whose health was causing concern. While the usual jollity at Molteni now came and went in inverse synchrony with the aches in '*capitan* Motta's' groin, all had seemed well at Faema as Guido Reybrouck sprinted to victory in Alba at the end of Stage 3, and Merckx 'loaned out' the pink jersey to the Italian Michele Dancelli in accordance with Adorni's grand plan. '*Tranquillo, tranquillo*,' Adorni had reminded Merckx again before the start in Novara. The message, by the look of things, was finally getting through.

Reybrouck's victory, just a few weeks after his positive dope test in the Tour of Flanders, crowned a memorable few days for Faema manager Vincenzo Giacotto in his native Piedmont. A more stylish, less bumbling version of the Peugeot directeur-cum-*bon viveur* Gaston Plaud, Giacotto was, says Marino Vigna, 'the man who brought a bit of civilisation to cycling, and taught riders how to behave in hotels at races, in the bars and lounges'.

True to form, Giacotto had wanted to celebrate Reybrouck's win and Faema's rip-roaring start to the Giro with a dinner amongst friends. The guests were to include the Faema team doctor Enrico Peracino and Professor Giancarlo Lavezzaro, the chief cardiologist at the Italian Institute of Sports Medicine in nearby Turin. Before the meal, though, Giacotto had invited Lavezzaro to meet his two star riders, Merckx and Adorni, and also to submit them to a cardiogram. The two riders had duly acquiesced, undergone the tests, and Lavezzaro was now examining the results. He didn't have to look very hard to notice that something in one of the graphs wasn't only amiss, it was downright alarming. He immediately found Giacotto; the young Belgian chap's cardiograph, he informed his friend, was that of a man in the middle of a heart attack.

Lavezzaro says today that, in their concern, he and Giacotto had agreed to repeat the tests the following morning. All they gave Merckx was the false pretext that Lavezzaro wanted to analyse the effects on the heart of several hours' sleep. After a nervous night, Lavezzaro had knocked on Merckx and Adorni's door the following morning and performed the test. He waited and watched. To his dismay, Merckx's graph was still that of someone whose next journey ought to be to hospital, not the 162 kilometres of the Giro's fourth stage.

This wasn't the first time that someone had said there was something not just unusual, but genuinely faulty about Merckx's heart. Prior to the amateur World Championships in Sallanches in 1964, the then 19-year-old, and anyone else in contention for a place in the Belgian team, had been summoned to Gent for routine medical checks. Merckx would later refer to their outcome as the first 'hammer blow' of his career: the tests had supposedly revealed that Merckx had a problem with his heart and therefore wouldn't be available for selection.

When his mother called the Belgian Cycling Federation to query the results, she was told: 'You're putting him on a pedestal...He can't climb a mole-hill.' Selector Oscar Daemers then said that her son could perhaps be accommodated in the four-man 100-kilometre time trial team. Jenny Merckx demanded to know why Eddy's heart was considered fit for this, most aerobically exacting discipline, and not for the road race. 'You stubborn old woman!' Daemers snapped back. Now she was convinced that something fishy was going on. A few more phone calls, between Jenny Merckx and the family doctor, then between him and the man who had examined Eddy in Gent, and it quickly transpired that Daemers didn't want Merckx to race in Sallanches, most probably because he hailed from Brussels and not Flanders, and had apparently 'engineered' his exclusion. Merckx's heart was, as the Merckxes' GP Dr Fesler had always said, 'strong like his father Jules's'. Shamelessly, Daemers 'atoned' by sending the first telegram of congratulations that Jenny Merckx received after Eddy's victory in the Sallanches road race.

Four years on at the Giro, Giacotto and Lavezzaro faced a genuine dilemma: did they tell Merckx about his condition, or even pull him from the race? Lavezzaro remembers Merckx 'making vague noises about his cardiograms always being funny' but also seeming completely blasé. Lavezzaro was terrorised – but didn't insist. Instead he returned home to Turin and every day for the remainder of the Giro feared that he would return home from work in the evening, start asking his wife what had happened in the Giro, only to see a pallor in her face. Every day he braced himself and every day, it seemed from his wife's summary, Merckx was becoming stronger.

'Now,' Lavezzaro says emphatically, 'Merckx wouldn't be allowed to race. At the time we could see that he had a problem but couldn't make a precise diagnosis without doing a cardiac catheterisation, which obviously wasn't practical at the Giro. We just knew that he was at risk. Later I wrote to Merckx's doctors in Belgium but they said it couldn't be anything because he was still winning on the bike. The next year, the brother of the president of Torino football club had exactly the same thing and we went to Houston in the USA to get it diagnosed properly, because we didn't have the right apparatus in Turin. It was a non-obstructive hypertropic cardiomyopathy. Nowadays, you pick it up straight away in the electrocardiograms that, for instance, professional cyclists have to pass to get their licence. And someone with that diagnosis wouldn't be allowed to race. There are no symptoms…but there is a risk of sudden death. In 1977, an Italian footballer called Renato Curi with this problem dropped dead in the middle of a match… But no, there were no aerobic advantages and nothing Merckx could feel. There was just this sword of Damocles above his head every time he raced.'

By the time Merckx had failed for a second time in four months to win on San Remo's Via Roma at the end of Stage 5, narrowly losing out to his mate Italo Zilioli after their attack on the Passo Ghimbegna, one problem in the Faema camp was at least nearing its resolution. With Dancelli still comfortably leading the race but expected to struggle in the mountains, and Merckx over two minutes clear of every other contender for the Giro title, Zilioli's win had 'saved the Giro from becoming a one-man show', according to *Tuttosport*. There appeared to be nothing, however, which could stop precisely that happening at Faema.

Luckily, in Adorni, Merckx had a clever and pragmatic tutor and former co-leader. Eclipsed by his pupil on the road, Adorni now did exactly the opposite of Van Looy at Solo-Superia, resolving to pass on as much of his *savoir faire* as possible before the end of the Giro.

The 'Corsa Rosa', as the race was known, was the perfect context in which to 'Italianicise' Merckx, just as Giacotto had wanted.

'You could tell straight away that Eddy wanted to learn. It took him no time. But the Belgians were totally different from us,' Adorni remembers. 'At the Giro, on the first night, the Belgians were all congregating in a room, sometimes ours, and eating biscuits and drinking beer after dinner. For a few days I just watched them, quietly shaking my head. It happened once, twice, then on the third or fourth night, they all came in and I said, "Right, no more! Everyone out! This is no way to spend evenings at a stage race. Eddy, you have a camomile tea, you go to bed early, and you look at tomorrow's stage map. That's how you recover in stage races. You can't go around Italy drinking beer and eating biscuits for three weeks." Maybe at first he was sceptical, but then he saw that I was talking sense.'

Sure enough, within days, Merckx had a new routine. A phone call to Claudine back home in Belgium, some ribbing from Adorni about the frequency of their conversations, perhaps a mug of tea, then it would be down to business and the map of the following day's stage. 'He wasn't cold or clinical, and neither did he really know what he was capable of, so he needed someone helping him,' Adorni explains. 'If his legs felt good on a climb a hundred or a hundred and fifty kilometres from the finish, he'd want to attack. But the system we came up with was that I'd basically tell him when to go and when to sit in. Later, he performed these amazing exploits in the Tour and Giro, so we knew he could hold everyone off for a hundred kilometres or so, but in 1968 we didn't know how he'd last over three weeks.'

Meanwhile, at Salvarani, Gimondi was getting very little right except his predictions: he had said Stage 8 to Brescia would give vital pointers and Merckx had duly dropped everyone on the Colle Maddalena, this in a stage which passed through both Gimondi and

Motta's home villages, Sedrina and Groppello d'Adda. That pair both crossed the line 48 seconds behind Merckx. Motta was then penalised a further second for holding on to his car on his way to greet family members in Groppello, with the permission of the peloton.

Years later, it would be remembered, scarcely, as a Merckx victory like hundreds of others. Merckx, though, had noticed an unusual but soon-to-be familiar sound as he rode into the Brescia velodrome eight seconds ahead of Adorni: the crowd was booing.

Alpine folklore has it that there are six 'great north faces' in the range, each so high and so challenging that they remain the preserve of only the most daring – or foolhardy – mountaineers. Of the six, the most vaunted and infamous are the Eiger and the Matterhorn, both in Switzerland, and the third member of the so-called 'Trilogy', the Grandes Jorasses in the Mont Blanc massif. The Petit Dru in France and the Piz Badile on the Italian Swiss border are barely less terrifying.

This leaves one, great north face, and the only one whose name is also inscribed in cycling folklore. The Tre Cime or Three Summits of Lavaredo are a trio of adjacent pinnacles tucked high in the north-west corner of Italy in one of the most visually beguiling mountain ranges anywhere on the planet, the Dolomites. To give them their individual names, those summits are the Cima Piccola, Cima Grande and Cima Ovest, and it is the north face of the 2,999-metre Cima Grande, specifically, that represents one of the stiffest challenges in European climbing. Such was the adulation reserved for Emilio Comici when he took three days to conquer the vast, overhanging wall in 1933 that he claimed soon afterwards that his life had become 'unbearable'.

The Giro d'Italia's own mountain trailblazer, race organiser Vincenzo Torriani, had hoped that the first ascent by professional cyclists would cause equal hysteria in 1967. He was right – but not in the way that Torriani had wanted: Stage 19 of the '67 Giro, finishing outside the Rifugio Auronzo in the shadow of the Cima Grande, had been utterly ruined by fans pushing riders up the brutal, four-kilometre climb. Torriani was left with little option but to declare the stage null and void. The first man to the Rifugio Auronzo, Felice Gimondi, wept. The following day's *Gazzetta dello Sport* dubbed the Tre Cime 'The mountains of dishonour'.

What many had forgotten on the night before what Torriani hoped would be his and the Giro's redemptive voyage to the Tre Cime in 1968 was that, 12 months earlier, Eddy Merckx had crossed the line in second place. Many, but not Gimondi; in the Salvarani hotel, he, his sponsors and directeur sportif Luciano Pezzi looked nervously ahead to the following day's 213-kilometre stage. 'It's now or never,' Pezzi told him. The general classification, with Michele Dancelli still in pink but certain to surrender, and Merckx in second and over three minutes ahead of Gimondi, indicated that Pezzi was right. The same perhaps couldn't be said about journalist Gigi Boccacini, who in *La Stampa* described Merckx as 'a strong athlete in the mountains, yes, but not really strong'.

High in the Italian north-west, Merckx woke to sullen skies and more calls, in the local papers, for the fans or *tifosi* to avoid a repeat of the previous year's debacle. He had slept well, or at least much better than the night before Brescia, where he had been kept awake by the high temperature. Peracino, the Faema doctor, was feeling less refreshed. The cardiogram that Merckx had taken in Alba was still on his mind, and Peracino had tossed and turned all night. After breakfast, he went to find Adorni and Merckx. Adorni informed Peracino that his roommate had already left to prepare for the day's stage. Peracino told Adorni that it didn't matter and that he would catch up with Merckx later.

The scene now shifts several hours and a couple of hundred kilometres, from past to present, a memory to the Faema directeur sportif Marino Vigna's mind's eye. 'I can still see Eddy on the climbs before the Tre Cime di Lavaredo, in the snow. Every time the road goes up, he always goes off the front of the bunch by accident – he can't contain himself. He has magic in his legs.'

On the Passo Tre Croci, just before Misurina and its lake (said to have formed from the tears of a spurned maiden), nine riders, survivors from an earlier 13-man break, are still clear. The peloton, heaved along by Faema's Martin Van Den Bossche, is still seven minutes behind. The temperature is around three degrees. Adorni moves to Van Den Bossche's shoulder, glances at Gimondi, then turns to Merckx. Since the start of the stage in Gorizia, if not since the start of the Giro in Campione d'Italia, written in those doe-eyes has been the same plaintive expression, the same question: 'Can I go now? Is it time?' And all day, all race, the old stag has been telling his young fawn the same things: 'Not yet!', '*Calmo*!', '*Tranquillo*!'; 'You won't win the Giro at the Tre Cime di Lavaredo...'

But maybe, seeing that magic, now even Adorni isn't sure. Merckx is still watching him; Adorni decides to nod. Merckx goes; Gimondi pounces.

They all regroup. The sleet turns to snow, and Merckx turns again to Adorni. He is almost begging. Adorni nods again. The time to process what's just happened, and the gap is a hundred metres.

Merckx is now en route to what he will one day call his greatest-ever athletic performance. This moment has been coming for three years, some would say 22 years, 11 months and 15 days. It is nothing more, nothing less, than the precise second when Eddy Merckx rides off on his own into the distance.

For the foreseeable future, there will be fleeting instants when a rider appears at his side, as Adorni does now, having realised that Gimondi is beaten, then they, like the Italian, will come to the same conclusion: 'I'm just a cyclist – he's a motorbike.' And they will leave Merckx to his own rabid, sanguinary pursuit of whatever it is that he finds so compulsive about victory, just as Adorni does at the foot of the final, awful ramps to the Rifugio Auronzo.

Merckx will have left fellow pretenders trailing, and one by one he will slash through the relics of former glory with names like Anquetil or Van Looy – or today Galera and Polidori, who are the last to be caught a kilometre from the finish. Faster than himself, he will exhaust superlatives similar to the ones that will appear in tomorrow's newspapers: 'marvellous', 'irrepressible', 'unreal', 'fantastic'. He will give endless interviews like the one he conducts in the Rifugio Auronzo, peeling off clothes but revealing little or nothing of what makes him *different*. 'I attacked at the bottom of the climb after a long pull by Van Den Bossche, and I continued with a regular cadence, pushing a 42x26, the same that I used on the Colle Maddalena. This is the hardest climb I've ever done, so I tried to never change my rhythm. I kept catching riders but I had no info on what was happening in the race, either behind or in front of me. When I crossed the line and not before, I realised that I'd won.' He will continue to sound exactly like other riders, and equally banal, and look as different from them on a bike as he did on a cardiogram.

He will also go on making his victims despair, like they do when they realise he leads the Giro by nearly four minutes from Adorni and over five from anyone else, and sometimes driving them to tears. Having crossed the line today six minutes and 19 seconds after Merckx, for the second time in 12 months under the Cima Grande,

Gimondi is sobbing. Among the fans on the four-kilometre, 12 per cent corkscrew to the finish line, there were a group of his boyhood friends from Sedrina, and seeing them has caused his already frayed nerves to snap. For 15 minutes, while Merckx takes all the plaudits, the Rifugio for Gimondi has been exactly that – 'a refuge'. 'I saw people crying for me and now that's all I can do,' he blubbers, surrounded by the men with whom he plotted Merckx's downfall just last night. 'My fans and my teammates believed in me. How could I have betrayed them?'

Just when you think that things can't get any worse for Gimondi, a door opens and Gianni Motta, the rider he most loathes, steps into the improvised changing room inside the Rifugio. For one day, though, the sworn enemies are united in their dismay. Two years ago, they had the world at their feet. Now, they see an abyss.

Motta picks his way through the small crowd of journalists and Salvarani staff and places a hand on Gimondi's shoulder. 'Come on, chin up,' he says. 'You've had a bad day, but that's all it is – one bad day. Look at me: I've been going from one disappointment to the next for the past ten months!'

It wasn't that bad, Motta wanted to tell Gimondi. What neither of them knew is that it could, and would, get a whole lot worse.

The boos rang out all across the Bay of Naples, over the Mediterranean and around Vesuvius like the toxic fumes of a first eruption since March 1944. In Brescia a fortnight earlier, the jeers had all been for Merckx, but now they echoed towards the tall, frowning figure to Merckx, the Giro winner's right. Poor Vittorio Adorni. Three years ago, that time in Florence, he'd tossed back his head, closed his eyes and allowed his ears to soak in the applause of the countrymen and women who had seen him turn the 1965 Giro into a procession around Italy. He had won by 11 minutes – more than double his deficit from the champion Merckx in this year's final standings. This was what the Neapolitans couldn't understand: how could an Italian capable of winning the Giro sacrifice his chances in favour of a foreigner?

No one, though, was better placed than Adorni to know just how dominant Merckx had been, and how much more pain he might have inflicted. On the night of Merckx's masterpiece at the Tre Cime, for the first time in the race, Adorni was happy to see the pink jersey draped over a chair in their hotel room. He had even joked, 'Hey, Eddy, you'd better watch out. I'm going to attack you and come after that tomorrow,' and Merckx had laughed.

Similar room, similar scenario a few days later, only this time the one mucking about was Merckx. At least that's what Adorni assumed when he heard, 'Hey Vittorio, come and have a look this' and looked up to see Merckx's head buried in a map of the next day's stage, and his arm beckoning Adorni. 'Look at this nice climb after 60 kilometres. We could light it up there.'

Adorni's expression was now one of complete stupefaction. 'Are you serious? What on earth are you talking about, *light it up*? The Giro's over. What's the point of attacking? Forget it. Just stay calm and you'll win the race...'

'Well, you know, I thought...I just thought that we could have some fun...' Merckx muttered as he walked away.

The final days of the Giro had, in all truth, passed off in a strange, sombre atmosphere. As it wended south through the Appenines, abandoning the Italian cycling heartlands of the north, the race had also left a trail of shattered ambitions and disappointment. That photo from Milan–San Remo and the Via Roma in 1967, with Bitossi and

Motta and Gimondi fanned across the road and Merckx millimetres ahead of them, now looked less the harbinger of an impending gold rush than a sepia souvenir of former fantasies.

The catcalls for Adorni, Gimondi's tears – above all, from an Italian point of view, it had felt like an *undignified* ending. After some disastrous days in the mountains, 'Crazy Heart' Bitossi had salvaged some pride with a stage win in Umbria, but also found himself unwittingly embroiled in a controversy over dope testing. After Stage 19 to Rome, Bitossi claimed, he had seen Merckx's teammate Vic Van Schil emptying the contents of his drinking bottle or *bidon* into the container he had been asked to fill with his urine. Bitossi and a teammate who had witnessed the same thing later filed a formal complaint. So much for the rumours that had been doing the rounds for several days, and which were never substantiated, that the Faema team was using some miracle, mystery drug made all the more remarkable by the fact that it was perfectly legal.

If the Giro's denouement had been bad, its epilogue was to be more unseemly still. A week after Merckx's coronation in Napoli, the Union of Italian Professional Cyclists (UCIP) announced the names of the nine riders who had tested positive for 'doping' during the Giro. Given what Bitossi had seen and reported in Rome, the least surprising name was Vic Van Schil. The most shocking were Gianni Motta and Felice Gimondi.

Exactly a fortnight after their brief reconciliation in the Rifugio Auronzo, Gimondi and Motta again found themselves side by side. They were supposed to be in Castelgrande, a small town in central Italy, for a money-spinning circuit race, yet here they were, in the front room of an ordinary punter who had offered up his house as the venue for an impromptu press conference. Once again, Gimondi was devastated, Motta more sanguine. 'Fifteen years of work and it's all collapsed,' lamented Gimondi. 'What bugs me is having ridden the Giro for nothing,' said Motta.

While both men confirmed that they would appeal against their one-month bans, one dilemma had at least been taken out of their hands: neither, it was now sure, would ride the Tour de France in July. This gave them one thing in common with Merckx. The previous winter, Merckx and his pal and fellow world champion, track ace Patrick Sercu, had been granted an audience with the Belgian Prime Minister Paul Van den Boeynants. Clearly aware of the already growing lobby for Merckx to make his Tour de France debut in 1968, Van den Boeynants had advised him not to succumb to the public clamour. Faema boss Vincenzo Giacotto was of the same opinion. Merckx had then stood firm the following spring when a delegation from the Tour organisers visited him at Paris–Roubaix and again, reportedly, when Coca-Cola offered him one million Belgian francs to line up in France. In the second instance, Merckx's manager, Jean Van Buggenhout, had understandably wavered before reaffirming that his client's no was a no. He was too young, it was too early.

For the second year in succession then, riders divided into national, not trade teams, set out on their journey around France. The Italians were without Gimondi and Motta but at least had Bitossi. 'Franco, if you want to win the Tour de France, you'd better make it now, because next year there'll be Merckx,' the agent Daniel Dousset whispered in Crazy Heart's ear before the start in Vittel. Bitossi went on to enjoy by far his best ever Tour, and possibly his best ever major tour. He would win two stages and the green jersey of the points competition and finish eighth on the final general classification.

The winner was the wily Dutchman, Jan Janssen, who had stolen the Tour from under Herman Van Springel's nose in the race-ending time trial. Van Springel, too, admits today, 'I knew that it would be my last chance. I knew Merckx was coming...'

An old ghost came back to haunt Merckx towards the end of 1968. In truth, Rik Van Looy had never really been away. As he got older and weaker, the now defrocked Emperor had become more and more preoccupied with Merckx and stalling his ascent, particularly in the one-day races that Van Looy had dominated. The most prestigious of all for a Belgian was the Tour of Flanders, and in 1968, once again, Walter Godefroot's victory in a Classic had been overshadowed by a perceived injustice to Merckx. Simply put, Van Looy seemed to have ridden the whole race glued to Merckx's wheel, apparently only interested in making him lose.

The brilliant 2010 documentary *De Flandriens* and its narrator, Michel Wuyts, tackled the issue head on in a rare interview with Van Looy.

WUYTS: You said that you never rode on Merckx's wheel just to make him lose.

VAN LOOY: How can you ride on someone's wheel to make him lose? If they can explain that...

WUYTS: By making him nervous.

VAN LOOY: Yes, well you shouldn't get nervous. There is always someone on your wheel.

WUYTS: But if it is a Van Looy...

VAN LOOY: But Van Looy was already 35 years old. You shouldn't be scared of a 35- or 36-year-old.

Wuyt: But you still had your very good days.

[Van Looy nods]

Wuyts: In the '68 Tour of Flanders, did you ride on Merckx's wheel?

Van Looy: [pauses for five long seconds] In '68…yes that was the case, yes.

Racing in the same Belgian team and national colours as Merckx, not even Van Looy would have the audacity to attempt the same trick at the world championships in Imola in central Italy, on 1 September 1968. What he could do instead was attack with Adorni, of all people, with 58 kilometres gone and 219 remaining. Did Van Looy really think he could win, or was this just his latest ploy to cripple Merckx? The second explanation looked plausible when, having collaborated with the Italian and seven others to take the group out of the peloton and Merckx's reach, Van Looy wilted with 85 kilometres remaining. From there, Adorni rode unchallenged to win by over 10 minutes, with his Faema teammate and the defending champion, Merckx, resigned or at least happy to repay Adorni for his help at the Giro d'Italia by not chasing. Even having sacrificed his own chances, Merckx still finished eighth.

'I'd told Eddy in the run-up to the race – the Worlds were in my home region and I couldn't and wouldn't help him there,' Adorni recalls. 'Van Looy and I went away with a few others but the race had barely started. I said, "Rik, what do we do now? We've two hundred kilometres to go. We're going to die out here in this heat." Rik just looked at me. "Are you scared of dying? You and me are old anyway." So on we went. To be honest, I wasn't afraid that I wouldn't be able to drop Van Looy, which is what I did. I wasn't worried about

Merckx or what it meant to him that I was away with his big rival, either. I heard later that he hadn't really made any effort to catch me. I never asked him why. I didn't want to know.'

Adorni may have preferred blithe ignorance, but the Italian press the next day had more than an inkling that the two riders' association with a certain Italian coffee-machine maker, Faema, night explain Merckx's passive approach.

The *Gazzetta dello Sport*'s headline: 'A coffee aroma in Adorni's world title'.

4
eddy, ciao

'He came at us from every angle, slaughtered every one of us,
like some rabid wild man, some barbarian.' DINO ZANDEGÙ

It's amazing what you can learn about the lie of the land in international cycling towards the end of 1968 on an afternoon at the Giro d'Italia...in 2011.

From one mythical mountain to another. From the Matterhorn, lightning rod for Nino Defilippis's 'electrocution', to the Cima Grande of Lavaredo and now the Monte Rosa. The Rosa's eastern face, the highest in the Alps, appears so enormous from its base in Macugnaga that the summit may as well be an extension of the sky. Even when the clouds roll down the mountain and into the valley, as they do today, it's not hard to see why the first president of the Alpine Club, John Ball, declared this valley the most beautiful mountain canvas on the planet.

The rain has finally stopped. In its place is a man-made percussion not unique to the Giro but maybe more disorderly and cacophonous here than at other races. A surprise winner, the Sicilian Paolo Tiralongo, will cross the line in under two hours, yet banners and barriers still have to be erected, cars still need to be parked, the corporate crowd still has to be fed and fans entertained. In every direction, there are *carabinieri*, volunteers or men and women in fleeces emblazoned with the race organisers' logos, pointing, shouting, gesticulating flamboyantly.

Three or four hours ago, at the stage start in Bergamo, Giancarlo Ferretti had taken shelter from the approaching storm under a gazebo in the hospitality village. The once fearsome 'Iron Sergeant' of team managers, 'Ferron' has lost some of his aura, as well as his job, since an internet scammer tricked him into thinking that emails from a Hotmail address were promises of a multi-million-euro sponsorship deal from Sony-Ericsson in 2005. His five foot nine frame is still as lean, his posture just as proud as when he rode with Gimondi at Salvarani in the 1960s, but some of the old gunslinger's steel has faded from his eyes.

At times, like now, it is replaced by a misty nostalgia.

'The Tre Cime di Lavaredo was just one of the first of endless exploits,' he says. 'After that, Merckx just got faster and faster. He would be riding on the bunch, taking it easy, or so he thought, and the group would start breaking apart behind him. Or he'd attack 120 kilometres from the finish and we'd think he'd gone insane, then the next time we'd see him would be at the finish. There were things which the general public didn't see and no one remembers but which gave us all nightmares. He went tack tack tack and swept through professional cycling like a forest fire, burning everyone and everything in his path. He made us suffer, he beat us, he humiliated us, yet we still had an inestimable admiration for him. More than for his strength; for his courage, his *fantasia*, that imagination to dream up things that no one else believed possible...'

Ferretti draws breath.

'I was Gimondi's domestique until 1970 then three years later I became his directeur sportif. Felice fought, he battled, he pretended, but finally even he got despondent. At the Volta a Catalunya in September 1968, a week after Adorni won the World Championships, it hit him. Merckx and Felice were going at each other every day, the leader's jersey was going from one to the other, then we got to the time trial. I had already finished and was watching on TV back in the hotel. Felice is a born time triallist, but Merckx made him look like a pantomime horse. Half an hour after the race, I hear the door creak open and see Felice standing there, shaking his head. He peels off his gloves and throws them on the bed, cursing. "*Porco cane!*" he says. "How the hell am I going to beat this guy? I have to beat him. If it's the last thing I do before I give up, I have to beat him in a time trial!"

'Well,' Ferretti says with a chuckle, 'it took him five years...'

Up the road in Macugnaga, a moment of serendipity.

In a VIP enclosure overlooking the finish line, Felice Gimondi reminisces about the same afternoon in the same Volta a Catalunya in 1968. A small crowd has formed at a respectful distance from our table. From its midst, a smartly dressed, strapping man in his 60s steps towards us. He takes the chair next to Gimondi.

It is Eddy Merckx.

'Merckx was so strong,' Gimondi has just been saying, 'that you had to take it in turns to follow his wheel!'

Gimondi now turns away from the recorder and towards Merckx, who gives the impression of wanting whatever is about to be said to remain a private conversation, without necessarily wishing to change the subject. When he looks at his old mate, his old rival, Gimondi, he smiles. When he looks in our direction, with head and body at 45 degrees, Merckx is nigh on expressionless.

'Eddy, when was it that we first met? Bruxelles–Alsemberg in 1963, when we were still amateurs?'

'You beat me. You made me suffer like a beast.'

'It was the only race he let me win! All the others, you won after that...'

They both laugh. Gimondi shakes his head.

'That time trial in the Volta a Catalunya still burns. I still think about it now. At midnight, I was still down on the beach, the Playa de Rosas – walking up and down, up and down – trying to figure out how I'd lost. Because it was the first time that you'd beaten me in a time trial...'

'I'd broken my wheel. I broke two spokes. I had to change a wheel.'

'You? In that one, too? *Merda*, I didn't know that...Anyway, it took me two years to swallow what happened that day and finally understand why he'd beaten me.' Gimondi stops and points to Merckx. 'He just was stronger.'

'But do you remember the war we had in that Volta a Catalunya?' Gimondi continues. 'This huge battle, knives out in every stage. One day, I had a problem after five or six kilometres, and on they all went, into battle. The next day, you had a problem, and off we all went. The jersey went back and forth two or three times that week. And then, in the end, as always, you won.'

And with that, Merckx gets up from his chair, without warning or a word, walks away and the interview continues with its main subject matter no longer present.

'*Dino! Dino!*'

Another former Salvarani rider, Dino Zandegù, is shuffling down the mountain and towards us wearing a dark blue raincoat and a smirk. It's now gone four in the afternoon; by his own estimates, that means 90 per cent of what he's about to tell us is going to be true.

*

Dino, Dino, tell us about Merckx. When you finally realised what you were up against, I mean after 1967, what was it like, racing against him?

'He came at us from every angle, slaughtered every one of us, like some rabid wild man, some barbarian. He could have been the greatest footballer, the greatest skier, the greatest boxer of all time, only he chose cycling. But Merckx also had this great drama in his life: he couldn't stand, couldn't tolerate losing. And it was a real drama for him.'

And a drama for you and the rest of 'em, eh, Dino?

'Oh, he used to drive me nuts. When he was racing, you knew that he could put you out of the time limit any time. It was a constant, breathless chase. You'd see Merckx's team on the front ready to make the race 150 kilometres from the finish, Van Den Bossche, Van Den this, Van Ben that – they all surged to the front – and he'd be pawing the ground like this big tiger. He couldn't wait for the moment, kilometre X, when he would attack and smash us all to pieces. I used to tell him to go stuff himself. When you're hurting, you turn nasty. I'd be shouting from the back of the bunch, *"Vaffanculo, Merckx! Bastardo!"* Half of the peloton detested him despite thinking that he was an OK bloke.'

But you got on well with him too, eh, Dino? He had a sense of humour. You used to sing for him…

'"O Dolce Paese", that was his favourite. We used to talk, you know, at the criterium races. We'd get there and eat three hours before, then the crit would start at eight and at ten we'd all be together in a restaurant again. After one of these crits, we'd maybe had a drink or two and Eddy started telling me to sing him this song he'd heard in Friuli one time, which he'd loved, this "O Dolce Paese". I sang it that night, and every time I saw him after that, it was *"Dino, Dino, sing me that song, that 'O Dolce Paese'!"*. I said, "Merckx, who do you think I am? Father Christmas?" But because he was even more important than that, because he was Merckx, I always sang.'

5
new world order

Two days before the 2011 Giro stage to Macugnaga, another mountain-top finish, this one at the Nevegal ski resort near Belluno, throws up another brief encounter with shrill echoes of 1968.

After all these years, *Il Processo alla Tappa*, the post-stage review show enlivened by Dino Zandegù's singing in the sixties, is still going strong, and this year acquires extra gravitas thanks to Merckx. Every day for a week he sits on the stage, drowning in blandishments from the female presenter and dispensing his nuggets of insight and anecdotes. At Nevegal, though, he isn't the only guest and former rider introduced as a 'Belgian legend'. The other man is leaner, darker and noticeably younger. His facial features are smaller and neater. He also speaks good Italian. He is also smartly dressed. His young, blonde, gazelle-like wife, perhaps in her late 30s, and their son Eddy, watch from offstage.

He is Roger de Vlaeminck.

One day in May 1968, Merckx headed out for a pre-Giro training ride with a few of his teammates, and decided to drop in on the amateur Tour of Belgium. His influence was already such that he and manager Jean Van Buggenhout had largely taken charge of the Faema team's recruitment for the following season, and there was a young lad from West Flanders about whom Merckx was hearing great things. Spotting De Vlaeminck among the 18- and 19-year-olds making their last-minute adjustments and preparations before the start, Merckx climbed off his bike and ambled towards him. They shook hands. The conversation, as usual with Merckx, was brief and to the point: what would De Vlaeminck say to riding with Merckx at Faema the following season?

The response was instantaneous, unequivocal and unexpected.

'No. I don't want to ride with you. I want to ride against you.'

De Vlaeminck went on to win the race, and the significance of his words became apparent within a few months. The same would be true of the Merckx camp's efforts to reinforce Faema with another headstrong personality ahead of the 1969 season. At the Giro, with Merckx irrepressible, Van Bug had begun discussions with Guillaume 'Lomme' Driessens about joining Faema as a directeur sportif the following year. On first impressions, they had much in common: both were in their 50s, they were imposing in words, actions and physique, and both were considered big beasts, two of the kings of the Belgian cycling jungle. 'The difference between them,' says Marino Vigna, the Italian Faema directeur who would soon be Driessens's colleague, 'was that one was underrated, the other overrated.'

Van Bug's confidence in Driessens is interesting for what it says about how he regarded Merckx who, having turned 23 the week after the '68 Giro, was now his prize asset. If, early in 1967, there was a raft of other riders with their sights on domination, it had been definitively capsized and any doubts forgotten. As the 1968 season ended, this left Merckx exactly where he wanted to be in his life and career, yet also exactly where he was at his most uncomfortable: with the spotlight of his homeland and, increasingly, the rest of Europe, sting-ing his eyes. In a sense, he straddled the worst of all worlds: he was a Belgian, but a Belgian from bilingual Brussels, and therefore the public property of both French-speaking Wallonia in the south and cycling-crazy, Dutch-speaking Flanders in the north; he was excelling in a sport whose popularity owed in part, and still owes today, to a physical *proximity* to its people, whether they were fans at the road-side or journalists at races. Team press officers didn't yet exist, and this meant unbridled access, or intrusion, for reporters who would think nothing of knocking on his hotel-room door and demanding an interview. There was no top-secret compound in which to train, and the biggest star in Belgium could be witnessed at work on any morning when he wasn't racing. All an assiduous fan had to do was camp outside the spacious but hardly palatial four-bedroom house that Merckx bought with Claudine after their wedding. On the stroke of nine, come rain or, more seldom in Belgium, shine, the garage door would tilt open and Merckx would emerge.

As soon as pedals and wheels were turning, of course, Merckx was into his bubble. The faster he rode, the freer he felt. As the Italian Ferretti team's directeur sportif at the time, Alfredo Martini, puts it, 'This is the guy who said that, when he rode slowly, his legs hurt. The faster he rode, the better they felt.'

In front of cameras, microphones and notebooks, it was another story. These he didn't have the talents or the training to outrun or outride. 'He had no idea at all how he was supposed to conduct himself in the new situation,' one of the journalists closest to Merckx at the time, the late Robert Janssens, told Rik Vanwalleghem in *Eddy Merckx – De Mens achter de Kannibaal.* 'He was overwhelmed by it. He couldn't understand quite why he needed to give answers to the more diverse questions. He would have liked to have a good chat, but simply couldn't. His middle-class upbringing had taught him to do what was asked by his environment. But his nature was in direct conflict with his intent. He was not very well disposed verbally, he didn't read much, and he used few words to express himself. Moreover, he didn't really read the press.'

These were gripes, or observations, that would temper the media's admiration for Merckx throughout his career. The impression he gave was of seeing interviews not as an annoyance but certainly a distraction from the main business of racing, training or at least thinking about one or both. The issue was exacerbated by the fact that he hated to offend; hence, while he would rarely refuse an interview, out of simple politeness, he was incapable of offering reporters the incendiary or even insightful quotes that could have made him their darling.

To all of this was added another problem: while hailing from Brussels guaranteed interest and claims of ownership from both the French and Flemish-speaking halves of Belgium, it also placed Merckx in a state of linguistic limbo. The Merckx family had moved to Woluwe-Saint-Pierre in the south-east of Brussels when Eddy was one, attracted, like many, by the increased opportunities for employment. As well as being a born introvert, Eddy's father, Jules, didn't speak a word of French, while his mother Jenny's was competent if not quite fluent. The Merckxes were by no means the only predominantly Dutch-speaking family in the neighbourhood, but French was becoming more and more prevalent. The reason was that, since the Second World War during which many of the Flemish provinces had sided with the Nazis, speaking Dutch had been regarded if not as a badge of dishonour, then certainly as the least preferable option when language was a choice. French, on the other hand, could be an instant step up the social ladder.

Now, having grown up in a Dutch-speaking household, in a mostly French-speaking neighbourhood, and living with a Francophile wife, Merckx often just sounded confused. Even today, over forty years later, he admits that there are gaping holes in both of his vocabularies, French and Dutch.

Van Bug, then, was perhaps right to think that Merckx needed help. Where he had made a grave error was in enlisting Guillaume 'Lomme' Driessens to be a directeur sportif who was also a spin doctor – a brilliant motivator who all too often behaved like a hired thug.

Merckx disliked him instantly. At the 1967 Giro, Driessens had taken the trouble or liberty to point out his tactical errors on an almost daily basis, despite the fact that Merckx was riding for an opposing team. He had then told a journalist in private that the youngster would never measure up to Rik Van Looy. Driessens, of course, had quickly forgotten this when he finally joined Faema a year and a half later.

'I wasn't made to get on well for long with Guillaume Driessens,' Merckx wrote in *Coureur Cycliste, Un Homme et Son Métier* in 1974. 'His volubility and his sly way of talking just didn't fit my character. I often wondered, for example, why he always tried to keep the journalists away from me, telling them I didn't want to see them, when it was all coming exclusively from him. It was because of him that people started saying I was an unpleasant character. "Merckx is impossible – he couldn't be any less cooperative," the journalists who didn't know me well used to say, and they were right.'

If they weren't obvious before, Merckx's true feelings about Driessens weren't too difficult to decipher when his old directeur died at the age of 94 in 2006. 'When I heard of his death, my first reflex was to wish everyone could live as long as he did...Without any ambiguity, I would say that we weren't friends. He was forced upon me at an important time in my career. I tolerated him but we didn't have the same vision of cycling.'

That vision, Merckx discovered quickly in 1969, was to his mind a toxic mix of bluster, bullying and deception, but also the charisma and motivational capacities that seemed, in Van Bug's eyes, to make Driessens and Merckx a Belgian dream team. 'Cycling's Napoleon', as some had christened Driessens, had traded for years on his supposedly close association with the Italian *campionissimo* Fausto Coppi, whom he had met when Coppi came to Belgium on a hunting expedition in the late 1940s. To listen to Driessens, one would have been forgiven for thinking that he was the man who discovered Coppi, made him a world-beater, and masterminded every one of his legendary exploits. Boasts like these made it easy to see how he had earned another, even less flattering moniker : '*Guillaume le menteur*' or 'William the Liar'.

One rider Driessens had certainly been close to was Van Looy. Their partnership, though, had ended badly at the end of 1953, whereupon Driessens joined the rival Romeo-Smiths team and quickly exhibited another unsavoury characteristic – his quenchless thirst for revenge. 'Let's see what Van Looy's worth without me,' had been Driessens's sniffy parting shot from Van Looy's GBC team. For the next three or four years, as if the emerging generation spearheaded by Eddy Merckx wasn't enough to deal with, Van Looy had to cope with constant efforts by Driessens to undermine and frustrate him. 'Lomme the Liar's' favourite tactic was the one later employed, probably not coincidentally, by Van Looy against Merckx: stick to the stronger man, mark him, taunt him and under no circumstances help him, until finally either his legs or his nerve gave way. When it worked, as when Guido Reybrouck sucked like a leech on Van Looy's back wheel en route to Ax-les-Termes in the 1965 Tour de France, then beat him in a sprint, Driessens was insufferable. And when it didn't, Driessens was also insufferable. At the 1968 Giro, his Romeo-Smiths riders' abject performances prompted a withering tirade and, eventually, Driessens's departure for Faema. 'The way things are going, you'll all soon be back working in factories! I'm a directeur sportif and I want to be following races, not funerals!' Driessens ranted.

It was somehow apt that Driessens should mention funerals. In the 1948 Tour of Switzerland, then working as a masseur for Mondia, he had been sitting in the back of a team car that ran over and killed the Belgian rider Richard Depoorter. Driessens's contradictory statement in court and his fainting attack during cross-examination were typical of the antics Merckx could later expect at Faema. The driver of the car, the Mondia directeur Louis Hanssens, was convicted of causing Depoorter's death in 1957.

In football in the 1970s, the phoney war between two managers, Brian Clough and Don Revie, would grip the English public, but by that time Driessens had already served up an uncanny cross-breed of their most distinctive traits. Before his time in cycling, Driessens had also been a football manager, for the modest Vilvoorde in the northern suburbs of Brussels. To the same round face and frame as Revie, the same thick jaw and hooded eyes, and a similar reputation for dirty tricks and skulduggery, Driessens somehow added Clough's gift for the gab and his even bigger gift for self-aggrandisement. 'Driessens was an egomaniac of the first order,' confirms the journalist Walter Pauli. Another writer, the erstwhile *Tuttosport* cycling correspondent Gianpaolo Ormezzano, agrees that the same attributes which made Driessens poorly suited to Merckx also made him incompatible with the other top dog at Faema, Vincenzo Giacotto. 'Giacotto and Driessens were at the antipodes,' Ormezzano says. 'Vincenzo was a paragon of civility, Driessens more like a bandit.

Vincenzo was a bourgeois from Piedmont, Driessens was a peasant from Flanders...'

Observing from the outside, one of Merckx's main rivals in the Classics, Walter Godefroot, could see why Van Bug had brought Driessens in, but also why it wouldn't be plain sailing with 'Lomme the Liar'.

'Driessens was one of the best motivators, no, I think the best motivator in cycling at that time. But it doesn't work for some people,' Godefroot says. 'It works with Van Looy for a while but not with Merckx. Van Looy likes him because sponsors like him so he brings in a lot of money, but cycling at this time is changing. It's becoming more modern, more structured, and Driessens isn't an organiser. What he is, is an incredible motivator. That's why Van Buggenhout told Merckx to take Driessens: it was better having him on your side than against you. Driessens is very smart, plus he can talk himself out of any situation: if you kick him out of the front door, five minutes later he'll be climbing through the back window. When he wants something, he does everything to get it. I mean, when you were on top of your game, Driessens was great. If I'd have had him in my peak years I would have won more races... So he's great if you follow him blindly, but if you can think independently about bike-racing, which Eddy already could, it's not going to work.'

Godefroot pauses to search for the right analogy.

'Driessens is like...he's like the husband who comes home and asks his wife what's for dinner, and what time it will be on the table. At first she keeps doing what he says, but after a while, a wife with character tells the husband to sod off.'

Any expectation that Lomme Driessens had of being the 'star' at Faema evaporated about as soon as Godefroot et al.'s hopes of somehow getting the measure of Merckx in 1969.

At the beginning of the '69 season, Adorni had left for Scic, Driessens was in the Faema team car, but otherwise it was as you were – only with Merckx's supremacy growing exponentially. By the end of 1968, he had raced 129 times since the start of the year and won on 32 occasions, including the prestigious Italian semi-Classic the Tre Valli Varesine in August. It was getting to the point where all that seemed to matter in international bike racing now was whether or not Merckx was competing and, if he was, how or by what margin he would win. At the Spanish Vuelta a Levante in the first week of March 1969, he won three out of seven stages and the general classification. At Paris–Nice, the haul was identical: three stage wins and the overall title. In the final stage, the traditional last-day time trial up the Col de la Turbie above Nice, an estimated 50,000 fans witnessed a poignant changing of the guard. Once unassailable against the clock, the 35-year-old Jacques Anquetil heard the lethal drum of Merckx at his back as the crowd thickened 250 metres from the line. Anquetil had started a minute and a half before Merckx, but was now overtaken. Depending on your vantage point, it was either a fitting abdication to the new king or the grisly execution of someone who could and probably should have bowed out sooner. Merckx, incidentally, suspected the latter and told himself that he would never make the same mistake.

Sparing in his plaudits until then, Anquetil finally had the decency to recognise Merckx's true merit. Master Jacques now called Merckx the greatest, most complete rider that he had ever seen.

In many pundits' eyes, if that assessment demanded further accreditation, it came at Milan–San Remo a few days later. Again, more impressive than the victory per se, was the manner in which Merckx achieved it, breaking with the sequence of his sprint wins in 1966 and '67 to attack alone on the descent of the Poggio. Not only had he turned a weakness, his descending, into a strength, it now appeared that Merckx was merely enacting the races that he had already ridden and no doubt dominated in his own head. Before San Remo, he had asked his Milanese mechanic and framebuilder Mario Milesi for a bike four centimetres shorter than his normal steed expressly for the two-kilometre plunge off the Poggio hill. The plan had worked so beautifully that Merckx had ample time to raise both arms in celebration on the Via Roma – a gesture that led one wag in the Belgian press pack to inform Merckx that he had just broken article 196 of the Belgian Cycling Federation rulebook stating that both hands must be kept on the handlebars when a rider crossed the finish line. Merckx's response – 'It's worth paying the 200-franc fine to say that I can win' – was substantially less newsworthy than his claim that it had been a race 'without any difficulties' except for a brief scare when he struck a kerbstone with his leg at the foot of the Poggio and momentarily considered pulling out.

Amid talk in Italy that he already bore comparison with *campionissimo* Coppi, Merckx flew home to Brussels, where a large group of fans was waiting to greet him at the airport. An even larger one would of course be in Gent two weeks later for the start of the Tour of Flanders, Belgium's cup final, and one of a shrinking number of Classic races that Merckx had not yet won.

The days when Rik Van Looy's Red Guard could tease and toy with the peloton were long gone, but the old Emperor had suggested there might be life in him yet with a victory over Merckx at the E3 Harelbeke semi-Classic.

A week later, it was Merckx's turn to read a Flemish newspaper, specifically *Het Nieuwsblad*, and shake his head. Merckx, the newspaper's preview of the Tour of Flanders suggested, may not have the requisite qualities to ever win the Ronde. Merckx had triumphed before on flatter courses, hillier ones, in harder Classics, and easier ones, so the logic was hard to fathom. 'We'll see about that,' Merckx mumbled as he read aloud to his soigneur Guillaume Michiels. A few hours later, Hoban recalls, Merckx sparkled on the cobbles and hills, in the cold and rain of Flanders.

'By that point there were no tactics: everyone knew that it was just a case of following Merckx for as long as possible. In that Tour of Flanders he killed us off in stages. After his first attack, there were thirty of us left, and I thought I'd pick up some pocket money by sprinting for the primes [cash prizes] at the top of the climbs. On the Kwaremont, he hammered all the way on the front, and I just about managed to hang on for grim death and nip round him at the top. On the Kruisberg, the same. But then we got to the Kapelmuur and you could see that he was ready for the *coup de grâce*. He went up like a man possessed. I got to the top a few seconds behind, with Bitossi and Gimondi. "*On y va*" – "Let's go", I said to Bitossi…but, a few kilometres later, Eddy was already gone, and we knew by then that Merckx wasn't going to wait. Even with seventy kilometres to go.'

Not that Hoban or anyone else realised it, but there was one man capable of troubling Merckx on his procession towards Gent: Lomme Driessens. Merckx had charged clear like a bull, head low over the handlebars, nostrils flaring, steam rising from his throbbing ribcage, but now he slowed as Driessens drew alongside him in the Faema team car.

'*Verdomme*, Eddy! What do you think you're doing?! Committing suicide?! Are you crazy? There are 70 kilometres to go!'

Dino Zandegù was right when he said that a hurting rider is a nasty rider, and there could be no more unwelcome intruder than Driessens into the privacy of Merckx's pain. 'Go stuff yourself!' he told Driessens – and went on to ride the last 70 kilometres as though

Merckx's jubilation after winning the amateur World Championship road race in Sallanches in the French Alps in 1964. He was 19 at the time.

© POPPERFOTO/GETTY

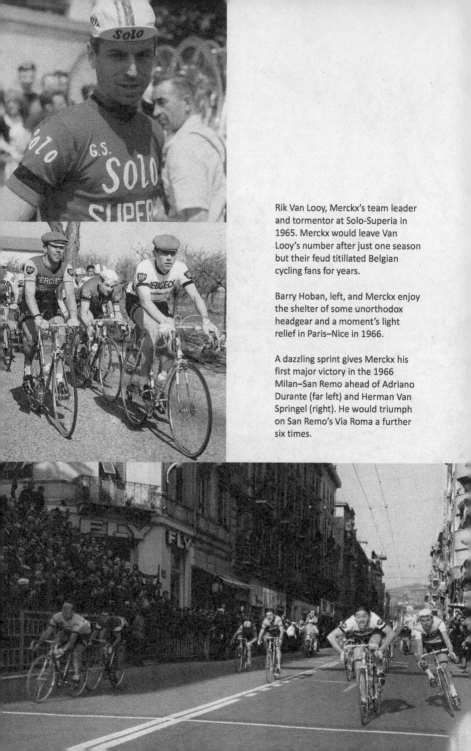

Rik Van Looy, Merckx's team leader and tormentor at Solo-Superia in 1965. Merckx would leave Van Looy's number after just one season but their feud titillated Belgian cycling fans for years.

Barry Hoban, left, and Merckx enjoy the shelter of some unorthodox headgear and a moment's light relief in Paris–Nice in 1966.

A dazzling sprint gives Merckx his first major victory in the 1966 Milan–San Remo ahead of Adriano Durante (far left) and Herman Van Springel (right). He would triumph on San Remo's Via Roma a further six times.

Riding alongside the Italian 'King of Cool' Gianni Motta on his way to victory in the 1966 Milan–San Remo. At this stage in their careers, the smart money was still on Motta becoming a dominant force in major stage races.

Merckx's inexperience caused the crash that ended his first Tour of Flanders in 1966. Barry Hoban escaped with the distinct impression that the Belgian wunderkind still had much to learn.

Merckx wins in a blizzard on the Tre Cime di Lavaredo in the 1968 Giro. It was, Merckx has claimed ever since, his greatest victory in the mountains of a major tour.

From left to right, Felice Gimondi, Merckx and Vittorio Adorni soak up the applause on the final Giro podium in Naples in 1968.

Merckx with his wife Claudine, who he had married the previous December, after his first victory in Paris-Roubaix in April 1968.

'Merckx, you're the strongest' says the banner on the Via Roma. No one could have argued otherwise by the spring of 1969.

Merckx is the first rider on the start ramp in his first Tour de France in 1969. He would go on to win the Tour by just under 18 minutes and take all four prize jerseys.

Hostility towards Merckx would take a while to infect the French public – and even longer to blunt the enthusiasm of schoolchildren like these ones awaiting the arrival of the 1969 Tour.

Showing the first signs of strain near the top of the Aubisque on his way to maybe his most famous Tour de France stage win in Mourenx in 1969.

'Cycling's Napoleon', directeur sportif Lomme Driessens, muscles in on the lap of honour around the Cipale velodrome at the end of the '69 Tour, riding the special yellow street bike he'd had prepared for the occasion.

Merckx lies unconscious in the middle of the Pierre Tessier velodrome in Blois after the crash that killed his derny rider Fernand Wambst in September 1969.

an imaginary red rag hung from the peak of his Faema cap. His final victory margin was five minutes and 36 seconds over Gimondi, who had finished second to win the race of the mere mortals.

Driessens's histrionics were not over. Under the podium, 'Cycling's Napoleon' proceeded to hold forth about how Merckx's attack had been a tactical masterstroke, Driessens's very own Waterloo. When he read the quotes in the following day's papers, Merckx was furious. The reality, which everyone in the peloton now acknowledged, was that cycling was turning into an Eddy Merckx biopic, and all besides the lead character were extras.

There were still defeats, near misses like at Paris–Roubaix the week after Flanders, but even they now came with caveats. These could then somehow be tweaked into further evidence for Merckx's genius. He had been suffering with a knee injury at Roubaix, yet *still* been beaten only by Walter Godefroot? The other Belgians were so afraid of him at Flèche Wallonne that they formed an anti-Merckx coalition? After that race, he had spent the evening with his mechanic, and the next morning with his doctor, because *something* must have been amiss for him to lose? Some efforts to shoehorn any race outcome into the now accepted canon of his invulnerability were risible. After Paris–Roubaix, one Italian newspaper suggested that Merckx would be 'relieved to have abandoned the excessive weight of his invincibility'. In Belgium, meanwhile, his same po-faced omnipotence was more sensibly held up as the reason for Van Looy still being the more popular rider.

If losing was what it took to relieve and ingratiate himself, Merckx was about to fail again at Liège–Bastogne–Liège, the hilliest, the oldest and the toughest of the Belgian Classics. Once more, Barry Hoban was among the stranded admirers as this time Merckx opened the throttle on the Côte de Stockeu, 100 kilometres from the finish. Only one rider could stay with him – his Faema teammate Vic Van Schil, he of the ham-fisted attempts to escape a dope test at the 1968 Giro. Merckx now seemed omnipresent, subliminal; even when he wasn't nearby, his influence was. In the wooded hills of the Ardennes, as much as a drubbing, it felt to Hoban like a haunting. 'I was chasing with Herman Van Springel, Gimondi and Jos Huysmans, and I kept wondering why they weren't riding. Of course, I couldn't know at the time that Huysmans and Van Springel were future teammates of Merckx. Eventually I pulled over and the gap got huge. It was scary.'

The scary margin by the time Hoban crossed the line in third was just over eight minutes. The world's most famous boxer and possibly sportsman wasn't fighting in 1969, self-exiled from the Vietnam War and so ostracised from competition, but Hoban says that he had found a worthy substitute in Merckx. 'It was now like Muhammad Ali. Even if Merckx wasn't saying it like Ali did, you could tell he was thinking, "I'll take the man in the fifth round!" In other words, "I'll drop them all on the Côte de Stockeu and win by eight minutes." 'Basically,' Hoban concludes, 'he was doing exactly what he wanted.'

Before the end of a spring in which Merckx and Faema had flirted with perfection, there was still time for Lomme Driessens to underline yet again why he was often more of a liability than an asset. After his antics in Flanders, he had already angered Merckx by insisting that he rode the Tour of Majorca with a sore knee and the leftover symptoms of an intestinal virus. Everyone had seen the effect of that decision on Merckx's performance at Paris–Roubaix. In the Omloop der Vlaamse Gewesten in the last week of April, with Merckx's appetite momentarily sated by his Liège masterclass five days earlier, the Faema riders agreed that Merckx's old Madison partner Patrick

Sercu would get his chance to shine on the road. Sercu appeared to be doing just that when the other Faema man who had made it into the key move of the day, Julien Stevens, attacked two kilometres from home. Incensed, Sercu joined the chase which ended with Stevens being absorbed with 400 metres to go, and was so tired that he could only finish third in the sprint to the line. And provoke another Driessens diatribe...

'We spend all day working for you and you can't even win the sprint! You're only a track rider!'

'OK, that's fine, that's sorted: I won't race in your team next year,' Sercu snapped back.

Sercu says now that the exchange 'summed up Driessens'. 'If you didn't win, it was all the rider's fault and you were useless. If Eddy won, though, Driessens could have spent the afternoon napping in the car, but you'd still find him next to the podium at the finish, kissing Eddy and taking all the congratulations.'

Driessens apart, Faema was now turning into almost as formidable a force as its leader. Liège had been their most intimidating display yet. Hoban was not surprised, having ridden in the same team as Joseph Spruyt and Roger Swerts at Mercier in 1967, before they left for Faema. 'Merckx was never on his own,' Hoban says. 'His team was phenomenal, because he'd cherry-picked the best from other teams. He'd already rewritten the rulebook about bike-riding, long before people were going to South Africa and Australia for training camps. On Monday, Wednesday and Friday, they'd all meet at his place and they did 200 kilometres, rain or shine. Then in the race, the red and white jerseys would surge to the front and it'd be a battle just to hold the wheels. If you're going at 40 kilometres an hour, anyone can attack, but if you're going at 43 kilometres per hour it's not so easy. Now, Eddy's team could go at forty-five, forty-six. He controlled the race all day long. You never saw his teammates at the back of the bunch.'

Others, though, watched the Merckx platoon – Spruyt, Swerts and the Van Dens and Van Bens, which for Zandegù blurred into one hellish red mist – and marvelled. They were all now over-performing. Meanwhile, the opposite appeared to be true of Merckx's rivals. For all that it had been mooted during the '68 Giro, few really believed that Faema and their doctor had access to some secret rocket fuel, legal or not. Anquetil had, it's true, briefly set tongues wagging during the 1967 Giro by revealing that a French doctor was submitting him to daily 'super-ozone' injections in a mobile laboratory that followed him around Italy. The treatment supposedly eliminated toxins from the bloodstream and muscles, thereby aiding recovery. It wasn't banned – but neither was it healthy or very effective. With interest in Merckx so hysterical that one Flemish newspaper, *Het Laaste Nieuws*, was about to send 13 journalists to the 1969 Giro, it was also inconceivable that daily visits by Merckx to some itinerant ozone Tardis could have passed unnoticed. The same would have applied to a needle-wielding Svengali entering his hotel, particularly if there was no shame in what he was doing.

Steroid use was already rife in weight-lifting, and was undetectable in urine tests, but the dosage was fraught with risk and the side-effects ugly. The 1960 Tour de France winner Gastone Nencini had a terrible reputation for 'experimentation', notably with morphine and hormone injections. He had also had the same team doctor as Merckx – Enrico Peracino. But no one was making the connection or thought that Peracino had encouraged Nencini. In fact, an old story went that Nino Defilippis asked Peracino to inject him with a doping product before a time trial at the 1957 Tour de France, and Peracino threw the syringe back in his face. This left the old bric-a-brac of amphetamines and stimulants which could be used with impunity in training but were a dangerous option for someone winning and therefore being tested as often as Merckx, if not for his teammates. Other theories were of the crackpot variety, like specula-tion at the 1968 Giro about a mystery Mongolian plant extract. Either that or they relied solely on dubious, anecdotal evidence. One story went that Merckx had already been 'warned' about the results of his dope tests on multiple occasions. More plausible, because Peracino had admitted it in Nencini's day, was that the doctor used needles to inject legal vitamins and rehydration solutions which aided recovery.

In interviews, Merckx's statements were neither especially reas-suring nor incriminating. 'It's a shame, a real shame,' was all he had said about Gimondi and Motta's positive tests at the '68 Giro. His regular lieutenants Swerts, Van Schil and Reybrouck had all failed tests before 1969, as had Vittorio Adorni at the 1968 Giro di Sardegna – but then so had dozens of riders.

So, no, there must have been something else going on, some other phenomenon. One of the journalists closest to Merckx, the Walloon television reporter Théo Mathy, reckoned that it was a logi-cal aggregation of several factors. They were the disciplined example set by Merckx, the intensity of training sessions with him, plus the dual incentives of success and money, whether through better wages or cash prizes.

Merckx himself probably put it better years later in his *Coureur Cycliste, Un Homme et Son Métier*. Here, he went into detail about the ideal team composition, its blend of riders able to make the pace on the flat and 'police the bunch', and climbers like Martin Van Den Bossche who could 'toughen up the race'. None of this was new or ground-breaking, but there were many interesting and intelligent observations in the four pages he devoted to the topic. What emerged was a profound awareness not only of Merckx's teammates' worth to him, but also of his to them. The reason for Spruyt's, Swerts's and Van Schil's marked improvement since joining Faema was, Merckx wrote, 'the effect of emulation'. In a team that works, 'everyone takes pride in not falling below the standards of their neighbour', he went on.

Of course, they also had to be talented. Even today, the leggy climber Martin Van Den Bossche is half confused, half insulted that his 10th place overall in his first Tour de France in 1966 barely registered with the Belgian public. 'Nobody talked about it! Nobody talked about it! People had been spoiled by riders like Rik Van Looy and Rik van Steenbergen. The rest of us just didn't exist,' he laments. Asked, however, whether he didn't consider himself too good to sacrifice himself for another rider, in this case Merckx, Van Den Bossche immediately frowns and shakes his head. 'No! People would have laughed at the suggestion! The lead man was the lead man – and the lead man was Merckx.' The fact was that forsaking one's own ambitions also meant forsaking an awful lot of responsibility and pressure. Life on Merckx's team was straightforward. 'It wasn't a team of many words,' says Van Den Bossche. Literally and figuratively, on the bike and off it, 'keeping Merckx's head out of the wind, that was pretty much it,' he adds. With time, Van Den Bossche would come to feel that he and his teammates weren't only burying their egos and ambitions, but also their personalities in the name of the Merckx cause. For the time being, though, he suited the job, and it suited him fine.

What was interesting was how perceptions of Merckx and his band had changed in 1968 and early '69 and started to assume a harsh edge. Driessens's siege mentality hadn't helped, but really they were all a victim of Merckx's success and his rapacious hunger for more of the same. In the years from '66 to '68, he had been a 'budding star' then a 'young champion' and finally a '*campionissimo*'. Since the '68 Giro, from around the time of those boos in Brescia, the rhetoric had shifted to the point where Merckx was now 'unbeatable', a 'matador' or even 'a monster'. For many, he would soon be 'The Ogre of Tervuren' – the Brussels suburb bordering Woluwe-Saint-Pierre and Kraainem where he and Claudine now lived.

It wasn't Merckx's fault unless, as he said, the object of racing was no longer to win. Roger Bastide put the sniping in context in his *Eddy Merckx Cet Inconnu*, published in 1971. 'It'd be exactly like saying about Beethoven or Mozart: "He always wants to compose a *chef d'oeuvre!*"'

The difference in cycling was that only one masterpiece could be created at any one time, and by one person. Merckx was giving no one else a look-in. In the past, the custom of 'gifting' victories to other riders had arisen not from altruism but the knowledge that somewhere down the road, some day, the donor would need a wheel, some shelter, a favour or a contract himself. What some riders forgot was that this wasn't some sacred code or etiquette, but often a quite cynical mechanism of survival; Merckx was good enough not to rely on it and therefore felt no need to respect the protocol.

To this, of course, was added that 'real drama in his life' – his intolerance of losing or, more precisely, of not winning. Guillaume Michiels, his masseur-cum-confidant-cum-motorpacer on training rides, said that Merckx's patience had a time limit: after ten days without a win, he became fidgety, nervous, sometimes unbearably so. On average, he pinned on a race number about once every three days throughout the year, which meant that he had to win one of every three races to keep the gremlins at bay. A bad sleeper at the best of times, a winless week was enough to give him nightmares, or have him tip-toeing down to his garage to tinker with one of the 30-odd bikes, 300 tyres and 100 wheels that he kept there. After his first pro season, Merckx had bought one well-known mechanic's entire tool kit for 80,000 Belgian francs. Within hours of one Classics win, he would already be fretting about the next one, those melancholic eyes frozen in concentration as he twisted, tightened or gouged with screwdriver, spanner or allen key in hand.

Such perfectionism, again so alien to the carefree *sprezzatura* that geniuses were supposed to exhibit, but on closer inspection never did, was easy to confuse with ruthlessness. Decades later, Lance Armstrong would describe a Tour de France peloton thus: 'It is completely ghetto. Everybody looks at the other person and thinks that they're either trying to fuck them over or they're getting fucked.' On a practical level, despite all the mutual back-scratching, the politics and machinations of international cycling were such that the same conclusion was even harder to avoid in Merckx's era. He and his team not only had the strength to condemn any attack, and consequently a season or career; no one was accusing Merckx of being vindictive, certainly not yet, but he and Van Buggenhout could, in theory, dictate to any organiser of any of the lucrative, aforementioned criteriums. Upsetting Merckx or Van Bug raised the threat if not the real consequence of missing valuable paydays. The position of '*patron*' or boss of the peloton was a de facto one, and for Merckx it was involuntary. But it was his nonetheless.

'He wasn't a bully...but he was a Mafioso in one sense,' says Patrick Sercu. 'If Eddy said the first hundred kilometres had to be easy, they'd be easy. But you can only do this if you are the best. The strongest. The chiefs are always the strongest.'

At the end of his career, Merckx would bequeath his mantle to the Frenchman Bernard Hinault. The two had very different interpretations of the role of '*patron*', says Walter Godefroot.

'Hinault would turn up to criteriums and say, "Right, I win today." He was so intimidating that no one questioned it. Whereas Merckx wants to fight, he wants to beat everyone. Hinault is not interested in small races. But Merckx wants to win everything, for himself, for the public, for the organiser.'

It was no wonder that Merckx seemed to have mutated before everyone's eyes. The young fawn who had started the '68 Giro had grown horns – big spiky, ferocious-looking antlers – that he was now using to preserve the natural order. Whether he liked, wanted, knew it or not, he *was* a kind of Mafioso. He was the Godfather who in 1969 had come to life in Mario Puzo's novel. Merckx was Don Vito Corleone. It was no wonder, either, that his teammates had undergone the same transformation. Looking at photos of the anvil-jawed, sombre-eyed Joseph Spruyt, journalist Walter Pauli is now reminded of Don Vito's top killer Luca Brasi. 'Spruyt was the big henchman that Merckx would send to do his dirty work...' Pauli observes with a grin.

The other question that needed addressing was why Merckx's opponents were not inspired to emulate him, unlike his Faema teammates. The answer to that, too, was simple: since the summer of '68, that enemy of motivation, fatalism, had started to grip. They now all knew and had their seatbelts fastened for what would be a long and morale-sapping ride. Even Gimondi who, according to his teammate Ferretti 'never gave in, always fought', was eyeing up the path of least resistance. His loss to Merckx at the '68 Volta a Catalunya had been a bitter pill, but also one which had kick-started the process of letting go. It was painful but also, in a certain sense, liberating.

'It had been like banging my head against a wall,' Gimondi says. 'I did that for months, no, two years before I figured it out. Then the penny dropped. I put my ego to bed and started to become realistic.

I realised that I needed to adapt. I needed to change the way I rode. The first golden rule was – try not to take a beating, then maybe attack at the end. Whatever you did, you could never attack first, because he'd come looking for you, drop you and make you look like a fool.'

Gimondi shrugs.

'It was the hardest phase of my career – no longer thinking I could beat him at his own game, and realising that I had to adapt, beat him with my head, because it was no use trying with my legs. I had to change my style of racing completely, all because of Merckx.'

Others, too, seemed to have realised that the game was up. Walter Godefroot had turned pro with all guns blazing, determined to fight Merckx's fire with his own, but now the pair were increasingly friendly.

Another Belgian, Herman Van Springel, had finished second in the '68 Tour and the Worlds. He had also beaten Merckx in the Tour of Lombardy and the season-long SuperPrestige Pernod rankings. But not even Van Springel's *annus mirabilis* had raised his hopes.

His biographer Mark Uytterhoeven agrees. For Van Springel just like everyone else, the summer of 1968 had an air of *fin d'époque*. It had felt like an ending, not of their careers but of their excuses, yearnings and illusions – of everything, in short, that represented their youth. There was no need to kid anyone any more. Not themselves, not each other and not Merckx.

'Everyone knew that it had been thirty years since the last Belgian win, Syvère Maes's in 1939, and everyone knew that '69 would be Merckx's Tour, the Tour of the Belgian revenge,' Uytterhoeven says. 'Herman knew that '68 was his only chance. Everyone knew it. Even I as an eleven-year-old and a Van Springel fan knew it. I was quite sure.'

There was only one man in Belgium, says Uytterhoeven, who hadn't yet yielded to the evidence, and indeed never would. He was the man who had met Merckx at the amateur Tour of Belgium in 1968 and told him, albeit in more polite terms, to stick his offer of a contract for the following year somewhere even less sun-kissed than Flanders. He was the man who had been and still was a fervent supporter of Rik Van Looy. He was the man whose first professional race had been the coveted Omloop Het Volk in February 1969, and whose first win had been...the Omloop Het Volk in February 1969, with Merckx in 12th place. He was the man who would soon become the Belgian national champion, again well ahead of Merckx. He was the man we would see 42 years later on a mountaintop in Italy. He was Roger De Vlaeminck.

Before too long, another stubborn resistance fighter would step out of the cowering hordes. A Spanish *caballero* of hot blood, sultry visage and a smouldering, fanciful ambition: to beat Eddy Merckx.

For now, though, Merckx was on his own. And he would never feel more lonely than at the 1969 Giro d'Italia.

6
end of the world as we know it

'I don't understand anything. I didn't take anything.'

EDDY MERCKX

Of all the flowers, there were gladioli in reception, the symbols of moral integrity. Someone from Faema had handed them to the receptionist in the Hotel Excelsior the previous evening, and now there they were, poking pathetically out of a faux crystal vase like leftover, burnt-out candles.

On the first floor, in room 11, big Martin Van Den Bossche looked at his empty bed, then to the one at its left, where Merckx lay, sobbing uncontrollably. Fed up with the constant knocks at the door and interruptions to their morning routine, he had joked just a few minutes earlier to Merckx that the next person who disturbed them was 'going to get it'. When the Faema manager Vincenzo Giacotto pushed the door, Van Den Bossche had thrown a pillow that struck Giacotto in the face. The giggles had quickly subsided when Giacotto's stony expression didn't change.

What could Van Den Bossche say now? There was nothing. So he said almost nothing.

In any case, many more gifted linguists had now arrived in the room, like *La Gazzetta*'s Bruno Raschi, who had come with Giacotto. In a few hours, Raschi would pen one of his more unusual reports from a Giro stage. 'I can believe that they've found Merckx drugged, but I'm sure that someone put the dope in his broth,' will be his instinctive conclusion.

For now, Merckx himself is too upset to formulate a hypothesis. He can barely make out the silver microphone tended by RAI TV's Sergio Zavoli a few inches from his nose through the tears and his long lashes, and barely blubber a few words of faltering Italian. 'I don't know what to say. I don't understand anything. I'm sure I didn't take anything. Sure.'

Then more sobs.

If the words don't flow, the thoughts and memories must surely cascade. First, the previous day's stage to Savona, when, with an innocuous breakaway down the road, for once he'd cruised along in the middle on the pack, chatting to his former teammate Vittorio Adorni. It had felt like old times, and for a minute they'd forgotten the trials of the previous fortnight: the banners that Adorni had seen in the south – 'Adorni, think of Italy' and 'Adorni, become a Belgian citizen' – and their clear implication that he was riding so poorly because he was still riding for Merckx; Merckx's claim that he would have quit the race had a bottle thrown by a fan in Napoli on Stage 9 hit him and not missed by two centimetres; the grandstand that had collapsed in Terracina and crushed an 11-year-old boy who had gone to write about the Giro for a school project; the endless strikes and protests they had encountered on the route, about the cost of the race to hospitals, the state of the roads, wages in Napoli, and who knew what else. They had forgotten even about the fact that Merckx had won four stages and had the '69 Giro sewn up five days before the first real mountains. Then, two kilometres from Savona, a motor-bike had shunted the pink jersey from behind and all those nagging suspicions that someone or something was out to get him, that this Giro was cursed, had come rushing back.

Those images may then have segued into the last time he'd felt the world caving in, a few days after his World Championship win in Heerlen in 1967. Merckx had been in his parents' grocery store, a family friend had mentioned something about two positive tests from the Worlds, then a few hours later his mother had interrogated him. 'Come on, Mum! Don't tell me you're thinking that!' he had snapped. He perhaps also thought back to the times when he'd assured Jenny Merckx that he would never go near the stimulants for which other riders were testing positive. He said it again before the Giro, and they had even talked about how accepting bottles from fans at the roadside was a bad idea.

He peered again through the tears in his eyes and saw his friend Italo Zilioli, then felt the Italian's hand on his own. Zilioli was also crying. They both remembered when Zilioli had been in the same predicament a year earlier, and how Merckx had supported him. Zilioli looked around the room and saw genuine sympathy intermingling with crocodile tears.

Adorni, Bitossi and Gimondi had also entered the room. Gimondi had been here too, a year earlier, when he had taken the same substance that appeared to have triggered Merckx's positive test: fencamfamine. The substance itself was not banned but had similar effects, and caused similar 'spikes' in urine analyses, to amphetamines. 'I don't understand anything. I didn't take anything,' Merckx repeated.

Who knows, maybe Merckx thought back to a few evenings earlier, when a rider from another team had appeared at his door clutching a briefcase full of money. What would Merckx say to letting this one, you know Eddy, nudge nudge, slide by? He'd left disappointed – Merckx had a reputation for never selling races, and had told the rider, 'Just don't tell me how much is in the suitcase. That way I won't regret my decision later on.' But there were no hard feelings.

Maybe Merckx was so distraught – and he seemed it – that he wondered whether it was all worth it. Not just the Giro, but cycling in general. He could have thought back to the days when, aged four, he tore around the leafy suburban streets of Woluwe-Saint-Pierre on his bike and people shouted out, 'Are you riding the Tour de France, laddie?' That – 'Tour de France' – had soon become his nickname in the neighbourhood. At age eight, he had been given his first second-hand racing bike. Guillaume Michiels, who later became Merckx's masseur, and whose brother and mother used to help out in the Merckxes' shop, told the young Eddy that his backside was too fat for him to be a cyclist. Years later, when Merckx was selected to take part in the Olympic Games road race in Tokyo, he reminded Michiels, 'You said my backside was too fat...and now I'm going to the Olympic Games.'

That had been another injustice: Tokyo. The cramps in the last kilometre, Godefroot claiming that he would have won gold, not bronze if Merckx had helped him. But that all paled now. What would the newspapers write tomorrow? Would they interview Van Looy? What would he say? 'If you're really the greatest, you'll be able to do it on your own' – that was his favourite line in criteriums. Would tomorrow's remark be an even snider variation? Something like 'If he was the greatest, he could do it without drugs'?

The memories, the recriminations, the fears – were they all now swirling in vortexes, cogs spinning out of control in Merckx's head?

Perhaps he was praying, like he had at mass in the Duomo in Parma before yesterday's stage. He had arrived on his bike, parked it outside, then headed off in the direction of the stage start as soon as the service was over. As he did every day, he had then crossed himself before the race began.

More replays – of the test, that strange mobile cabin in the main *piazza* in Savona where it was carried out, flashes of things and people seen over the past few days: a waiter skulking near the door of the hotel room that Merckx and Van Den Bossche shared; the minutes that Merckx had left his bike – and water bottle with it – outside the Duomo; the odd jeer from the crowds in Parma, the home town of Gimondi's sponsor Salvarani; the fan who had leaped out of the crowd on Stage 11 to Scanno and grabbed his saddle – yet more evidence that he was *persona non grata*.

Maybe now the faces assembling in his imagination, as though in a jury box, were his family's – the twins brother Michel and sister Micheline, born four years after Eddy, mother Jenny and father Jules. This was all eerily like being transported 15 or 20 years, to one of Jules's tellings off. He always seemed to blame and vent his anger at Eddy, like the time when Michel threw a pair of scissors at his elder brother, and it was Eddy who got smacked. Once a suspicious-looking character had been spotted roaming the streets in Woluwe while Eddy was out with his friends, and when Eddy finally bundled through the door, Jules had given him such a row that a customer in the grocery store had complained. 'Madam, it's my family,' Mr Merckx had told her. This was the Jules Merckx that Patrick Sercu would get to know when he visited the Merckxes years later. Sercu saw 'a very strict man, like an army major, who never expected to say the same thing twice'. Michel thought that he could be like a tyrant. At least Jules practised what he preached: hard work and respect of the rules. Eddy had inherited his anxiousness, his rigour, his fairness and his introversion. Both were good with their hands – Jules at DIY, Eddy when it came to tinkering with bicycles. Jules had also played football and been a decent runner in his youth. Physically, there was little resemblance except for the eyes and the slim, athletic frame. The hair, the facial profile, they both came from Jenny.

Again, that scene in the grocery shop in 1967: if he had cheated, what would Jenny say to him? On any other day, he could think about the grief he caused her when he was a kid and laugh. On his seventh or eighth birthday, he couldn't remember which, he had gone to the hairdressers, not much cared for the result, and declared that he wouldn't leave until the barber shaved off everything. For some reason, he had wanted to look just like the convicts he'd seen working on the drains in Woluwe. The barber had finally obliged, and when Eddy arrived home, Jenny cried, and Jules applied a clip around the ears.

As with many couples, Jenny and Jules had been opposites in so many respects, but united in their core values. Théo Mathy, the TV journalist, said that Eddy was 'his dad on a bike, and his mother in everyday life'. Jenny was warm, invariably smiling in photographs, yet also as safe and sensible. Merckx had heard the stories about his birth: he had been overdue and the family doctor had arrived at his grandmother's farm in Meensel-Kiezegem, an unremarkable Brabant village encircled by dreary fields, in the nick of time. Even in the womb, Eddy was already proving a stubborn customer, and the doctor had reached for the forceps to pull him out. He still bore two faint scars on his forehead.

What would Jenny say to him now? And Jules? It wouldn't be difficult to imagine what his father thought of drugs. Cigarettes were bad enough – if not for him then at least for his children, and he barely touched alcohol. Merckx remembered the time he'd been caught puffing on a Zemir. His dad had hauled him in front of the mirror and said that he looked 'as white as a piece of stale cheese'. Then came the obligatory clout.

Eddy was always up to mischief, most of the time outside the Merckx family's store in the Place des Bouvreuils or in the park in Woluwe, where the ponds were fantastic for finding frogs and tadpoles. At school, the teachers would see his attention wandering or his chair shuffling towards the window and the noise coming from the street. Even when he played cards, he would want to play in the open air. About the only time he could bear to be indoors was for rare games of billiards in the Cheval Blanc Inn next to the grocery store. When, as they often did, Jules and Jenny asked him to lend a hand in the shop, it went without saying that he'd always be happier doing the bread deliveries than stacking shelves.

'It doesn't matter what you do, as long as you do it well,' Jenny always used to say; if he had learned anything from his parents, it was that hard work would always be rewarded. That, whatever his detractors said, explained his success until Giacotto and Raschi had appeared in the room Merckx was already pulling the braces of his bib shorts over his shoulders. In the time it took Giacotto to utter that sentence, everything had been tarnished for ever. The sound of Merckx ripping off his gloves as the first tear rolled down his cheek had made Giacotto flinch.

All he'd ever wanted to do was this – ride his bike. From before he knew it, when Stan Ockers was finishing second in the Tour de France in 1950 and 1952, and certainly when Ockers did the Ardennes 'double' in 1955, before Eddy's tenth birthday. The next autumn, Ockers had died in a crash on the track in Antwerp, aged 36. Eddy was inconsolable when one of his friends broke the news as they walked to school.

At the time he was still playing football, tennis and basketball, and showing promise in all three. After one football match in which he'd scored a double hat-trick, when he was eight or nine, the coach of his team, White Star, had asked him to stay behind after the other kids. 'Well played. Here you go,' he said, handing over a large pile of official club kit as a reward for Eddy's Man of the Match performance. So why hadn't he stuck at it? Why the obsession with cycling and not another sport? No one knew, because it didn't run in the family, and the residents of Woluwe were a little too bourgeois for such a low-brow sport to have any traction there. The best cyclists were sons of factory workers, miners, not social climbers like the Merckxes had become. Sure, everyone listened to the Tour de France on the radio in summer, and everyone had heard of Rik Van Looy, but that was as far as it went. This wasn't Flanders. For years Eddy didn't even know what the Classics were because he spent Sundays with his grandmother on the farm where he'd been born in Meensel-Kiezegem. His obsession had been and, even now, still remained the Tour de France.

The Tour...Would he even ride it now? Only this morning, perhaps a little complacently, his thoughts had skipped ahead to June and how he would prepare for his first crack at the big one. 'I already feel like I'm in training. I've already established my programme for between the two tours. I'm going to race nine times, then I'll be ready for the Tour,' he had told a journalist. Those comments now seemed as pitiful as the flowers wilting downstairs. The sanction for a positive test was a one-month ban. The test had taken place on

1 June, today was 2 June, and the Grande Boucle would begin in Roubaix on 28 June.

Maybe, back home in Woluwe, the same people who had called him 'Tour de France' as a kid would be remembering the times when they told him that cycling wasn't a career. He hadn't stood out in his very first races, that much was true. Before the first, unofficial one when he was 12, his only 'training' had been mucking about with his mates and riding to school up the steep incline of the Avenue du Kouter. Then, one weekend in Meenzel-Kiezegem, he had tagged along in a race for unlicensed riders and been lapped several times. Two years later, Jules rigged up a TV for the road race at the Rome Olympics and Eddy watched, transfixed. A Soviet, Viktor Kapitonov, won and Eddy swooned at the white jersey adorned with the five Olympic rings that they gave him on the podium. 'The next Olympics are in Tokyo in four years. I'd better hurry up,' he said aloud. Then, in July 1961, Jenny had gone off on holiday to Middelkerke on the north coast with the twins, and Eddy had mysteriously asked to stay behind to help his father in the grocery store; Jenny discovered later, and wasn't particularly amused, that he had an ulterior motive – his first official race. It had taken place in Laeken, and Eddy finished sixth of 33 riders, on the same afternoon that Jacques Anquetil rode into Paris as a Tour de France winner for a second time. Eddy had raced 11 more times between then and 1 October, the date of his first victory. That had come in Lettelingen, appropriately, a few hundred metres from the Flanders–Wallonia border. He wore a black leather skullcap and shorts that barely skimmed his thighs.

In 1961 he had ridden 14 races, the next season it would be 55. At school he was so distracted that his grades had dipped from an already low baseline. He had failed in every subject (including the

Latin in which, according to one paper, he was suddenly fluent at Milan–San Remo in '66) and had to repeat the year. Jenny despaired. Sometimes she cried. Eddy saw her and worried – but he knew what he was doing. He knew that a future in professional cycling was now not only a dream but a compulsion. In the winter of 1961, now aged 16, he had gone training one Sunday with Michiels, the professionals Emile Daems and Willy Vannisten and a couple of other strong, local riders, and Daems had struggled to hold Eddy's wheel when they all sprinted to the top of a cobbled climb. In the classroom, things continued to deteriorate, until on the day before the 1962 Easter holidays, Merckx was sent to see the headmaster about an unfinished essay. 'Have it done on the first day back or there won't be a second,' he was told. That had made up his mind; now he just had to persuade his parents. As strict as he always was, Jules loved seeing Eddy succeed, and had given his blessing to him racing in Halle on 1 May. Now Eddy went to see his mum. 'If it really upsets you that much, I'll stop riding my bike and concentrate on school. But I'd like to become a cyclist,' he said.

'There are thousands of cyclists, but only Rik Van Steenbergen and Rik Van Looy make decent money…' she replied, feigning some knowledge of the subject. 'But if that's your decision, you'll get our support. Just think of what I've said to you today when you're racing,' she said finally.

On the evening of 1 June, Jules called from Halle to tell her that Eddy had won the race…by over four minutes. His prize was 400 Belgian francs for coming first and 450 in the bonus sprints. Two months later, on a wet day in Libramont, he became the Belgian national junior champion and all doubts in everyone's mind had been, if not totally erased, then at least suspended for the time being.

The headmaster's offer to postpone his exams until September if he returned to school was politely declined.

On another day at around this time he had turned up to a race, seen a fellow competitor looking him scornfully up and down, and heard: 'Hey, little kid, you've got no chance here. Didn't you know? *Le grand Eddy Merckx* is riding today.' Being admired felt good, but not as good as winning. The morning after that first ever win in Lettelingen, he had opened his eyes, seen his mother in the room, and beamed. 'Oh, Mum, winning is such a great feeling,' he said.

Le grand Eddy Merckx. That's what everyone had been calling him for a couple of years now, but he'd soon see whether they changed their tune in the next few hours. The Giro would be leaving Savona, the journalists would go with it, and then what? Giacotto was already talking about second opinions, getting some tests done at some Medical Institute in Milan. They might bring some clarity, but by then it'd be too late, at least for this Giro. Faema had even organised the inauguration of their new factory in Zingonia around the Giro's arrival there in two days' time. Some party that would now be. Giacotto was talking about the whole team, minus Merckx, flying home from Milan's Linate airport tonight. Meanwhile Gimondi had said he wouldn't wear the pink jersey, out of respect. That was a nice gesture. The *maglia rosa* that should have been in the peloton today, the one belonging to Merckx and with Faema stitched on the breast, was draped over the bedside table, destined never to be worn.

Merckx looked up now and saw Claudine and the Faema vice president Paolo Valente shuffle through the door. He embraced her. She had arrived at the race two days earlier, on the rest day in Cesenatico. Together with Van Bug, she was the one who always stepped in when Eddy was in above his head, when he wanted to say 'yes' to everyone, but, really, for his own sake, ought to have told them 'no'. Had he read that bizarre article in the *Corriere della Sera* a few days ago which said that Claudine 'managed his career'? Unlikely – he seldom read papers, books or magazines. He knew that it was bad, that he ought to make more effort, that he'd maybe have more to say in interviews, but the urge just wasn't there.

There was a cyclone in his head, and now every weakness, every character flaw was blowing up in front of his face. He knew that he could be selfish, even self-absorbed, but then which athlete, or at least which champion, wasn't? He tried to atone with generosity, sensitivity, politeness – not that it earned him much credit with the press, or one or two of his rivals. Merckx had always let his legs do the talking, or, on one occasion, when he had passed and turned to glare at Van Looy in the La Turbie time trial in Paris–Nice in 1966, his eyes.

Then Driessens – what would he now say? No doubt something ridiculous and self-important. 'This wouldn't have happened if I'd been at the Giro.' Yes, that's probably what Driessens would say.

As time went on, more and more, Eddy was noticing that the directeur sportif's role was a 'problem position' in his teams. His last real 'coach' had been Felicien Vervaecke. Vervaecke had himself been one of Belgium's best ever riders, a Tour de France King of the Mountains in 1937 and a runner-up on general classification in 1938. Guillaume Michiels knew him and had introduced Vervaecke to Merckx. Before long, as well as constantly reminding Eddy to be more economical in races, Vervaecke was telling friends and acquaintances that he had the next Belgian Tour de France winner on his hands. He had realised after a while that it was impossible to curb Merckx's attacking instinct, his sheer zest for racing his bike, and that the best approach was therefore just to limit the consecutive efforts which might lead to burn-out. Eddy had done just one stage race as an amateur – the Tour of Limbourg in 1963, which he'd won, the day before he met Jean Van Buggenhout for the first time. Vervaecke was still his coach and personal mechanic when he turned pro with Solo-Superia in 1965, but they drifted apart the following year when Eddy rode the Six Days of Gent, and his partner Patrick Sercu's mechanic worked for both of them. Vervaecke had taken that badly.

Merckx hated upsetting people almost as much as he hated losing. Increasingly, though, it had become unavoidable, an occupational hazard. On the bike, his competitive spirit and the way that it manifested itself had always ruffled feathers, even if he always tried to be as '*réglo*', as fair as they came. 'Come on, we're not risking our lives out here,' Walter Godefroot had said to him after one rambunctious sprint when they were amateurs. Godefroot was no shrinking violet himself – hence the occasional nickname, 'De Vlaamse Bulldog' or 'the Flemish Bulldog' – but there had always been an intensity, a single-mindedness about Merckx on a bike that inspired not just fear but a sort of repugnance. In a way there was insecurity in what Godefroot had said, and in what people kept complaining about Merckx's ceaseless will to win: they wished they were as linear, as motivated as him, but there was always a worry or a weakness or a reminder of their own mortality which intruded. Take Zilioli. He had seemed unbeatable in the summer of 1963, then 'frozen' as soon as that success created the expectation of more. It stopped being fun. Merckx, on the other hand, was *only* enjoying himself when he was fulfilling that premonition, that vision of his ideal future self as a winner, a champion. He couldn't explain it and couldn't comprehend the need to excuse it. Sometimes the others talked as though his victories *invalidated* everything they did.

It was now after lunchtime, and all those continuing their journey, their Giro, had left Merckx behind. The cycling world that seemed to spin like a basketball on his fingertip had stopped turning at ten o'clock that morning. Claudine, Van Den Bossche and Valente remained in the room, their attention all on him. 'Milan' and 'this afternoon' were among a handful of words that penetrated the daze when Valente spoke. Van Den Bossche pulled on a grey turtle-neck sweater, Merckx his zip-up tracksuit top and they began gathering their things.

Gladioli – the symbols of moral integrity, but also of a gladiator's sword piercing the heart. They were still in reception when Merckx left.

7
benefit of the doubt?

'Eddy, if I hug you, it's because you're an honest lad.
I don't make a habit of embracing Judas.' ADRIANO RODONI

Professor Genevose, who had watched Doctor Cavalli perform the 'B' test, agreed there could be no doubt: the concentration of the offending substance was '*altissimo*' – extremely high. And yet for hours, days, weeks and years after Vincenzo Giacotto had delivered his mortifying verdict, doubt is what continued to flourish.

If it hadn't been for the clear empirical evidence staring him in the face, not even Genevose would have believed it. He was on the race as the riders' medical representative, and had got the call at four in the morning: one of the five riders tested the previous day – Roberto Ballani and Marino Basso, respectively first and second in Savona, Merckx the *maglia rosa*, and the randomly selected Enrico Paolini and Luciano Luciani – had tested positive. Genovese threw on some clothes and hurried to the mobile laboratory where Cavalli was waiting to test the second sample. Only four hours later, when the second test was complete and had yielded the same conclusive result as the first, had Genovese discovered that the sample belonged to Merckx.

'I left no stone unturned before accepting the result of the analysis. I didn't know who the test concerned, but I pleaded with Doctor

Cavalli to keep checking *ad nauseam*. I can tell you that we were even more careful than on Gimondi's case [in 1968], so horrified was I by what had happened. I can rule out any imperfections in the analytical procedure. Everything was done technically perfectly.'

The professor's reaction was no different from anyone else's: how and why now, in Merckx's ninth test of the Giro and at the end of a stage almost devoid of difficulty? The Ferretti team's directeur sportif, Alfredo Martini, called the idea of Merckx cheating in this context nothing less than 'a joke'. Martini pointed out that the hardest climb on the road to Savona had been the three-kilometre, 2 per cent Piani d'Invrea – barely a ripple on the Ligurian coastal cruise. And as the race leader and holder of the pink jersey, Merckx knew that he would be tested.

Everyone, indeed, had greeted the news with disbelief and disgust. Not at Merckx but whoever or whatever was responsible for what was surely a grave miscarriage of justice. The most outspoken were those who had already encountered the same 'problem'; yes, it was amazing how their language could change, and the euphemisms flow, months after the event. Adorni had had his own little 'mishap' at the Giro di Sardegna in Faema colours the previous year. 'It's impossible. We should all protest and go home,' he fumed now.

The chorus of discontent contained many variations on the same refrain.

Gimondi, himself positive the previous year: 'It's impossible. I know Merckx as a rider and as a man. Now we should protest and all go home.'

Motta, also shamed in the '68 Giro: 'You would have had to be stupid…and Merckx is extremely intelligent.'

Altig, nicknamed 'The Cycling Pharmacy' after his admission in one French cycling magazine in 1969 that he was smart enough to use products that didn't show up in urine tests: 'We're exposed to the actions of some stranger who offers you a drink, and you don't know what it is that you're swallowing.'

Gastone Nencini, the directeur sportif of the Max Meyer team, whose injections had so appalled doctor Enrico Peracino in his racing days: 'The riders shouldn't start today, out of solidarity with Merckx.'

The handwringing was understandable coming from either current or recently retired riders. Part of it was sympathy – if not for what they all seemed to think were improprieties in the test, then at least with Merckx for getting caught. Their outpourings also reflected the power he and Faema now wielded – not least their capacity to mete out suffering in the bunch. Because there was another thing that no one believed: Merckx's affirmation, in the rawness of his distress, that he might give up cycling. They all knew that he would be back in the peloton and inflicting pain as soon as his ban had ended.

As far as his countrymen were concerned, within hours, that had become the key issue: if not clearing Merckx's name, then how to get him back riding in time for the Tour. The Giro had left Savona with a new leader, Gimondi, who tomorrow would finally pull on the pink jersey relinquished diplomatically today, erasing all trace of its previous incumbent. The Giro was over – at least for Merckx. His father, Jules, had asked an Italian journalist who called the house shortly after the news broke whether Eddy could still be readmitted to the race once his innocence was established. Jenny seized the phone out of her husband's hand and roared, 'It's a scandal!' She then reached for and puffed on a cigarette for the first time in her life.

No, the priority now was to have the sanction lifted and Merckx's good name restored in time for the Tour. Giacotto had set about the task even before leaving Savona. The Faema manager summoned the journalists Gianpaolo Ormezzano, Michel Seassau and René Jacobs to witness Merckx give a urine sample, which was then taken to a private laboratory in Milan for analysis. Faema were also soon studying other options, or perhaps 'loopholes' was a better word: Giacotto recalled that every team had been asked for its written consent to the testing arrangements presented to them on the eve of the race, and that Faema had agreed only verbally. He informed the race jury, who immediately called the Italian Procycling Cycling Union (UICP) in Rome. There was nothing doing – as far as UICP were concerned, Faema knew and had agreed to the rules like everyone else.

It was now late in the afternoon. In Savona in the morning, an impromptu gathering of senior riders had mooted the idea of a strike, before finally deciding that the show would go on for any other rider and so should for Merckx. Under cold and grey skies, their speed in the first hour had been that of a funeral cortege. Normal service and a brisk pace had then resumed before the Dane Ole Ritter's decisive attack on the run-in to Pavia. It was impossible to know whether some of the banners at the roadside had been prepared before or after the rude awakening of a few hours earlier. 'Merckx, you're greater than Charlemagne' said one.

Merckx's 'best friend' in the peloton, Italo Zilioli, was covered in his blood when he crossed the line. Somehow, a huge shard of glass from a jar had embedded itself in one of his sandwiches and shredded his lip as he ate. As often seemed to be the case with Zilioli, when it rained, it poured.

Merckx and his downfall monopolised RAI's *Processo alla Tappa*. As Italians often do, the panel seemed to voice identical opinions while at the same time bickering furiously. The consensus above the racket was that Merckx was clean and had been wronged. The issue had already assumed such proportions that the most famous Italian journalist of all, on any subject, Indro Montanelli, was asked to wade in. 'The other

riders should go home and boycott the rest of the Giro. Merckx's innocence is proven by common sense, if you ask me,' he sniffed.

Again, contempt was directed not at the alleged crime, but, somewhat bizarrely, at the anti-doping institutions and procedures. The
president of the Professional Riders Association, Fiorenzo Magni, had
stated rather alarmingly that, 'Merckx's problem has always been anti-
doping.' Magni went on to explain, 'Other riders have said that they
don't feel protected. It's true: anti-doping lends itself to deception.
We'll get to the point where we have to flee the hotels, where we'll
have to eat in a caravan outside. The anti-doping law is a scam.'

Merckx, of course, had already 'fled' to Milan, more precisely the
Hotel Royal. He was still crying intermittently, between threats to
abandon cycling. At eight o'clock, his teammates left for Belgium
from Linate airport. The telephone lines between the two countries
had been humming all afternoon as the case rapidly turned into a
major diplomatic incident. A telegram was already on its way to the
Faema bosses from the Minister of Flemish Culture, Franz Van
Mechelen, saying that he was saddened and had already demanded a
full investigation from the Italian authorities. Another was winging
its way from the Belgian Foreign Minister Pierre Harmel to his Italian
counterpart Pietro Nenni, calling for a resolution of the 'mystery of
Savona'. Hundreds more, almost all expressing solidarity, had been
picked up by the cleaning lady at Merckx's home in Tervuren.

Speaking of diplomacy, Driessens had already excelled himself.
'Eddy was the victim of a plot dreamt up by jealous people,' he blus-
tered. 'What did he eat and drink on the rest day? Someone must
have put a banned product in his food or drink. In Italy you can't
trust anyone or anything.'

Meanwhile, in the Hotel Royal, Merckx tossed and turned in his
bed as Claudine slept next to him. He replayed everything that had

happened in that mobile laboratory in Savona for what seemed like the hundredth time in his head. He, Giacotto and Marino Vigna, Faema's directeur sportif, still had many questions. Why had the officials not informed Merckx that his A-sample was positive, or for that matter waited for his authorisation to open and test the B-sample, as per the protocol? How was it that some teams had known that Merckx was positive on the night of his test, hours before the rider concerned had found out – this, at least, according to Vigna? Who was behind the rumours that had circulated since the start of the Giro that Merckx would be 'eliminated' before Milan? What did that person know about what had occurred in the last 48 hours?

The night had brought no rest and the morning came abruptly. Merckx rose wearily from his bed and pulled on grey slacks, a light green turtle-neck, and blue jacket. At nine o'clock, he and Claudine drove in their white Mercedes to the airport to collect the secretary of the Belgian Cycling Federation Maurice Moyson, and took him back to the Hotel Royal.

At around the same time, all over Europe, people were waking up and opening their newspapers. In Belgium, Merckx may not yet have equalled the popularity of Van Looy, but there was nothing like a foreign conspiracy to whip up a bit of patriotic fervour. In Francophile Wallonia, *La Dernière Heure* spoke of 'a Machiavellian' affair and the high probability that someone had spiked Merckx's drink or food. The other big Walloon paper, *Le Soir*, questioned the legitimacy of the mobile lab unveiled amid such fanfare before the Giro. *Le Soir* pointed out that only three labs were officially recognised by the International Cycling Union, and they were in Rome, Paris and Gent. The French paper *Le Parisien Libre* also noted that, in France, A and B tests also had to be carried out in different laboratories, which hadn't been the case here.

La Gazzetta dello Sport's Bruno Raschi had been the unhappy witness of a 'bitter episode', having gone with Giacotto to break the news to Merckx. *La Gazzetta* ran a picture of Merckx in tears on the hotel bed on their front page, the headline 'Merckx forced out (positive in a medical test)' and six pages of reports. *La Stampa* led with the more dramatic 'Merckx disqualified: requiem for cycling'. Italian writer Giovanni Arpino complained in an editorial that 'Because of an error or maybe even some ploy concocted by a third party, that greatest rider of our age, Merckx, a man as clean and pure as water, has to abandon the Giro and in all probability the Tour. Let's say *grazie* to the organisers and the doctors.'

The centrepiece of that paper's coverage was a photograph of the product believed to have been found in Merckx's urine. It contained the banned substance fencamfamine, was sold commercially as Reactivan, and was produced by a pharmaceutical company called…Merck.

Midway through the second day after cycling's apocalypse, Tuesday 3 June, a routine had already started to set in. It consisted of meetings, interviews, more tears, multiplying conspiracy theories, sleepless nights, postponements of Merckx's return to Belgium and more threats to abandon cycling – and it lasted three days. It was also utterly inconclusive except as a gauge of Merckx's standing in Belgian and in international sport. That and, possibly, as a challenge to the received wisdom that dope testing was a force for clarity and credibility in a sport dogged throughout its lifetime by cheating.

Merckx's problem was that with every fanciful new theory, every unwavering yet seemingly unfounded pronouncement of support by an official or leading commentator, old resentments began to spawn. At times it could all look and sound like a conspiracy to absolve Merckx, not to condemn him. Shortly after he had fetched Moyson on 3 June, the president of the International Cycling Union (UCI) Adriano Rodoni flew in from Switzerland. He immediately wrapped an arm around Merckx, who was again sobbing. 'Eddy, if I hug you, it's because you're an honest lad. I don't make a habit of embracing Judas,' Rodoni whispered in his ear, within earshot of Belgian reporters. The next day, one Flemish paper issued a heartfelt '*Grazie signor* Rodoni' on behalf of its readership, while another railed against Giro organiser Vincenzo Torriani for not turning a blind eye, even if Merckx's sample was positive. The weekly magazine *Sport 69* alleged that Torriani had orchestrated Merckx's demise out of spite towards the Tour de France and its director Félix Lévitan, who would again be deprived of the sport's biggest star in July. There had been talk of Lévitan postponing the start of the '69 Tour by three days, until after Merckx had served his one-month ban. Alas, this would be 'impossible', the Tour chief admitted.

On 3 June, the University of Liège carried out a sociological study measuring the impact of the scandal on the Belgian public. Its conclusion was that, of recent 'world events', only the assassination of President John F. Kennedy six years earlier had been of a similar magnitude.

As a pure soap opera, a true Italian *telenovela*, it was utterly gripping, and by the hour the tales were becoming more and more outlandish and tantalising. Some stories were old, like talk of an ancient and undetectable Oriental plant that had been fuelling Merckx and Faema for months, while others briefly spiked curiosity before losing the interest of even those who had peddled them in the first place. One went that Merckx's urine had been borderline positive after his time trial win in Montecatini Terme on Stage 4. The sample that Faema had taken themselves in Savona and sent to the Istituto di Medicina Legale di Milano, meanwhile, had come back negative. The experts said this couldn't be explained by the normal degradation of the fencamfamine in the original sample, as its concentration had been so high that the Milan tests should also have been positive. The second opinion, though, had been mandated only by Merckx and Faema and had no official value.

One minute Merckx was comparing his case to that of the Bologna football team, four of whose players had tested positive in 1964 then later been absolved. The next he was recalling that he had filled a test-tube labelled with the number 6 in Savona, and wondering whether it hadn't been mistaken for a 9. He was then distracted by talk of a traitor within his team, whom Van Bug had supposedly identified. The culprit, said some, was a masseur due to leave Faema at the end of the season. Others, including *La Gazzetta dello Sport*, referred to but didn't name a Faema rider who had already won several Classics himself, and had privately announced in the days leading up to Savona that he would 'wage war against Merckx in the future'. The only man who fitted that description was Guido Reybrouck. Merckx claimed that he had 'specific suspicions' and was considering legal action against one individual, but wouldn't reveal who this was.

The juiciest morsel of all came from a priest. He had watched Merckx arrive for mass at the Duomo in Parma on the morning of his positive test and park his bike outside. Noticing that the bottle cage on Merckx's bike was empty, the priest assumed that Merckx had taken his drink inside with him, safe from would-be saboteurs. The next time he looked, he was startled: a bottle had appeared, yet Merckx hadn't stepped outside the cathedral. Some form of skulduggery – and not, for instance, an innocent member of the Faema staff going about his normal duties – could be the only explanation.

It was all enough to give anyone a headache, and indeed the maelstrom in Merckx's mind wasn't abating. Peace could elude him even in the midst of success beyond other riders' wildest imagination; in times of crisis, his brain became an infestation of dark thoughts and anxieties. Van Buggenhout said that he was 'almost a broken man'. On Thursday 5 June, after three infernal nights at the Hotel Royal in Milan, he and Claudine finally began the car journey back to Brussels with the intention of arriving in Tervuren almost 'incognito' the following day. There was little chance of that: 24 hours later, on the first sunny day of the week in Belgium, the white Mercedes was cheered as it pulled into the Merckxes' driveway. *La Gazzetta* called it a reception 'worthy of a cosmonaut'. 'He needs more rest than if he'd finished the Giro,' Claudine told journalists as she wrestled him through the herd and through the front door.

At around the same time, Felice Gimondi was applying the finishing touches to his second Giro d'Italia victory in the mountains above Trento. The last week of the race had been ridden in a wretched ambiance, with the riders climbing off their bikes on the stage to the Marmolada and effectively forcing its cancellation due to bad weather. This led to their own directeurs sportifs branding them 'whingers' and much worse, and others claiming that this had been a belated gesture of protest after an ultimately limp reaction in Savona.

'I don't care who wins the Giro,' Merckx had said – and neither, it seemed, did anyone else.

From a strictly practical point of view, the situation as Merckx returned to Belgium was that he was banned from all races and awaiting the outcome of UCI president Adriano Rodoni's 'personal' investigation. Once Rodoni had admitted, in an interview with the *Corriere dello Sport*, that the now infamous mobile laboratory laid on before the Giro by Hewlett Packard did not conform to UCI regulations, the die appeared to be cast. In France, a group of riders led by Jean Stabilinski had already announced that they would go on strike if Merckx received preferential treatment. While in Belgium, Georges Vanconingsloo and Emile Bodart, among others, demanded to know why there had been no fuss about their apparently very similar cases. Jan Janssen in Holland said much the same thing. Merckx was in an 'alarming state of depression', 'even lower than in Savona and Milan' according to Van Bug. But intuition – as well as Rodoni's embrace in Milan, plus the incongruous fact that he was the president both of the UCI and the Italian Cycling Federation who had officially imposed the sanction – proved the best guide. On 14 June, after a meeting with the Belgian cycling federation, the members of the UCI's board of directors announced in a communiqué that they:

- Accepted the results of the tests carried out by the Italian doctors.
- Granted that the Italian Federation had the right to suspend the rider Eddy Merckx according to the results of their tests.
- Considered the irreproachable record of the incriminated rider and the negative results of tens of tests that he had undergone in the past.
- Doubted that Merckx had wanted to dope voluntarily.
- Gave him the benefit of the doubt and immediately lifted the suspension of which he was currently the object.

And so on and so on…

In Tervuren, Merckx read the statement and felt a surge of relief. Then he looked again, digested, and the anxieties returned in torrents.

Benefit of the doubt?! He knew which three words the public and his peers would retain, and what was their implication: Merckx had been 'let off' because he was Merckx. Not because the test had no validity, and should never even have been carried out in conditions like the ones in Savona. Not because he had never cheated. His instinct was correct, and at the Tour of Luxembourg, the peloton manifested its discontent in a mini-strike, while the defending Tour de France champion Janssen vented his frustration at the Tour of Switzerland. 'I have nothing against Merckx. I actually have a lot of admiration for him. But this decision is an injustice towards Adorni, Motta, Lucien Aimar, myself and lots of little riders who were punished without being able to defend themselves,' Janssen argued. Today, incidentally, Janssen's summation is more succinct. 'He cried like a baby so they let him off,' the Dutchman says.

Merckx was wounded but, as Walter Godefroot had already noted, he was never more dangerous than when he was down. 'When everyone else is hurting, they slow down. When Merckx is in trouble…he attacks,' Godefroot says. With the Tour de France just a fortnight away, and his pride throbbing, Merckx now pummelled his bike like rarely before. He had recommenced training on 10 June, four days before his ban was officially overturned, and now alternated 220-kilometre training sessions behind Guillaume Michiels's scooter with criteriums in Caen in France and Bruges. At both, the cheers outnumbered the jeers. He then finished a weary 32nd in the Belgian National Championships won by the new prodigy Roger de Vlaeminck, having bashed his left knee on a gear lever. The next day, he rode a 110-kilometre criterium in the afternoon and a track-meet in the evening; on Tuesday, he reported for the start of another criterium but caused such an onrush of autograph hunters that he missed the start and had to withdraw; on Wednesday, he rode

160 kilometres with teammates; on Thursday, Merckx covered 270 kilometres alone; Friday was speed work behind Michiels's scooter, cut short to 50 kilometres by a torrential rainstorm; and on Saturday, he rode '*à bloc*' for 40 kilometres in the morning, '*tranquille*' for another 40 in the afternoon, then readied himself for what would be his third outing of the day in the evening: the Tour de France prologue time trial in Roubaix.

8
first man on the moon

'That bloke needs to be...handicapped. They should stick a
25 kilogram weight under his saddle.' GILBERT BELLONE

One of the first to notice the change was the new Giro champion
Felice Gimondi. '*Oooo, ciao Eddy, ciao!*' Gimondi had called to his
old *bête noire* from the other end of the lobby where both of their
teams were staying ahead of the Tour de France prologue time trial
in Roubaix. Merckx had looked over, smiled sheepishly, then carried
on walking.

It was normal after what had happened, explained Lomme
Driessens. Those words – 'benefit of the doubt' – still grated loudly
and painfully in Merckx's mind, along with the less-than-charitable
statements of one or two colleagues over the past four weeks. There
was no malice towards Gimondi in particular; Merckx had even used
the column he was writing in *La Dernière Heure* to urge his fans on
the first stages of the Tour in Belgium not to direct their anger about
what had happened in Savona at the Giro winner. No, Merckx's was
simply the dazed air of a man who had woken one morning to a
world different from the one he'd known for the previous 24 years,
and who was still tip-toeing into his new reality.

Marino Vigna, the Faema directeur sportif, had not seen him since Savona. Vigna emerged from a contentious meeting about dope-testing procedures on the Thursday before the race with the news that there would be three tests after every stage at the Tour. Depending on the day and what the Tour doctor Pierre Dumas had written in a sealed envelope labelled with the number of that stage before the Tour, he would summon either the top three riders on general classification, the first three finishers that day, or three riders picked at random. Dumas had declined Merckx's exceptional request to test his urine every day, no matter where he finished, but confirmed that the sanction for a first positive test would be just a 15-minute penalty rather than a disqualification and ban. 'Well, that means you'd better win by over fifteen minutes, in case they stitch you up again, like in Italy,' Vigna told Merckx.

'I meant it as a joke, but I think it actually explained quite a bit about how he ended up riding in that Tour,' Vigna says.

Thirteen teams of ten men had reported to Roubaix for the Grand Départ of the 56th Tour. As per tradition in prologue time trials, one man from each of the 13 teams would start their race in a predetermined order, before the roll-call was repeated for their second rider, their third and so on. Custom and conventional wisdom also dictated that teams would leave their leader until last, for reasons of theatre but also, above all, so that his teammates' and the majority of the field's finishing times could serve as reference points. The prior knowledge that most, if not all, teams would adopt the same policy also afforded a degree of security: if it happened to rain, a team leader could at least be sure that he was starting within a few minutes of his direct rivals for overall victory, in similar weather, and hence in much the same boat.

The Tour was cycling's grandest stage, Merckx's big moment and Belgium's – but also an important three weeks for Lomme

Driessens. Driessens had realised in the spring that Merckx's brilliance was about the only thing in cycling that could eclipse or even efface his inflated impression of his own genius, and it was therefore paramount that he reaffirmed his value early at La Grande Boucle. As it turned out, this was one of Driessens's better ideas: having picked the number one out of a hat to secure the first of the 13 starting positions for Faema, he selected Merckx as his team's and the Tour's first rider. That way, Driessens told Merckx, he could dodge the commotion of fans and journalists which would build throughout the day, return to his hotel in good time, eat early, then get a good night's rest. So went the infallible logic: in the event, with Merckx poised on the start ramp at 16h48, the race commissaires noticed that there were publicity vehicles still on the course, panicked, and imposed a five-minute delay. A frown, a shake of the head, an emergency second warm-up and Merckx was finally en route. Thirteen minutes and seven seconds later he crossed the finish line. Only Rudi Altig would cover the ground faster, by seven seconds. Altig was the Tour's first leader.

The second day was to be the first key rendezvous, not because anyone expected decisive racing on either of the two 'split stages', but because they were taking the race to Woluwe-Saint-Pierre on the outskirts of Brussels, where Merckx had grown up. This partly explained his nerves before both the flat 147-kilometre stage in the morning won by the Italian sprinter Marino Basso, and the 15.6-kilometre team time trial in the afternoon dominated by Faema, which had given Merckx the race lead. Even in the yellow jersey, and in his dream scenario of a triumphant homecoming, Merckx seemed edgy. 'Only Gimondi is riding sportingly,' he griped. 'Most of the others seem to be in league against me. They're marking me, watching me, sucking my wheel; when I chase down attacks that I think are dangerous, my main rivals refuse to do their share of the work. I feel like a train dragging along a bunch of heavy and useless carriages.'

The next morning, for once he seemed able to lose himself. Perhaps relieved by Claudine's presence at his side, he posed smilingly for photographers in front of the Woluwe town hall, then rode ahead of the peloton to lap up the adulation of folk who were normally just neighbours in Tervuren. The route then pointed south-west into the forests and former battlefields of the Ardennes – and a savage combat.

Neither the average speed of just under 40 kilometres an hour – nor the fact that Merckx's Faema teammate Julien Stevens had won the stage in a breakaway and inherited his leader's yellow jersey – offered any clue as to how torrid the day had been. Almost as fancied as Merckx before the race, Roger Pingeon already seemed to have lost his head as well as precious energy as he strained to regain touch after a puncture. Pingeon's fellow French hope Raymond Poulidor and Poulidor's domestique Raymond Riotte were also reeling.

'I had ridden the Tour that Pingeon won in 1967, and Jan Janssen's in 1968, and I swear that everything felt 10, 15 kilometres per hour quicker right from those first stages in 1969,' Riotte says. 'The difference was, it was…*c'était terrible*. His team was strong too, of course, but they'd become strong riding for Merckx. Maybe it was the effect he had on them, or the salary wasn't the same. We didn't know what had happened. All I know is Swerts, Van Schil and Spruyt were with me at Mercier, and they weren't that strong when they were riding with me for Poulidor.'

Poulidor himself was also shocked. An aspiring winner before the race, the three-time podium finisher had been disarmed to the point of publicly admitting that he could barely hold the wheels – this on terrain where finishing in the main peloton ought to have been a formality. Stage 3 back into France and Charleville Mezières offered no let-up. The Bic team's directeur sportif Raphaël Géminiani, the so-nicknamed 'Grand Fusil' or 'Big Gun' who had nearly signed Merckx when he left Solo-Superia at the end of 1965, was among those who thought that Merckx was showing his naivety about the Tour de France. 'Merckx is bluffing,' Géminiani said. 'The way he's riding is pure cinema. This Tour has started at a breathtaking pace. I don't know how Merckx will last...' The same evening Gimondi admitted that it had been an 'ultra-rapid' start and would consequently be a 'terribly hard' Tour. 'A race unto death', *France Soir* called it.

Perhaps contrary to appearances, the only man beginning to enjoy himself, in his own, idiosyncratic, self-flagellating way, was Merckx. Géminiani had miscalculated if he thought that the novelty of the Tour would rekindle his old impetuosity. That much was clear when Rik Van Looy escaped on Stage 4 to Nancy, and Merckx resisted the temptation to personally hunt down his old tormentor. The greatest insult of all was indifference. Van Looy's build-up to the Tour was also more liable to inspire amusement than fear or a reaction from Merckx; the 'Emperor's' participation had been uncertain up to the last minute, and hinged on him finding a stable-lad to look after his horses in Herentals. Van Looy had identified a suitable candidate hours before the Tour was due to start, and so hopped across the border to Roubaux. He was now rewarded with what would be his final stage win in his final Tour.

Where Géminiani had been right was in thinking that Merckx's rip-roaring start had been that classic old crock, rule one of Sun Tzu's *Art of War*: appear strong when you are weak, prepared when you are not. If they wanted to exploit it, though, it was already too late. Merckx broke the bad news in Nancy: 'I needed five stages to really get the engine burning. I was afraid that I'd lost my legs after the Savona affair and the time I had to spend off the bike...If I attacked on the first two days of this Tour, it was partly to make people think that I was stronger than was actually the case. Show my strength so I didn't have to use it. Tomorrow we get to the mountains and now I know that I'll be fine.'

The breath of a nation, one that hadn't won the Tour for thirty years, was bated. Merckx sounded confident, relaxed, but within hours the old agitation was back. Stevens lost the yellow jersey on the first stage through the Vosges. The Faema troops gathered themselves that night in the Hotel Bristol in Colmar. When the lights went out, Merckx's eyes remained open. No sooner had he finally fallen asleep than the nightmares began. A repeat of Savona. Sabotage. It could happen again. Every precaution had been taken, but it could happen again...

He was still twitchy when a journalist from one of the Antwerp papers approached him near where the Faema cars were parked in the place de la Réunion the next morning. The reporter was angry that Driessens had installed a blockade in front of Merckx's hotel room the previous night. Merckx apologised. Sometimes he thought journalists imagined that he went out of his way to inconvenience them, but really saying 'no' made him cringe. He could remember being mortified when he double-booked interviews on the rest day of the 1967 Giro, and the journalist who had been squeezed to a later time confronted him. 'I don't want to speak to you any more,' he'd snapped. Merckx had got straight on the phone to Claudine, who then called the newspaper's sports desk to say sorry again on Eddy's behalf.

At the summit of the Ballon D'Alsace, Merckx would upset another journalist, but this time there was no need to ask forgiveness. Pierre Chany of *L'Equipe* watched Merckx maraud across the line over four minutes ahead of Gimondi, Poulidor and the rest, turned to his colleague, the Tour co-director Jacques Goddet, and sighed.

'Oh well, that's us screwed.' As if to say, the Tour was over after six stages and one relatively straightforward day in the Vosges. What were they going to write for the next two weeks?

Merckx said simply that it had been 'time to get serious and land a big blow'. The ever-contrary Pingeon was the only man who refused to admit that, barring accident, Merckx was already unassailable. 'His superiority is more apparent than real,' Pingeon opined live on French TV the next morning. 'He took minutes off us on the Ballon D'Alsace, but that wasn't down to his pure strength. The difference between him and us is that we didn't believe the Ballon would be that important, and we kept a bit in the tank, dare I say. We'll be like cats on hot tin roofs now, and it's no foregone conclusion that Merckx will be able to prolong his domination in the Alps.'

It was funny that Pingeon should mention cats. Well, not funny, but at least coincidental; in a very roundabout sort of way, Merckx would be grateful for one as he staved off the Frenchman in the Alps.

Martin Van Den Bossche has just turned 70. He sits in a big leather chair in the sparkling office at the back of his sparkling tile showroom in Bornem, not far from Antwerp. 'Big' Martin is still an imposing figure, well over six feet tall, and with a booming voice that delivers sentences like volleys from a bazooka. He has lost most of what in 1969 was already just a spur of brown hair, but the eyes that slant down at the edges, the narrow chin, and the protruding ears still fit together at familiar angles. Not much is all that different from the giant mosaic of the owner in action at the 1970 Tour de France that looms over the shop-room floor.

Anyway, Merckx, that cat...

'It was the June 1960,' Van Den Bossche announces. 'The Tour de France was passing through Belgium, and we'd got a half day at the metal factory to go and watch the race. My brother was a year older than me, he'd been a cyclist, but he'd fallen and broken his collarbone, and I'd inherited his bike. I'd started racing and realised quickly that I was pretty fast. You start riding in age-group races and you hear and see people breathing hard and dropping back when the pace is high and you're following easily. Those guys disappear, and you stay. That way you go from a thousand to a hundred, then from a hundred to the ten best in your area. From there, from reading about Jacques Anquetil and Charly Gaul at the Tour de France, to having a career in cycling, though…well it doesn't even occur to you.

'Anyway,' Van Den Bossche continues, 'we're on this half day, and we ride and watch the Tour at Willebroek. After the race, we have one of our own. A cat runs out into the road and I crash into it. Smash! Broken arm. Three weeks off work. By now my cycling's going well, and I'd already won a junior national title in 1959. It hits me that I have to make a decision: it's either riding to and from the factory twice a day, from Hingene to Boom, 40 kilometres on ash and sand roads, because I do two shifts, or it's riding in professional races. At the end of the three weeks I go back to the factory with my mind made up: I'm going to become a cyclist.'

A powerful climber with a penchant for churning huge gears in the mountains, Van Den Bossche continues to improve and earns a pro contract in 1963. Riding for Wiel's-Groene Leeuw, he turns heads by finishing third in the 1965 Liège–Bastogne–Liège. The same year he rides Paris–Luxembourg and witnesses the first on-the-road skirmishes in Rik Van Looy and Eddy Merckx's war of succession. While he sympathises with Van Looy, 'who had to fight for years against Van Steenbergen, then is finally on his own and sees Merckx arrive', Van Den Bossche is mainly impressed by the youngster. 'You could see he was a huge talent. When he was pacing the peloton, you just felt it,' he says.

If Van Den Bossche rates Merckx, the feeling isn't necessarily mutual, despite him being in the first wave of riders signed by Vincenzo Giacotto for Faema in 1968. Nonetheless, in the Giro, on the famous stage to the Tre Cime di Lavaredo, it is the leggy Belgian who shreds the lead group on the approach to the final climb before Adorni and Merckx take over. At the end of the year, Jean Van Buggenhout negotiates on Faema's behalf and offers Van Den Bossche the same terms as in 1968. Van Den Bossche rips up the contract theatrically in front of Van Bug's face. Van Bug promptly apologises and draws up a new, much more lucrative one. Van Den Bossche is again in the Giro line-up in '69 and also Merckx's roommate, including in Savona. Nothing in those primitive dope tests surprises Van Den Bossche any more. He recalls one occasion when a teammate locked a tester in a hotel room after Milan–San Remo, dangled the key out of the window and threatened to throw the tester with it if he didn't leave immediately having recorded that the test had been performed and the rider was 'negative'.

'We were used to having to pee for dope tests, but your urine wasn't sealed or anything. Nor did you have to sign any kind of paper! There was no fridge!' he sniffs. 'They could do with the urine sample whatever they wanted. In a courtroom nowadays those tests would have had no value at all.'

What about the rider who allegedly 'visited', and was turned away from, his and Merckx's room a couple of days before Savona, with briefcase in hand? Does Van Den Bossche remember that?

He laughs but doesn't seem inclined to answer.

Martin? Do you remember?

More laughter. The soupçon of a smirk. 'Who knows? There are so many stories.'

*

By the time that Van Den Bossche had begun grinding on the lower slopes of the Col de la Forclaz on Stage 9, the peloton had already been extensively pruned. Merckx, of course, was comfortable in Van Den Bossche's giant silhouette, but there weren't too many others like him. Near the top of the climb, big Martin's work was done and he made way for the boss. Merckx accelerated but could immediately feel that he lacked his usual zip; the extra-long pedal cranks that he'd asked his mechanic to fit that morning had been a mistake. Pingeon led him over the climb, then beat him to the stage win in Chamonix under the immense awning of Mont Blanc. In their respective post-race interviews, Pingeon said, 'I told you so' – or words to that effect, while Merckx paid tribute to Van Den Bossche.

The next day, over the 2,645-metre Col du Galibier, which Merckx had never climbed, they all rode cautiously. Herman Van Springel, another Belgian who had already strewn his ambitions of overall glory all through the Vosges, Jura and Alps, was allowed to escape on the descent off the Galibier and win the stage, but there was no change to Merckx's five-minute, 21-second advantage over Pingeon on general classification when they reached Briançon. An old Tour adage went that he who wore the yellow jersey in Briançon wore yellow in Paris. Merckx wasn't sure about that but the 'race unto death' that his attacks had instigated on the first two days had already claimed some illustrious victims: Roger de Vlaeminck, the 21-year-old Belgian champion who some had believed might turn the '69 race into a battle of the Tour rookies, him and Merckx, had climbed off his bike.

Merckx's tactics on the Galibier were interpreted by some as proof that, nine days in, he had reconciled himself to the difficulty of the Tour. Jacques Goddet spoke in *L'Equipe* of his 'passivity' and him riding 'like the most common of champions'. Goddet spoke too soon: on the final Alpine stage to Digne, Merckx attacked incessantly, uphill and down, and finally left Pingeon trailing on the descent into Digne before beating Gimondi in a sprint. The next day, an innocuous attack by a rider 53 places behind on general classification, Jacques De Boever, was temptation enough for Merckx to cast off his shackles 60 kilometres from the finish in Aubagne. Only Gimondi could follow and earned a stage win for his troubles, nipping around Merckx at the end to show that he was learning his lesson. Pingeon, meanwhile, had floundered on a superlight bike ill-suited to the terrain. He was still second overall but more than seven minutes behind Merckx.

Now Goddet nuanced his analysis, and in doing so hinted that intelligent observers at least were zeroing in on the *essence* of Merckx's riding. His almost unprecedented aggression for a Tour favourite in the first dozen stages perhaps wasn't about revenge for Savona, or even his 'fear of disappointing people' as Raymond Poulidor describes it. Neither perhaps, as Goddet wrote in *L'Equipe*, did it necessarily come from a 'determined desire to massacre his adversaries'. Felice Gimondi is observing not explaining when he says of those hellish afternoons with Merckx tugging on his leash in the Southern Alps and Provence: 'He was angry at the start of the Tour – he did probably want revenge – but then Eddy was always like that, like he wanted to attack someone, physically. He was always aggressive, always up for it. You were always chasing him, because he never really rode on tactics – it was all power and instinct.'

The reason, Goddet concluded, seemed almost to be a sense of duty – to his fans, to the contest, and to his own natural talent. The Tour is many races within a race. Broadly speaking, it consists of four types of stage – the mountains and time trials where ground is made or lost by the overall contenders, sprint stages where they keep out of the way, and 'transition' stages in which stray dogs who excel in none of the above can have their day. Most if not all other aspiring Tour winners would have seen a lowly rider like Jacques De Boever's attack, 60 kilometres from the end of one of these 'transition stages' like the one to Aubagne, as an irrelevance. Not Merckx. To him it was a race like any other, an opportunity, and a win by an inferior rider would be, to his way of thinking, an incongruity or even an affront. The much-discussed, much-mythologised 'politics of the peloton' to him sounded more like the convenient excuses of those uncomfortable with the idea of sport as meritocracy. 'May the best man win'; more often than not, the best man was Merckx, on flat or hilly terrain, and finishing first was just his way of respecting, in both senses, the verdict of the road.

What this meant for other riders like Raymond Riotte was that, nearly two weeks in, the 1969 Tour already felt radically different from what had come before. Merckx's disregard for the status quo and for the others' cruising speed – what Alfredo Martini had said about his 'legs [hurting] when he rode slowly – the faster he rode, the better they felt' – manifested itself in his almost constant presence at the front of the bunch. 'I like hard racing for a good reason,' he said. 'It's that, if I ride hard, I'm the master of my own rhythm, espe-cially in the mountains. I make the others hurt and, at the finish, I'm no more tired than them.'

This made perfect sense to Merckx but ensured misery for the rest. Way down the field, the French debutant Robert Bouloux was cursing Merckx and Faema's every pedal stroke. Later, having strug-gled to Paris in 55th position, nearly three hours behind the winner,

Bouloux lamented, 'I would have ridden a much better Tour if Merckx hadn't been there. With him, it's different. He's too superior to us. You lose morale and it's hard to get it back.'

Another journeyman, the Bic rider Gilbert Bellone, was similarly downcast. 'Every day, we're already beaten before we start,' Bellone said. 'Even here on my own patch, in the south of France, I'm out of my comfort zone. And that's all Merckx's fault. That kid needs to be…handicapped. They should stick a 25 kilogram weight under his saddle.'

The four-day interlude between the Alps and the Pyrenees threw up few surprises, a further strengthening of Merckx's hegemony in a short time trial in Revel, plus one or two interesting dispatches. The sprint stage to La Grande Motte on the Mediterranean coast had a curious winner in Merckx's teammate Guido Reybrouck. Curious in the sense, first, that Reybrouck had been selected for the Tour and, second, that Merckx had helped him to win. Hadn't the Italian press supposedly identified Reybrouck as the enemy within, the saboteur of Savona? That was now inconceivable, for all that Reybrouck seemed sure to leave Faema, which he would indeed do, in 1970.

Rudi Altig, the German who had won the first yellow jersey of the Tour in Roubaix, had also become the first rider to test positive. His urine sample after Stage 14 to Revel contained traces of amphetamines. Altig was scandalised, the German media too – not so much by his cheating as by their own belief that he was a sacrificial lamb in a big cover-up presided over, they said, by the Tour's official doctor Pierre Dumas. In the *Frankfurter Allgemeine Zeitung*, Helmer Boelsen quoted Dumas saying that '60 per cent of riders now and again use products on the banned list'. Meanwhile, another German journalist, Ulfert Schröder, wrote that 'Dumas knew very well that Van Looy was doped after his stage win [in Nancy], but he exonerated the Belgian because he needed a stage win.'

None of this was of any concern to Merckx, Van Den Bossche and the rest of the Faema men. The Tour may have been wrapped up, but it was still the Tour – the hardest endurance event in sport, demanding maximum concentration and resilience. While Merckx's attention to detail and professionalism were already changing cycling, there were some things that not even he had the influence or foresight to alter. Van Den Bossche remembers, 'No one had a fridge or freezer in those days. Even in the feed zones in stages, things were lying open in the sun on a white blanket. If you were unlucky and the feedzone was exposed to the sun, the rice tarts were only fit for the bin. You were only allowed to drink after 30 kilometres and before the 50 kilometres-to-go sign. We drank water and back then the idea was that the less you drank, the longer you lasted. There was no science about recovery, and hotels were sometimes terrible. If you were unlucky and your room was on the fourth floor for three days in a row, the stairs just killed you.'

If the Tour doctor Pierre Dumas's colleague Lucien Maigre was to be believed, Merckx could have been staying on the top floor of the Montparnasse Tower, then under construction in Paris, and still be raring to ride. Maigre had been astounded when he examined Merckx after his time trial win in Revel and 20-kilometre ride back to the Faema hotel. 'It's like he hasn't raced and has been resting for the last few days,' Maigre gasped as he prodded Merckx's thighs.

After another late, downhill attack on the first Pyrenean stage to Luchon, Merckx woke the next day with no intention of attempting further heroics. He had promised Jean Van Buggenhout. A journalist had also approached him that day with the opening gambit, 'Merckx, old chap, you're killing the race. It's no fun.' The 214-kilometre stage from Luchon to Mourenx Ville-Nouvelle, over the passes of the Peyresourde, the legendary Tourmalet and the Aubisque would therefore be about consolidation, defence, following the wheels.

Of course it would...

The Col de Peyresourde climbs out of Luchon like aroma from a kitchen, its wisp of road rising slowly and serenely towards the pass 13 kilometres away. One rider in the peloton in 1969, Jean-Marie Leblanc, said years later that it was the kind of climb which made you want to pull to the side of the road, spread a picnic blanket on the grass and lie all afternoon among the cows. Maybe whistle a tune. Perhaps that was why the young, pocket-sized Belgian climber Lucien Van Impe was cheeping away almost as soon as the peloton left Luchon.

'On the Peyresourde, people were jumping around, attacking left, right and centre,' Barry Hoban, who was riding for Poulidor and Mercier, recalls. 'I was riding next to my mate, Gerben Karstens, both pretty comfortable, but muttering under our breath that anyone attacking this early was a stupid idiot. Van Impe was whistling away. It was his first Tour and he was so cocky – climbing mountains was a doddle for him. Someone else went up the road, then suddenly we heard Merckx, in this deep Belgian accent: "Martin!" Then we see Van Den Bossche, big Martin, moving forward to the front of the bunch. Martin was the only guy I knew who would climb mountains in the big chainring. He's powering away at the front, setting this tempo so that no one can attack, then about three kilometres later he swings across the road and turns around to face everyone. "R-r-r-right," he said, with his slight stammer. "I-i-i-f p-p-people keep attacking, h-h-h-alf of the field will be outside the t-time limit tonight. D-d-d-do you understand? A-a-a-a-s for you, Van Impe, i-i-i-f you don't stop whistling, I-I-I-I'll knock it down your head!" Karstens and I nearly fell off our bikes laughing.'

From behind his desk in Bornem, Van Den Bossche disputes this version…but only slightly.

'All true except the last part!' he declares. 'I told Van Impe, a nice fellow, "Children should be at the back!" If you start threatening people, that's not cycling any more…'

As far as Merckx was concerned, all that mattered was that order had been restored in time for the Tourmalet, the 2,115-metre ceiling of the Pyrenees. He appeared to be honouring his self-imposed cease-fire when Van Den Bossche pulled clear of what was now just a nine-man group in sight of the summit. The prize for being first over the Tourmalet was not only a few more points towards the King of the Mountains competition which Merckx led, but also prestige of the kind that wouldn't matter to a rider with as rich a past and future as Merckx, but might to Van Den Bossche. Merckx didn't care; he accelerated past his domestique to cross the summit first.

A photograph immortalises the moment when Merckx appears over Van Den Bossche's right shoulder. Van Den Bossche's head is turned to face Merckx's, whose gaze is fixed, lazer-like, on the road ahead and the summit. Years later, the actor Michael J. Fox would star in a much-lampooned yet much-loved film about a normal college kid and amateur basketball player who acquires miraculous athletic abilities the day that he discovers he can morph into a wolf. His previously hapless basketball team becomes unbeatable but also increasingly irked by his ball-hogging. This culminates in a scene when the wolf runs from behind one of his teammates, robs the ball from out of his hand, and proceeds to score yet another basket. The teammate looks on, dejected.

More or less, this is what happens on the Tourmalet.

Merckx said later that he didn't originally intend to prolong his attack; at the foot of the descent his advantage was just 45 seconds. Driessens pulled alongside him in the Faema team car and told him to eat and wait for the group coming from behind. Merckx nodded. Moments later, Driessens's vehicle had punctured, and Lomme the Liar was hopping up and down at the roadside, trying to thumb a lift. Merckx ate a rice-cake, sprayed his face with water, then turned around to scan the mountainside for Van Den Bossche and his group. He saw nothing but bare rock and road. 'At that point, for the first time, I thought it might be worth attempting an exploit in the context of such a beautiful mountain stage. I pressed on and I dug deeper than ever before,' he explained later.

Merckx gained an incredible six minutes on Pingeon, Van Den Bossche and company on the ascent of the Col d'Aubisque. They were eight minutes behind at the summit. From there 70 kilometres lay between Merckx and the finish in Mourenx. Driessens had finally jumped in with the journalists from the *Gazet van Antwerpen*, but his balding dome and clenched fist were now mere background ornaments. Merckx was out on his own, in every sense. After 15 tricky kilometres in which he let slip nearly two minutes, he recovered and began gaining time once more. Within minutes of him crossing the finish line, Driessens had of course pounced and planted a kiss upon his cheek. He then turned to the press and announced that only his intervention had prevented Merckx from abandoning the Tour when his legs had started to burn with 50 kilometres to go. Later, he deco-rated that version further: 'Eddy came close to the car and screamed,

"I want champagne!" So I took some fruit juice, added a bit of sugar, then shook the bottle. Eddy drank it thinking that it was the elixir of victory and off he went again, stronger than ever.'

The road-kill, dragged home by the Italian Michele Dancelli, seven minutes and 56 seconds behind Merckx, alternated stupor with black humour.

'Now we know why he's so much fresher than the rest of us: he's back at the hotel resting and we still haven't finished the stage,' quipped Raymond Riotte. The Frenchman has since tweaked this to, 'He was in the shower and we still had 15 kilometres to ride!'

Barry Hoban also saw no other option but to laugh. Hoban was widely attributed with the joke which did the rounds over the subsequent stages before Paris.

'Did you know that Poulidor and Gimondi both copped a 50-franc fine? They hung on to the wing-mirror of a lorry and climbed the Tourmalet without even turning the pedals?'

'Oh yeah? And what was Merckx doing in the meantime?'

'He got fined 50 francs as well. He was towing the lorry.'

In the television commentary box, the former rider René Vietto's analysis was harsh but possibly accurate. He called it a 'Tour *de résignés*' – a 'Tour of resigned riders'.

There was now no mystery about the outcome of the Tour, or probably the three or four to come, but some were still puzzled by Merckx's attack and more specifically its timing. Why, in particular, had he denied his teammate Van Den Bossche the privilege of being the first man over the Tourmalet? Speaking to Rik Vanwalleghem over 20 years later, Merckx went into more detail about a secret he would reveal a few weeks after the Tour. 'I still feel guilty about not letting Van Den Bossche go over the top of the climb first that day. But on the previous day he'd really got my back up. He came up to me and, straight out, told me that he had received an offer from the directeur sportif of Molteni, Giorgio Albani, and that he would be leaving our team [in 1970]...It was a pretty inappropriate time for Van Den Bossche to do what he did, and it really annoyed me. That is what made me think only of myself at the top of the Tourmalet. I knew I had done wrong, but in the situation, it proved stronger than I was.'

So, Martin Van Den Bossche, is this true?

'It's a lie as big as the Mont Ventoux!'

He shakes his head, then continues, 'Nobody knew! I had signed for Molteni the night before in Superbagnères, where we slept, but nobody knew!' he says. 'My monthly wage was going to be four times what it was with Faema. But, again, nobody knew! Why would I have told Merckx? After that Tour, we even met in Kampenhout and he thought I was going to sign for Faema, but they weren't offering me a rise, and I already had the contract with Molteni...'

On a night when the world was already hailing Merckx as greater than Fausto Coppi, and his ride to Mourenx as one of the finest ever seen in the Tour, Van Den Bossche went looking for his captain.

'I said, "Eddy Merckx, today a small rider expected a big gesture from you." He didn't respond and I never brought it up again. It didn't change the relationship as far as I was concerned, but I can't speak for him. It was just that I kind of expected a gesture at that point. I wasn't complaining. It was just that Eddy was so far in the lead [in the King of the Mountains competition]. He didn't need to take the points. There are so many cols in a Tour, but the Tourmalet is such a monument. I don't know if a helper wasn't supposed to say something like that. I just don't know, and I don't really know what the others in the team thought, either. We never spoke about such things. Eddy himself didn't talk much. He almost never talked about personal things. I almost never went to his house. There was no problem, either before or after Mourenx, but I could never get close to him.'

The next day's media coverage was a litany of superlatives, which has been reproduced often enough. The flavour was now familiar: Merckx was going where no man had been before, just like Neil Armstrong was about to do in a few days' time.

The most famous homage of all came from Jacques Goddet in *L'Equipe*. 'Merckxissimo' was his headline.

The 'Martian', as his mate Crazy Heart Bitossi now called him, gained more time at the Puy de Dôme. Two days later, before the race-ending final time trial, Merckx's former teammate Christian Raymond says that his wife and daughter Brigitte came to visit him in Créteil in the southern suburbs of Paris.

'My daughter asked me why Merckx always had to win, and I tried to explain that it was normal, because he was the best rider. She went quiet for a minute, then looked at me quizzically and said, "Well, then, he's a real cannibal…". I liked that name, "The Cannibal" straight away, and mentioned it to a couple of journalists that day. They, evidently, liked it too.'

Merckx was poised to live up to the new moniker and win the time trial into the old Cipale velodrome when, suddenly overwhelmed by the noise coming from the track, he almost rode straight past the entrance and into the crowd. The next few seconds, as he regained composure to win the stage by nearly a minute and the Tour by close to 18, would be and forever remain, by his own reckoning, the sweetest of his career. After a kiss from Claudine, one from mother Jenny and another smacker from Driessens, Merckx thanked his teammates one-by-one then joined them for a lap of honour. 'Eddy, Eddy!' chanted 25,000 spectators. The Faema ensemble circled the track two or three abreast with Merckx and Driessens, riding the special yellow street-bike he'd had prepared for the occasion, waving to the crowd on the front row.

In Belgium, special trains had already been chartered, and would ferry thousands to greet the hero in Brussels the next day. In previous Tours, the Walloon radio reporter Luc Varenne hadn't even been allowed a press motorbike; before the 1969 Tour, sensing the nation's excitement, his bosses had laid on an aeroplane.

At just gone nine o'clock French time *Apollo 11* prepared to make its landing on the moon. Belgian state TV would be blessed with a pundit *par excellence*, having scheduled a double video link-up – one to Armstrong and Aldrin on the Moon's surface and another to Merckx in a studio in Paris. Unfortunately, Jean Van Buggenhout had forgotten to pass on the message, and Belgium's most popular citizen was celebrating with its Prime Minister and his teammates in a restaurant on the other side of town. Merckx's friend, the TV journalist Théo Mathy, was dispatched to find him, a terrifying slalom through the Paris traffic ensued, and Merckx finally arrived on set, like a superhero, having cleaved his way out of a broken elevator.

'One small step for man, one giant leap for mankind...' said Armstrong.

If Savona had supposedly marked the Belgian public to an equal degree as the assassination of JFK, TV and radio networks were now faced with an on-the-spot dilemma: for some, if not all, Merckx was the first news item and events in outer space the second.

The following day, what seemed to Merckx like the entire Belgian population congregated in Brussels to see the prodigal son return and ride through the city in an open-top car. He and his Faema team-mates were then received by King Baudouin and Queen Fabiola at the Royal Castle of Laeken. With tears in his eyes, Merckx presented Baudouin with one of his yellow jerseys from the Tour before the gathering moved inside.

'It was a quiet thing,' recalls Martin Van Den Bossche. 'The king asked us a couple of questions: were you thirsty, that kind of thing. We were there about two hours. Then the queen asked whether every-one there was married. I was the only one who wasn't, so she wished me a lifetime of love and prosperity. After that they started handing out cigarettes. I was the only one who really smoked, but only cigars, so they went to get cigars with the royal crest on them. I got two. After that it was thank you, thank you, thank you and goodbye.'

9
down and out?

'I looked at the blood coming from Merckx's ear and thought that it was over for him, that he was a goner.' RAYMOND RIOTTE

The rough translation is 'full throttle!', the literal meaning more convoluted and cryptic. All that matters for now is that Claude Lair keeps saying it, over and over...

'*A fond la caisse! A fond la caisse!*'

Lair is talking about a different crash from the one we're in Blois to relive, but this clearly doesn't faze him. And neither should it. As athletic and up-and-at-'em a 77-year-old as you're ever likely to meet, Lair is explaining that our car is approaching the spot where the American David Zabriskie fell and lost the yellow jersey in the first week of the 2005 Tour de France. As he does so, he breathlessly interrupts himself with assorted observations on the topic that for the last seven decades has quite clearly been his *raison d'être*: cycling.

'*A fond la caisse! A fond la caisse!* He was coming down here, down here...there's the château on our right, the Château de Blois... Oh no, you must never stop cycling! *Never!* Never stop! I do 300 kilometres a week. We do 90 kilometres in three and a half hours! Three and a half hours! So he's coming down here, Zabriskie, the American, *à fond la caisse*! Then, hup, on that manhole cover! Down he goes! Down he goes! The yellow jersey, on the floor! It was there, *there*, not where the newspapers said the next day...'

But like Lair, we can't stop. Moments later we're crossing the Loire on the Pont Jacques Gabriel – 'there are three bridges in Blois! Gabriel, De Gaulle and Mitterrand!' – and bearing down on our final destination, the real reason for our visit. Given that the previous night he had been racing in Brittany this, in all likelihood, is also the route that Eddy Merckx and his soigneur Guillaume Michiels took out of town and towards the Pierre Tessier velodrome on the afternoon of 9 September 1969. It was going to be a post-Tour track meet, a night like any other.

At least so they thought.

Claude Lair was in the velodrome that night, as he had been hundreds of times before and has been maybe thousands since. Shortly he'll be standing on the spot where he heard the clatter of bodies and bikes.

'It wasn't just the worst crash I've ever seen, it was the worst crash there's ever been,' he says, his characteristic vim draining from his voice. 'Awful, just awful.'

Merckx couldn't say that Jacques Anquetil hadn't warned him. Twice. First about the toll taken by the second tour of France, which began immediately when the first one ended, and consisted mainly of mammoth drives across the country followed by a circuit or track race in the evening. When it wasn't France, it was Belgium. The races were traditional, they were lucrative and they were also more competitive than the rigged costume balls that later became the norm, and were inevitably won by the most popular rider. 'Yah, it was a real race,' says Patrick Sercu, Merckx's track partner and teammate at Faema in 1969. 'They were only 80, 90 or a 100 kilometres, but it was serious.

A lot of the peloton wasn't getting a wage, or a very small one, so they had to make their money in the criteriums. You were on the max from the first lap to the last.'

With a sizeable slice of Merckx's appearance and prize money going to Jean Van Buggenhout, it was clearly in Van Bug's interest to accept as many offers as the calendar allowed, and so he set Merckx a punishing schedule. Between the end of the Tour de France on 20 July and his appearance in Blois on 9 September, Merckx rode a staggering 36 criteriums. On 17 August, while Jimi Hendrix and Crosby, Stills, Nash & Young performed at Woodstock, Merckx raced in the afternoon in the Dordogne and in the evening in Moorslede in Flanders.

The races on home soil, and the volume of the Merckx supporters there, were the best possible barometer of how Merckx's popularity had now definitively outstripped Van Looy's. Numerous and intense, they also served as the ideal theatre for some of the pair's final, bitter and bloody conflicts. Two days after the Tour, no more than a kilometre from the family grocery store in Woluwe-Saint-Pierre, Van Looy enraged Merckx by leeching his back wheel on the pretext that he was 'dead', then rocketing out of his slipstream to beat the Tour champion in the closing metres. Three days later, in Denderleeuw, the rivalry reached its zenith, or possibly nadir, when Merckx dropped off the back of the peloton and allowed both himself and Van Looy to be lapped in protest at the 'Emperor's' perpetual wheel-sucking. 'You dirty old goat!' Merckx screamed at him, his patience finally snapping. Both were given suspended eight-day racing bans for their 'insufficient appetite to race'. This only made Merckx hungrier in Rijmenam the same afternoon. With Van Looy again ensconced in his slipstream, Merckx produced a rabid performance, sprinting into every corner until Van Looy was unhinged.

Quite how anyone, and more precisely the Belgian selectors, thought the pair of them could dovetail in the national team at the World Championship in Zolder two weeks later is beyond comprehension. The ovation reserved for Merckx was, if anything, even more magnificent than the one he had received in La Cipale at the end of the Tour. That was at the start of the race. When Van Looy's Dutch Willem II-Gazelle teammate Harm Ottenbros won in a breakaway to cause one of the biggest upsets in World Championship history, Merckx rode off the course 500 metres from the line to avoid the boos. Earlier in the race, staying onside with the fans and preventing Merckx from winning had appeared to be Van Looy's only objectives. 'Whenever Merckx accelerated, Van Looy jumped on to his wheel. But he did it very smartly, immediately, so that the fans didn't notice and start booing,' revealed the Italian Vito Taccone. While Merckx took refuge in a hotel and refused to speak for 90 minutes after the finish, finally emerging to say that Van Looy had been his 'worst enemy', even Lomme Driessens was speechless. 'What Van Looy did doesn't merit any commentary,' he said.

Naturally, Merckx was soon back to his winning ways, including at Châteaulin in Brittany on 8 September. That night, as was often the case after criteriums and particularly this one, the drink and the camaraderie flowed at a banquet laid on by the race organiser. A legendary *bon viveur* even in his Tour-winning days, Jacques Anquetil was in the last weeks of his career and completing his final lap of honour around France in a daze of demob happiness. The one arena in which Anquetil could still give Merckx a run for his money, he felt, was in the bar. He took Pingeon to one side before the meal and winked towards Merckx. 'Let's see if the young lad can take a drink,' he whispered. After several glasses of champagne, one or three of white and red and multiple invitations to 'Have another one, Eddy',

Anquetil was leading the woozy congregation towards another marquee where more whiskies were waiting. Round one had been equal on points, Merckx was still standing steady, and the bell sounded for round two.

More whisky. Doubles now. Through the booze-addled blur, what looked like a photographer. The flash of a camera, a lunge by Anquetil, the sound of a lens smashing on the floor, a slur of expletives, and finally the intervention of Anquetil's wife Janine. She had stopped both fights; Merckx had won his by technical knock-out. Janine now took her husband by the arm and headed off in the direction of their hotel, while Merckx rounded up Pingeon, Lucien Aimar and Jan Janssen and went in search of food. Pingeon was now semiconscious, or at least thought he was dreaming when Merckx ordered a bowl of onion soup liberally topped with grated cheese, a breast of chicken, then an enormous steak. The tales of Merckx's elephantine constitution and invincibility in eating and drinking games were apparently true.

The following day, needless to say, Guillaume Michiels and Merckx enjoyed a calmer and more clear-headed journey through Brittany and into the Loire Valley than the Anquetils. With the nausea rising through his stomach, Jacques reached for the door handle and instructed Janine to pull over into a grass verge. The next noise wasn't Anquetil retching but the door smashing into a signpost. If Anquetil had a headache before, now he was in pounding agony.

Anquetil's second warning to Merckx came an hour or two later in Blois, once the crowds had started to congregate in the Pierre Tessier velodrome and with them the clouds overhead. Anquetil had ridden on the same 285-metre outdoor velodrome in an earlier meet in May, alongside Walter Godefroot among others. 'This track is narrow, so let's not ride more than two abreast at a time,' Anquetil now instructed his five opponents for the night, Merckx, Jean Graczyck, Raymond Riotte, Francis Perin and Jiri Daler. The congestion and danger would be exacerbated by the fact that tonight's was a 'derny' meet: each man would be riding behind a motorbike or derny, and the pace would be blistering.

It was on nights like these that Merckx cursed Van Buggenhout, as he looked again at the dismal skies, the poky velodrome and the 3,000 fans supposedly massed around the track, expecting a performance worthy of a Tour winner.

He reached for his leather skullcap, then stalled, without quite knowing why. He picked up his reserve helmet and unbuckled that before hesitating again and going back to his first choice. He then changed his mind again and reverted to his back-up. He chuckled to himself. Claudine always said he was indecisive.

If neither Merckx nor Anquetil was relishing what lay in wait, the local press had been doing its best to whip the people of Blois into a frenzy. *La Nouvelle République* had declared that the meet promised to be 'sensational' and would see the first ever head-to-head encounter between Anquetil and Merckx behind a derny. 'The Normand has the advantage from an aesthetic point of view, but he'll have to reckon with the fighting spirit, the panache and efficacy of the Belgian champion,' said the paper's preview.

In 1970, Claude Lair was to inherit the position of velodrome director, but for now worked as a mere mechanic and track supervisor. A fine amateur racer himself, he idolised Merckx, but didn't dare to approach him as the Belgian ummed and ahed over his headgear. 'He was the president, the *grand patron*,' says Lair. 'I didn't speak to him, but I heard Anquetil harping on about the track: "Don't ride three abreast! Don't ride three abreast!" The track here's narrow – only four metres. When you're going at 80 kilometres an hour, which they do behind a derny, that doesn't leave much room for manoeuvre.'

The evening programme consisted of three 'legs' of 50 laps, all ridden behind a derny and with various sprints and spot prizes distributed throughout the races. Merckx, as usual, had pepped up as soon as he climbed on to his bike and won the first leg. He then set off behind his French derny rider, 56-year-old Fernand Wambst, for the second match. The other riders and the pacers buzzed around them like hornets. The skies darkened. The 3,000 bayed.

Claude Lair is now positioned exactly where he was that night, midway down the home straight.

'One of the riders, I can't remember who, and his derny man had punctured, and I was here trying to get him going again. Then, BOOM!'

Lair swivels and points to a corner of the track 50 metres away, next to the tiny changing rooms. 'There!' he says. '*There!* The Czech rider Daler's derny man, Marcel Reverdy, touches the balustrade there, falls down the track and Wambst can't avoid him. BOOM! They all fall down, and I run over to try to get Reverdy's derny off the track. I see Wambst and you can tell that he's dead. Then I see Merckx...'

Raymond Riotte and his pilot managed to avoid the crash and completed another lap while looking fretfully over their shoulders at the carnage behind them. When they swung into the home straight again, the track was still littered with bodies and bikes, and it was clear that the racing was over. Riotte pulled up close to where Merckx and Wambst lay and gulped.

'It was so upsetting,' he says. 'I saw Wambst, then looked at the blood coming from Merckx's ear and thought that it was over for him, that he was a goner. That night we'd been all nervous as soon as we got there and saw the track. It was too narrow for the number of people racing. You were rubbing shoulders and touching the other people's pedals all the time. Then, when the crash happened, we all got the fright of our lives.'

First aiders from the Red Cross were quickly lifting an unconscious Merckx and Wambst's already inanimate carcass on to stretchers. Reverdy was also badly hurt, as was an eight-year-old boy who had been watching from behind the balustrade that the derny had hit then scraped along. When he picked up Reverdy's derny, Lair noticed that a pedal was missing. He found it lying in the track 10 or 20 metres from where the pilot had lost control. Reverdy's own derny had been in for repair, and he had borrowed this one from a friend, Pierre Morphyre. A police investigation later ascertained that a pedal had been loose and became detached during the race, ultimately causing the crash. Reverdy was later fined 600 francs by the Tribunal Grande Instance de Blois for negligence, and Morphyre 400 francs. For his involuntary sins, Reverdy would spend over a week in hospital with a broken nose and fractured skull.

Merckx had also been rushed to the Hôtel Dieu de Blois hospital. When he regained consciousness, he was still oblivious to what had befallen Wambst. Guillaume Michiels had been standing in the track centre, five metres from where Merckx smashed into Jiri Daler. Merckx asked Michiels for news of his derny man. 'He's the same as you,' Michiels lied.

Merckx's life was not in danger. As for his cycling career, well, for a few hours it was too early to tell. The doctor diagnosed severe concussion and scalp wounds. Claudine and both of his parents hurried immediately from Brussels to see him the following morning, but visiting time was restricted to a few minutes. On waking, Merckx had worried about how Claudine would take the shock; she was pregnant and due to give birth to their first child early in the New Year. After a restful second night and more satisfactory checks from the doctor, she and Jean Van Buggenhout were both reassured, and informed local reporters that Eddy no longer feared for his future as a cyclist. In fact, in the warmth of the sunshine that streamed through the window, he could already feel the lure of the road.

The crash had occurred on Tuesday, and Merckx would leave hospital on Saturday. King Baudouin had dispatched a Pembroke military plane to fly to Blois and bring the nation's wounded hero back to his homeland. At 13h30, the priceless cargo flew out of Le Breuil aerodrome north of Blois, bound for the Melsbroek air base, where Lomme Driessens was among those waiting to greet him. A short ambulance ride home, a quiet afternoon among friends and family, and Merckx was soon heading to bed for another night of rest. Before the light went out, he turned to Claudine. 'Did they bring my bike back? We'll have to get it...'

Perhaps understandably in the circumstances, it had been the last track meet studded with stars of the road ever to be organised at the Pierre Tessier velodrome. Claude Lair as a coach and the same concrete track went on to nurture leading French sprinters Florian Rousseau and Frederic Magne, but very soon the site will have seen its last action. Its location on a flood-plain has forced the authorities to step in and build a substitute velodrome just a few hundred metres away, slightly closer to Blois's elegant town centre. The new track will be longer at 285 metres and significantly wider at seven metres.

If that sounds like one cyclist's paradise, Lair has turned his home into another on the opposite side of town. With his sick wife away in Lourdes, he had planned to ride 20 kilometres to catch the Tour de France on its way to Châteauroux and a second stage win in 2011 for Mark Cavendish. Instead, his ballbearing eyes will dart between the two television screens he has rigged up in his basement to watch the Tour, one tuned to the Eurosport channel and the other to French state broadcaster France 2. One of the three rooms on Lair's first floor is a shrine to professional cycling that would make museum curators jealous. He announces proudly that he has all 480 copies of *Miroir du Cyclisme*, the French bike fans' bible launched in 1961 and discontinued in 1994, and also a full collection of its nominal successor *Vélo Magazine*. Among his most cherished possessions is a photo of Merckx signed when he came to Blois during the 1969 Paris–Nice. 'The greatest champion of all time!' Lairs says, pulling the picture from one of his scrapbooks.

'Ah, yes, that made some noise, that crash,' he says. 'It was a shame that the track meets died after that. They started asking for too much money. They'd get to the velodrome, do a rough head count of the people in the stands, then think they were getting short-changed and ask for more in their envelope. They became too expensive. They shot the goose that laid the golden egg.'

Now slightly hard of hearing, Lair races these days on a tandem in the handisport category. At the time of writing he is the oldest competitive cyclist in France.

'I worked for thirty years in the Poulain chocolate factory in Blois, but now it's just cycling for me,' he says, surveying the shelves and cabinets crammed full of trophies and memorabilia. 'Cycling has been my life...I still ride! Three hundred kilometres a week! Oh, no, you must never stop cycling. Never! *A fond la caisse*!'

Twelve days after the crash in which, by his own admission, Merckx had 'flirted with death', it appeared to be business as usual as he completed and won a criterium in Schaerbeek on the north side of

Brussels. He was a little groggy, a little short of kilometres, but all seemed well given what had come before. Wambst's death had nonetheless upset and shaken him, and even more Claudine, who had known about the perils of derny racing ever since she used to accompany her father to the track as a young girl. As for the road, as Merckx had said in the clinic in Blois, he hoped that 9 September would soon be and remain in his career 'nothing but a bad memory'.

On 28 September, he excitedly watched Herman Van Springel win Paris–Tours from his living room in Tervuren. The following day he started and abandoned a criterium in St-Genesius-Rode. Merckx's next big test, his last of the season, would come at the Trofeo Baracchi two-man time trial in Bergamo, northern Italy on 2 October.

The Baracchi was a prestigious but strange event, ridden in pairings often irrespective of trade team allegiance and covering a mammoth distance of 120 kilometres. Merckx had won back-to-back editions in 1966 and 1967 with his Peugeot teammate Ferdinand Bracke. The 1969 race would be his first official competition since Blois – criteriums didn't 'count' – and Merckx had been due to partner his compatriot and Faema teammate Julien Stevens. Stevens, though, had also crashed at a recent track meet and been forced to pull out. Over several days at race HQ in Bergamo, discussions dragged on about who would replace Stevens as Merckx's partner, with Merckx requesting Van Springel. The final decision, though, fell to organiser Mino Baracchi, and he liked the idea of rewarding local lad Davide Boifava for a brilliant first season among the pros with the plum role of partnering Merckx. Merckx raised no objections.

Merckx had arrived in the Bergamo area two days in advance to prepare. On the eve of the race, he headed out for a final, intensive session behind a motorbike, which was briefly interrupted by strikers blocking the road in Dalmine. When they recognised Merckx, luckily, the picket line parted to let him through. He then flew back to Belgium for an awards ceremony on Saturday evening, before returning to a chilly Bergamo, briefly warming up, and discussing tactics with Boifava the next morning. When Merckx spoke of 'aiming for an average speed of 53 kilometres an hour', Boifava feigned nonchalance while shuddering inside.

A mismatch at least in reputation and experience, the Merckx–Boifava pairing in fact had the makings of a dream ticket. Boifava had won a stage in the Giro in May, was the Italian pursuit champion, and had excelled in the other recent 'unofficial time trial world championship', the Grand Prix des Nations in France. As he waited with Merckx for the starter's pistol, though, the wisecracks from a small gallery of 'well-wishers' were doing nothing to calm his nerves. 'Oh, youngster, you'd better watch or he'll drop you straight away,' was Vittorio Adorni's joshing send-off. Boifava's Molteni team directeur Giorgio Albani and his mechanic Ernesto Colnago cackled their approval.

True to his word, Merckx started, says Boifava, 'like a bullet'. As the route headed west out of Bergamo, skirting the hills of Brianza and towards Milan, Merckx bludgeoned his machine like rarely before. Fuelled by adrenalin, Boifava clung on, and at Robbiate after 28 kilometres, the duo was on schedule to smash Aldo Moser and Ercole Baldini's 1959 course record. At Monza, where the route swung back towards Bergamo, they still led Van Springel and his stand-in partner Joaquim Agostinho by 45 seconds. It was here, a moment or two after Merckx had peeled to one side, Boifava moved through for his next turn, and the road began gently rising that something very odd and unexpected happened.

'I'd been very nervous before we set off, because being paired with Merckx was such an honour and a responsibility,' Boifava recalls. 'My team actually weren't too happy about it because it was obvious that, if Eddy won, everyone would say "of course", whereas if we lost it would all be my fault. Anyway, we'd started at this crazy pace, but I was doing OK. Then in Monza we got to this motorway flyover, I was on the front, and I felt a hand on my hip. I looked around at Eddy and could see him gasping for air. I couldn't believe it. He said, "Slow down a bit." But it was obvious from his face that he was in a lot of trouble. I thought maybe it was just a passing crisis, but he never recovered. I had to ride on the front the whole way back to Bergamo.'

Eighteen kilometres from the finish line, the route took them through Zingonia. This was the site of Faema's new headquarters, an unholy breezeblock dystopia exhibiting the very worst of 1960s urban planning. Bruno Raschi had described it as 'a forest of prefabricated cement columns, huge expanses of nameless, ownerless factories and 70 kilometres without a single tree'. Here Van Springel and Agostinho finally took the lead, and Merckx's capitulation was almost complete.

As he and Boifava rode into the Stadio Atleti Azzurri d'Italia, Merckx cried and 25,000 people applauded. He crossed the line and could barely blubber a few words of apology in Boifava's ear. He then turned to the journalists and admitted, 'It went badly, really badly. I kidded myself about my strength. I started really fast, trying to beat the record, then I collapsed suddenly. Boifava was amazing...it was me who got it all wrong.' As his Faema directeur sportif Marino Vigna placed a hand on his shoulder, above the continuing ovation, Merckx mustered enough humour for a sardonic observation. 'You see, Marino, the only way I can get people to like me is by losing...'

'The Italian fans had turned on him a bit after Savona,' Vigna explains now. 'Gimondi's camp really destroyed a lot of the goodwill the Italians felt towards Eddy. Part of it wasn't their fault; the Italians were always going to resent a foreigner. But they also came up with a different excuse every time he beat them, instead of recognising his brilliant performances for what they were.'

Perhaps it was no coincidence then, that in Gimondi's home town, the *tifosi* warmed to the uncommon spectacle of Merckx suffering on a bike. Boifava conceded that he had 'probably lost my only opportunity to win the Baracchi', while also understanding that the race had come too soon for Merckx. Months later his own career would be badly affected by a crash in training which left him in a coma for ten days. He went on to win a handful of races before retiring at age 31 in 1978, but would forever be remembered as 'the man who made Eddy Merckx cry'.

As far as Boifava and plenty of others were concerned, Merckx would be back to his tyrannical former self, if not in the last criteriums before the end of the '69 season, then at least in the New Year. How could they be so sure? Merckx wished he knew, because that comment about Blois one day being 'just a bad memory' betrayed not only his, but every athlete's, gravest anxiety. In Bergamo, his head throbbed. Were these the occasional, permanent symptoms that doctor in Blois had warned him about, or just the born winner's psychosomatic rejection of heavy defeat? What if ignoring the doctor's advice to leave it a few more days, perhaps even weeks, before getting back on his bike had been a dire mistake? Hadn't people been telling him for years not to be so headstrong, so hasty?

The winter for a cyclist was the time to rest, but for the restless mind and body the long, cold months could be a purgatory of self-doubt. In Merckx's thoughts, the memory of the Baracchi, its thunderous first half and calamitous second, could quickly turn into a microcosm of two alternative versions of his future: the former, a continuation of the crushing supremacy he had reached at the Tour, the latter a sharp decline.

What Merckx didn't yet fully realise, but would soon find out, was that his life and cycling would never quite be the same after 1969. He would conclude years later that Savona had changed him psychologically and Blois physically. Whether and how those differences would manifest themselves in 1970, the world waited to discover with a mix of hope and trepidation.

10
a new merckx

'The crash had left physical and psychological scars...
To compound it, Savona was still on his mind. He had some
black days after what happened there.' ITALO ZILIOLI

By 1970, cycling had itself a sportsman who, later that year, would be voted the world's greatest in a poll of judges from 50 countries. In Mexico at around the time of the Giro, Pelé would orchestrate probably the finest team display in football history at the World Cup, and glitter as an individual, yet even he came up short of Merckx. Joe Frazier won the heavyweight boxing title of the world, Jack Nicklaus the British Open in golf, John Newcombe Wimbledon in tennis, but a 24-, soon to be 25-year-old Belgian cyclist seemed to tower over all of them.

And yet, as far as the man himself was concerned, the Eddy Merckx of 1970 and indeed every year thereafter was far inferior to another rider: the Eddy Merckx of 1969.

It is remarkable how many epoch-defining athletes have had their careers compromised by some, often widely unrecognised adversity or injury. The Spanish golfer Severiano Ballesteros is a pertinent example when discussing Merckx. According to one of his brothers, Ballesteros was already a shadow of his former self when he burst on to the international scene and almost won the 1976 British Open at 19 years of age. For three years in his teens, and until the onset of back problems that later bedevilled him, according to his sibling, Ballesteros played the best golf in the world and 'never missed a single shot'. If this raised the question of how good Ballesteros could and would have been, the same consideration could be made of Diego Maradona, who discovered cocaine at Barcelona in the early 1980s, peaked at the 1986 World Cup aged 25, and was practically finished as a footballer by his 30th birthday. Or about Ali, who lost three of his best years to the Vietnam War. Or about Fausto Coppi, who lost five shots at the Giro d'Italia and seven at the Tour de France to the Second World War. Or about Greg LeMond, who surely would have won more than three Tours but for his hunting accident in 1987. And so forth and so forth.

The prospect of Blois and its consequences hampering the remainder of Eddy Merckx's career was of course a remote one when the first signs appeared in the winter of 1969 to '70, but the fears would grow like a gangrene over the weeks, months and years that followed. If the Trofeo Baracchi had really only highlighted Merckx's lack of fitness and racing, a bout of tendinitis at the Six Days of Cologne a few weeks later was the first, true warning sign. Not that Merckx's partner in Germany, Patrick Sercu, could see or hear anything different from what he had become accustomed to with Merckx. 'Yes, he was complaining, but he was always like that,' Sercu says. 'Even when he was fifteen, he was always sick before the start, and it carried on when we did Six Days together. It'd be, "Ah Patrick, my stomach, my knee, my back. Take it easy tonight." Then we'd get on to the track, start the Madison, and on the first changeover he'd be asking me whether he should attack yet. On the bike he was another man. Cycling was the best medicine for him.'

To the outsider, there was nothing particularly new even in the way, that winter, Merckx was constantly tinkering with his bikes and his riding position. Only those in the very tight inner circle comprising family, Van Buggenhout and Guillaume Michiels perhaps began to notice a mounting unease – and even that largely relied on their powers of intuition or observation. The fact that he showed up one day at Jules and Jenny's to rescue two oblong mirrors from their shed, 'so I can look at my position when I'm on the rollers', might have confirmed nothing more than that Merckx was as focused as ever, despite the distractions of the previous few months and the impending birth of his first child. Added, though, just for instance, to Claudine one day finding the allen key with which Merckx adjusted his saddle height under a pillow in the marital bed, it would perhaps have been clear that, in Merckx's mind at least, his desire for Blois to one day be 'just a bad memory' seemed increasingly wishful.

What *exactly* was the problem? At first Merckx didn't know the name, only the feeling. In this first winter after the crash, it was mainly localised in his left leg, and was more a *discomfort* than a pain. When he climbed, the old fluidity, the way the pedals seemed almost to liquefy beneath his feet, was replaced by a clunking motion of equal power but nowhere near as satisfying a sensation. Sometimes his left leg would outright lock up. In time, his masseur Gust Naessens would come to refer to it as Merckx's 'little leg'.

One thing had changed over the winter: the Faema team had switched its name to Faemino, like the instant coffee the company had just launched. Their first, pre-1970 season training camp was to take place in Loano on the Ligurian coast, 25 kilometres from where old ghosts lurked in Savona. Merckx's old friend Zilioli was there for the duration, having moved to the team in the winter from Filotex. Merckx meanwhile would make only the briefest of cameos, having remained in Belgium for the due-date of what he and Claudine now knew would be a daughter. Little Sabrina, who would have been called Laurence had her parents not worried that it sounded too 'French' and therefore unpalatable to Flemish tastes, was finally born, well over-due like her father, on Valentine's Day. Sod's law: her birth immedi-ately contributed to the end of the love affair that had begun two years earlier between Merckx, Faema and their owners the Valente brothers. Merckx's late arrival and token appearance in Loano after the Milan Six-Days, which began within hours of Sabrina's arrival, didn't go down well with the local tourist board with whom the Valentes had arranged Faemino's stay. Over the next few weeks and months, the relationship would continue to deteriorate.

When they watched Merckx on the road, Zilioli and the other Faemino riders saw nothing unusual except that, in Zilioli's case, climbing wasn't quite the joy that it had been in training at some of his previous teams.

'Usually, after riding Six-Days over the winter, someone would give themselves a week or ten days to get used to their road bike again, but Eddy was out with us at eight o'clock the morning after arriving,' Zilioli says. 'As one of the better climbers, I always used to test myself on the hills. I said to myself that if ever I was going to drop Eddy on a climb it was now. So I accelerate and what happens? Eddy bullets past me and drops everyone.'

Zilioli, though, was one of Merckx's closest and most perceptive friends, and soon got a sense of the anxiety nibbling if not gnawing at Merckx. 'He was worried in that winter,' the Italian confirms. 'The crash had left physical and psychological scars. You should never underestimate what it's like to see a guy die in front of you, your derny rider…To compound it, Savona was still on his mind. He had some black days after what happened there.'

In some ways – and not that Merckx saw it – Zilioli was living proof of what lay on the other side of the precipice above which Merckx may now have been teetering. Zilioli's career had been sabotaged not by a physical weakness but a psychological one. People could and would speculate about how many more Tours and Giros Merckx would win, how many records he could break, but only the men looking down their own personal cliff-face, the riders, knew how precarious their footing was, and what a rocky landing awaited below.

No one felt the vertigo more acutely than Italo Zilioli.

'Eddy was sensitive, like me,' he says, 'but I suppose the difference was that he seemed to be able to express his emotions and worries or turn them into something positive. I on the other hand keep them bottled up, which isn't good. When you do that, eventually your head goes, or your liver, or your sleep... I used to get nightmares all the time when I was under pressure. Fortunately they stopped when I retired. It was because I couldn't handle the pressure. As soon as something was being asked of me, it started to get to me. I wanted to be instinctive. Eddy also had those worries, nightmares, but again he seemed able to use that sensitivity as fuel.'

The early indications were that, whatever Merckx feared or could feel, its impact would be bigger in his head than on the road. His final harvest in 1969 had totalled 43 victories from 129 races, and now he commenced 1970 in similarly ominous form. At Paris–Nice, he won three stages, including the traditional La Turbie uphill time trial, but finished in agony due to a delicately positioned wound caused by his constant shifting in the saddle. This prompted more tinkering, a phone call to Vincenzo Giacotto to warn him that his participation at Milan–San Remo could be in jeopardy, and finally the decision to ride with one pedal crank longer than the other in a misguided attempt to alleviate the pain. The night before the race,

Merckx called Zilioli into his hotel room and admitted that he was in no state to ride for victory. Instead, he promised, he would be Zilioli's domestique de luxe. Merckx was as good as his word, and Zilioli got fourth. Merckx congratulated him, stopped for a couple of minutes to answer journalists' questions, then rode straight up the coast, another 50 kilometres, to catch a plane from Nice airport. In total, that day, he had ridden 340 kilometres.

The next month, like every April, would be spent almost entirely at home in Belgium as Classics fever gripped the nation. Rarely had anticipation of a spring campaign been piqued like now, and not only because Merckx had shown chinks of vulnerability – or at least a lesser degree of invincibility. No, the reason was something, someone else, specifically the first of two major new challenges that would present themselves in 1970, together with the twinges in Merckx's left leg.

Later in the season Merckx would begin to gauge the ambition of the Spanish *caballero* Luis Ocaña, but his emergence would be slower and more *staccato*, despite victories in the Vuelta a España and the Dauphiné Libéré in the spring and early summer. The new and more immediate danger came in the Classics, and its or his name was Roger De Vlaeminck. The 22-year-old from Eeklo in East Flanders had justified his refusal to join Merckx's Faema empire with a string of victories in 1969 which patently established him as Van Looy's natural successor. De Vlaeminck was young enough and talented enough not to need his hero Van Looy's conniving, but a bullish refusal to accept Merckx's superiority was at least one similarity between him and the 'Emperor'. For all that Merckx's Tour win had sent his popularity soaring, De Vlaeminck also provided the dyed-in-the-wool Flemish speakers with a new totem for their linguistic, political or nationalistic hang-ups. Even some who weren't on the Van Looy bandwagon, and had no particular prejudice before, had turned on Merckx when he and Claudine exchanged French and not Flemish marriage vows in December 1967. This despite the fact that the decision had come, entirely innocently, from Merckx's mother Jenny, who assumed that she was sparing the priest the unnecessary inconvenience of translating two ways. 'They raked up my wedding hundreds of times. Ever since then, they have always been ready to pick up any mistakes I make with the language,' Merckx bitterly commented later.

While Merckx had spent the two or three subsequent years trying to redeem himself, taking immense care to give numbers of interviews in French and Flemish, certain sections of the public and press had continued to regard him as a divisive figure in an already bisected nation. At the 1969 Tour, three journalists from the Flemish Belgian Radio and Television network authored a Tour de France travelogue containing the following passage:

'Maybe it's too late to call the Flemish fans into action, but the fact is that this year we're only hearing cries in French, we're only seeing flags with French slogans. Brussels and Wallonia have adopted Merckx... Maybe it's just a reflex that makes the Flemish shout in French in France, but if that's the case they're wrong. Could we ask Flemish tourists to encourage Merckx in Dutch or, at least, in their dialect?'

Later in the same book, the authors lamented that De Vlaeminck had lost too much time on the first mountain stage to be considered a genuine contender. 'It would have been great,' they argued, 'if the first Belgian to win the Tour for forty years could have been "een Vlaeminck".' Or, their play on words seemed to suggest, anyone as long as he was 'een Vlaming' – a rider from Flanders.

Now, in April 1970, De Vlaeminck and his older brother Erik, the reigning cyclo-cross world champion, prepared to do battle with Merckx on the rutted roads and murderous, cobbled hills of Flanders that they considered more theirs than his. Roger was not only a thoroughbred Flandrian in name, extraction and upbringing, but also on a bike. Like Van Looy, he was speedy enough to beat all but the fastest finishers in a sprint and also among the best on the flat and short climbs or *bergs*. This made him the ideal candidate for victory at Gent–Wevelgem on 1 April, but it was Merckx who drew first blood in a repeat of his 1967 victory. Five days later, Merckx was beaten at the Tour of Flanders…but by the sprinter Eric Leman, not De Vlaeminck, who could only finish 13th.

Merckx's next competition was the Tour of Belgium, one of a shrinking number of races not yet in his palmarès. After three stages, the pain in his left leg was back along with the anxieties and, also, the old winning itch. The next morning, in Jambes, the weather was fit only for sled-dog racing, and De Vlaeminck was among a group of riders pleading with the race director to cancel the stage as they set off across Wallonia towards Heist-aan-Zee. Popular myth has it that Merckx took this as his cue to shoot immediately from the pack. Walter Godefroot says that, in actual fact, it was he who launched the first attack. What matters, though, is not who was the instigator, but the way that Merckx was about to force two-thirds of the field to abandon the race and set up overall victory.

'It started snowing and suddenly everyone starts shouting, "Stop! Suspend the race!" but I attack,' Godefroot remembers. 'I go up the Kruisberg in Ronse, and I remember that the derailleur is like a snow-ball. I had to pour some tea on the chain so it didn't jump. I get to the top of the Kruisberg, look round and see Merckx arriving with Erik De Vlaeminck on his wheel. Van Schil or Spruyt is also on the wheel. Not long after that, we come to a section of cobbles and we're down to three – me, Merckx and De Vlaeminck. Merckx didn't attack – he just accelerated slightly. A bit later, the weather is starting to change, De Vlaeminck is taking his leg warmers off, and Merckx looks at me and growls, "How's it going?" I say, "OK." But Merckx is now doing one, two kilometre turns on the front, while I can only do five hundred metres then pull off. Merckx is a motorbike. We keep going like this for a few kilometres, then he asks me again, "All OK?" I say "Yes." He then says, "OK, stay in the wheel and make sure you beat this prat."'

Godefroot's subsequent sprint win made it a double defeat and double-trouble for the De Vlaemincks: like everyone else in the main pack behind, Roger had been humiliated to the tune of 12 minutes.

Roger's fifth place in Paris–Roubaix the previous year, just weeks after turning professional, at least indicated that he could start the 1970 edition of the race known as the 'Hell of the North' with realistic ambitions of castling Merckx later the same week. With the rain teeming down and the notorious *pavé* cobbles at their most slippery, with 30 kilometres remaining, the lead group comprised Merckx, Leman and Roger De Vlaeminck, who looked perfectly placed. Then, disaster: a puncture. No sooner had he slowed for a wheel change, than Merckx was accelerating away on his own to a five-minute victory. Later, Merckx would admit that this was perhaps the only time in 1970 when his legs felt the same as before Blois. On the day he had the audacity or honesty to call it his easiest win over cobbles.

A few metres away, a furious De Vlaeminck was accosted by the same Flemish radio journalists whom Merckx had been careful not to spurn a few moments earlier. 'Let me tell you this,' he said. 'Next Sunday, at Liège–Bastogne–Liège, Merckx won't drop me. That, I promise.'

Erik De Vlaeminck listened to his brother and shook his head in exasperation. 'That what you said about Merckx not dropping you on Sunday... If you ask me, you're an absolute nutcase. You're setting yourself up for a massive fall,' he said as they headed for the showers.

Roger glared back in much the same way as he had at Merckx at the amateur Tour of Belgium in 1968.

'He is not dropping me on Sunday,' he repeated.

11

the gypsy and a nomad

'Ohohohohoho. "Who was the better player?!"
Dear me...I was much better.' ROGER DE VLAEMINCK

Roger De Vlaeminck sits behind the kitchen table in his farm in Kaprijke, watching intently as a small yellow sponge chases a puddle of coffee around the wooden surface.

'Dab! Dab don't wipe. Dab,' he says quietly, but with some urgency. When, a few seconds later, all trace of the liquid has gone, De Vlaeminck's gaze remains fixed on the spot. 'Dab, don't wipe. Always dab,' he says again.

De Vlaeminck looks much the same as he did a few months ago at the Giro d'Italia in Nevegal, albeit dressed for a lazy day around the house rather than preening on Italian television. He wears a white T-shirt, tracksuit bottoms and slippers. While the clothes aren't exactly fit for the catwalk, De Vlaeminck himself still has the lean, athletic physique of an active middle-aged man. All up the walls, there are framed photos of his 11-year-old son Eddy and 38-year-old wife Katty. Perhaps it's having a belle 27 years his junior that keeps De Vlaeminck looking youthful. Maybe that was also the main attraction of the model and actress Phaedra Hoste, whom De Vlaeminck began dating in 1987 when he was 40 and she was 16. Then again, perhaps there were other things.

De Vlaeminck brings his mug to his mouth and looks wistfully out of his patio window. Beyond the garden, where the llama guarding his livestock roams, the horizon ends after a few hundred metres of muddy, nondescript, quintessentially Flandrian field.

He shakes his head.

'London? How can you live in London? Look at this. Isn't it beautiful?'

The biggest challenge with De Vlaeminck proves to be keeping his mind and the conversation on the reason for our visit. Questions about, for instance, the now famous meeting with Merckx at the 1968 amateur Tour of Belgium, are inevitably cues to turn off at his favourite tangents, namely football or the mediocrity of current riders and races. The habit is manna for Belgian journalists on a quiet news day but also food for their scorn. Just this weekend, De Vlaeminck says, he was invited to the first cyclo-cross race of the season but didn't even stay for the race. 'I ate and then went home. I didn't miss anything. The top guys were paid really well to be there, but they were all thinking about the bigger race the next day. We never thought like that. I won Het Volk one day then beat my brother Erik in a cyclo-cross the next. As for the Tour de France, now, well, I come in here, turn on the TV, see there's 110 kilometres to go and then go and do some work in the garden for two-and-a-half hours. I watch the last 10 or 15 kilometres, no more. It's a different sport now from what it was when I was racing Merckx.'

And finally, we're back on message, the rivalry that, in 1970, threatened to stir and sever Belgium in a way that the unequal contest between Van Looy and Merckx had done only sporadically. At the heart of the matter, as already discussed, was a division of the Belgian landscape dating back perhaps even before to Julius Caesar's conquest of Gaul and Wallonia's gradual assimilation of Latin vulgaris, a precursor of French, as its mother tongue in the centuries that followed. Added to the old linguistic chestnut, though, was another factor: De Vlaeminck was not only a Vlaaming – from Flanders – but he was also a 'Flandrien'. The concept was a nebulous, often subjective one, but central to every definition was the idea that there was a sub-breed of riders from Flanders who were even tougher, stronger and more ferocious than the rest, and whose appetite for the most awful conditions was even greater. Merckx couldn't be ruled out on the second criterion – two of his biggest wins, the 1969 Tour of Flanders and the 1970 Paris–Roubaix, had been, after all, achieved on the hardest of courses in diabolical conditions – but the breadth of his repertoire, and of course the fact that he had grown up close to Brussels meant that this was one denomination, and one aura that he could never attain in the eyes of the Flemish purists.

De Vlaeminck, meanwhile, had flopped in his first Tour de France and, by default, reinforced his credentials as a man of the Classics and a pure Flandrien. Stories were also beginning to spawn about the 400-kilometre training rides which, he says now, he did 'every Wednesday when I was at home'. 'Merckx trained a lot but I don't think he trained more than me,' De Vlaeminck elaborates. 'Gent–Wevelgem used to be 260 kilometres. I'd get my friend to meet me with his motorbike at the finish and we'd do another 120. At other times, twice a week, I'd do 180 kilometres before nine o' clock in the morning. I had a 90-kilometre circuit that I'd do twice, then I'd get back home, eat, then go off for another 150 kilometres...'

He scoffs, 'These days they do the GP E3 Harelbeke on the Saturday and won't do Gent–Wevelgem on Sunday because they say it's too much!'

Interestingly, though, or maybe predictably given his temperament, De Vlaeminck takes a fundamentalist view of what constitutes a Flandrien, and in doing so excludes even himself.

'There was only one Flandrien and that was Briek Schotte,' he says. 'The others were false Flandriens. Schotte won the Worlds at Valkenberg in 1948 having attacked from the gun and ridden with a broken wheel for 200 of the 260 kilometres. You know the average speed? It was 37 kilometres an hour! Merckx could try to do that but I'm not sure if he'd manage. No, for me Briek was the only one. The first and only one. The others, me included, are all half-Flandriens.'

A half-Flandrien but, nonetheless, proudly Flemish. Like Van Looy before him, De Vlaeminck seldom if ever spoke French, but when he did, his Flemish fans felt somehow betrayed. 'You couldn't win with the fans,' he says. 'It was the same for me and Merckx. As soon as you said a word of French, you annoyed the Flemish fans. The difference was that I was Flemish so didn't need or even interest the Walloons as much as Eddy did. I didn't have to worry about speaking French. He had to try to please everyone.'

Whether the differences were real or imagined, it was easy to see why the clash seemed so appealing to both the public and the media. For all his tyranny on the bike, Merckx could seem docile, childlike and apologetic off it, while De Vlaeminck put sass and an edge into everything he did or said, like in those radio interviews after Paris–Roubaix. De Vlaeminck was mystified when the French rider Jean-Pierre Danguillaume appeared alongside him in the peloton one day in 1969 and said just, 'The Gypsy. You're the Gypsy' – but somehow the nickname seemed perfectly apt. He was dark, mean and streetwise. He had also been a brilliant young footballer, good enough to play four games for Eeklo in the Belgian third division at age 16. This was one apparent similarity with Merckx, about whom Dino Zandegù says, 'He would have gone straight into Serie C [the Italian third division].' Informal matches with journalists were common, and Zandegù recalls one in particular where Merckx 'scored four or five goals and absolutely murdered us – he had this rocket shot with his right foot'. These games were also among the best examples of the foaming competitiveness which was another characteristic of both Merckx and De Vlaeminck. Walter Godefroot remembers one occasion when all three were on the same team, fellow rider Ronald De Witte was in goal, and De Witte allowed a Godefroot back-pass to slip through his fingers and graze the post. 'They went crazy at him. I had to calm them down, remind them that we weren't playing in the World Cup final,' says Godefroot, still aghast. 'That was just their mentality. There was no such thing as playing for a laugh. You played to win or not at all,' he adds.

Having already been perplexed by Merckx's win-at-all-cost mentality on the Tourmalet in 1969, Martin Van Den Bossche decided to have some fun at his expense in one game between Belgian and Italian riders by deliberately giving away a penalty in the dying moments when Belgium led 2–1. Merckx was incandescent, and Van Den Bossche had to stifle a giggle.

Merckx and De Vlaeminck could both be as cut throat as each other, but who was the better footballer? When the question is put to De Vlaeminck, a series of low-pitched hoots echo through his kitchen, to be followed – if he's not careful – by the thud of him falling off his chair.

'Ohohohohoho "Who was the better player?!" Dear me...I was *much* better. Merckx was robust. You would bounce off him. But he wasn't technical. He was a big brute. "Who was the better player?!" Dear me...'

'Rivalries are good. I loved the battle,' he picks up, returning to the more pertinent matter of the 1970 Liège–Bastogne–Liège. 'I didn't mind. It only changed when, after a while, the others start to take advantage of our rivalry. Merckx would attack and the others would say, "Ah, De Vlaeminck will go after him and we'll get on his wheel. No problem." That changed things a bit. I then got sick of it and stopped bridging the gaps all the time. Before that, though, it was beautiful...painful but beautiful.'

On 17 April 1970, '*Le Gitan*', 'The Gypsy', kept his promise. Not only did Eddy Merckx not drop him despite endless, furious attacks, but De Vlaeminck was the first over the line and the winner of Liège–Bastogne–Liège. Merckx was disgusted, not so much by the fact he had dragged his rival through the Ardennes hills with barely any collaboration, but by the way in which, as he saw it, Roger's brother Erik had deliberately blocked him on the approach to the Rocourt velodrome. In September 2011, Roger De Vlaeminck still insists this wasn't the case, and, to prove it, uses three coffee mugs to reconstruct his decisive spurt on a right-hand bend, his brother's slight deviation to the left, and Merckx's position on Erik's wheel. 'In Formula One, that's perfectly fair, isn't it?' he protests. At the time, De Vlaeminck further irked Merckx, and made him change his mind about skipping Flèche Wallonne two days later, by telling the press, 'You see? Merckx can't drop me in a straight fight.' Meaning, 'He can't drop me without attacking when I've got a puncture', which is what De Vlaeminck believed had happened in Paris–Roubaix.

If that sounded like a gauntlet clunking to the tarmac, Merckx stooped to collect it at Flèche Wallonne. As he powered over the line in Marcinelle, neither of the De Vlaemincks, nor the rest of the field, were anywhere in sight.

The Classics season thus came to a conclusion: the unambiguous one that Merckx was still Merckx, in everyone else's judgement if not in his own. He had won two 'semi-Classics', Flèche Wallonne and Gent–Wevelgem, and one of the so-called 'monuments', Paris–Roubaix. What had changed was that he now had a talented, belligerent rival with greater longevity that Van Looy and more gumption than Godefroot. The former's spring had been a pitiful death rattle on his former hunting grounds, including abandonments at Paris–Nice, Milan–San Remo, Gent–Wevelgem, the Tour of Flanders and Paris–Roubaix. Godefroot had signed for Gimondi's Salvarani and immediately felt like the embarrassed guest in the home of a married couple now communicating only via hateful stares and thrown plates. 'We had our first training camp that winter in Alassio, on the Ligurian Riviera in Italy. There were only eight or nine of us – the rest were arriving later – and on the first morning we all set out from the hotel, down the little hill to the coast road. We came to the seafront and T-junction, and I saw Gimondi turning right and Motta turning left. I didn't know what the hell to do. I'd just joined the team, didn't speak a word of Italian, yet there I was, forced to make this decision in a split second, knowing that if you went right you were with Gimondi, in his clan, and if you went left you were one of Motta's boys. I had nothing against Motta, but I went right.'

Perhaps more to the point, like his feuding teammates, Godefroot had the world-weary air of a man whose best years had been the first of his career. The years, specifically, when Merckx still seemed mortal. 'I can remember [the Salvarani directeur sportif] Luciano Pezzi coming up to me one morning that year and saying, "Ah, I've heard Merckx isn't going well, so we'll put the hammer down and attack him." I said, "Luciano, with respect, I've heard before that Merckx isn't going well, and it's usually a sure sign that it'll be him who's attacking." We tried anyway and the attack from Merckx duly came. And that was Merckx. You perhaps thought that he wasn't the same any more, or on a bad day, then he rammed it down your throat.'

Here, unwittingly exemplified in Godefroot's anecdote, was perhaps also a key reason why whatever Merckx had lost after Blois was imperceptible to his main antagonists. Merckx's then Faemino directeur sportif Marino Vigna explains it best: 'Maybe he wasn't quite as strong [in 1970], but then maybe it also didn't matter as much because by that stage he'd put the fear of God into everyone. They were scared of moving, because they knew what chaos Eddy would then unleash. They never wanted to give him any bait. The memory of what he'd done to them in those '68 and '69 seasons terrorised a lot of people for years.'

By 'people' Vigna means not only riders but also the press and race organisers who had begun to fear for the sport itself in 1969. The second group, in particular, were damned if they did invite Merckx and damned if they didn't, and so some resorted to striking a strange kind of bargain. The rumour was that the Giro d'Italia chief Vincenzo Torriani had overcome Merckx's reluctance to return to the race which, he felt, had betrayed him in 1969, by offering him 80,000 Belgian francs a day to compete. In return, Torriani asked Merckx to ride economically, holding back some of his own energy in readiness for the Tour de France and also some suspense in the battle for the pink jersey. As it transpired, he appeared to amuse himself by taking three stages out of the first nine to all but wrap up the general classification, then by ensuring that Felice Gimondi beat the Faema defector Martin Van Den Bossche to second place overall. That, at least, was how it looked from the outside. In truth, even Van Den Bossche understood then, and still understands now, that it was in the interests of the Giro and Italy that Gimondi should finish second. 'Merckx never spoke about that, but it was obvious. When there was an attack and Gimondi wasn't part of it, Merckx just wouldn't ride. It was all part of the game, however much the Flemish press tried to build it into a Flanders versus Brussels thing. I mean, even I tried to sell my third place to my [Molteni] teammate Michele Dancelli, but he wouldn't pay up, and tried to finish third in a sneaky, cunning way,' Van Den Bossche concedes.

Another, at first more open secret, was that Merckx was suffering in the mountains, and Van Den Bossche had precipitated a recurrence of his leg problems on the Passo di Crocedomini on the stage from Zingonia to Malcesine. When his lanky former domestique accelerated, Merckx tried to follow, but felt his left leg immobilise. He was over a minute behind at the summit, then regained touch on the descent, before falling back again on the next climb to the Bezzecca plateau. He had returned to the main peloton by the time they reached Malcesine, but knew some would already be hailing a landmark moment: Eddy Merckx had been distanced in a major tour mountain stage for the first time since the 1967 Giro. His irritation showed when he initially refused all interviews at the finish line, only later admitting that 'I haven't suffered like that for a long time.' Perhaps wisely, he chose not to mention Blois or the leg, and chose instead to attribute the crisis to a bad cold and sore throat. The following day, sure enough, normality resumed and the pink jersey was secured with a trademark solo win at Bretonico.

From that point on, if Merckx wasn't 'allowed' or wouldn't permit himself to crush the opposition as he had at the Tour, there were still plenty of other outlets for his competitiveness. Dino Zandegù remembers one in particular on Stage 15 between Casciana Terme and Mirandola.

Dino, Dino, they say Merckx used to go crazy even for the bonus sprints! Did you ever see that?

'Oh yes, that day in 1970, we were going over the Abetone in Tuscany, but on the way we were passing Luciano Tajoli's estate in Pontebuggianese, and Tajoli had put up forty flasks of Chianti for the winner of a bonus sprint there. You know Luciano Tajoli, the singer – "*Terra straniera, ho pianto per te, la, la, la….*" Him. Anyway, when there was wine involved, I was always particularly motivated for that kind of sprint, so there I am, we go round a big curve, over a little bridge, and I sense this big shadow looming over me. I see out of the corner of my eye that it's Merckx in the pink jersey, but I'm so motivated that I do the sprint of my life and I beat him! As always, Merckx is black with rage. I try to hide in amongst my teammates, but he's seen me, and he's throwing every kind of insult you can imagine at me. "You rotten scumbag! You scoundrel! Just you wait and see! I'll make sure that you never race a criterium again! That Chianti's mine!" Then, that night, all the teams are staying in hotels next to each other and he comes to find me with Rudi Altig. He likes a drop of wine, too, Rudi. Merckx says he's not leaving until I give him half of the bottles. A few hours earlier I thought he was going to kill me, so I daren't say no, and off he goes with half of the Chianti…'

Midway through 1970, Eddy Merckx had won his second Giro d'Italia, asserted his authority over Roger De Vlaeminck in the Classics, and was already beginning, perhaps even subconsciously, to accept and adapt to the legacy of Blois. 'After Blois, cycling became suffering, especially in the mountains, when previously it had just been fun,' Merckx would comment in his retirement. At the time he swore to Guillaume Michiels that he had lost 'fifty per cent of my power'. Even in 1970, though, public and private hints by Merckx to this effect were greeted with rolling eyes. 'If you were to look at his career, just the results out of their context, you couldn't say there was a "Blois effect",' argues the journalist Walter Pauli. That may be true, but it's equally reasonable to point out that the accident occurred when Merckx was 24 and, most physiologists would argue, still two or three years short of his peak. There may have been no discernible dip in 1970, but most would have conceded that there had been no improvement on the stratospheric performances of 1969, either. Whether that also was because he had matured, mellowed, and was beginning to heed the advice of everyone who had warned that he was heading for burnout – their sole remaining hope or commiseration – maybe only Merckx knew. An interview with Marc Jeuniau early in 1971 would certainly indicate that Merckx had at least considered the long-term impact of the hell-for-leather approach he had employed in the previous three or four seasons. 'I won't race beyond the age of thirty,' he said. 'My way of racing makes it impossible to last a long time. But the public likes the way I ride. The quality of the spectacle and panache count more than everything else. Anquetil used to say that he didn't care about public adulation. That's not true. No champion is indifferent to it.'

If Merckx was really to retire at age 30, that left six more Tours de France to ride and, based on the evidence at hand, probably win. While he rode with new frugality at the Giro, however, down in the Alps, a rider with similar pizzazz and ambition was staking his claim as the most credible 'anti-Merckx' to date.

Luis Ocaña had been born a week before Merckx and into a very different milieu. His native Priego was a woebegone hodgepodge of ruins dozens of kilometres from anywhere and 150 to the west of Madrid. As his biographer François Terbeen put it, it was 'a desolate land where only misery found shelter'. A small flock of sheep, their wool and a tiny olive grove were the family's only income, and scraps of bread sometimes their only nourishment. Even at age five or six, the young Luis would decline to eat, like his father, if he could see that there was too little on the dinner table to go around.

In 1951, when Luis was six and money still short, his father accepted a job in a mine in Vila in the French Pyrenees. It was a success, or at least an improvement, and soon Señor Ocaña was heading back to Priego to round up Luis, his mother Julia and brother Amparo, and take them to France. Six years later, one of Julia's brothers raved about the new life he had also created in Magnan, just up the road in Armagnac country, and the Ocañas moved again. While Luis felt more and more at home in France, he remained a foreigner to the bullies among his classmates. One day, apparently for this reason alone, one of them spat in his face.

Another move, this time a few kilometres to the east and Houga, coincided with the start of Luis's apprenticeship as a joiner, his first journeys to work on his new 'Automoto' bike, and the Spanish climber Federico Bahamontes's victory in the 1959 Tour de France. Soon, Luis was entering races in the colours of the local Stade Montois cycling club and winning with increasing regularity. In 1967, he rattled off victories in the amateur Grand Prix des Nations, the Tour des Alpes de Provence and the Tour of Majorca. One of the leading Spanish teams, Fagor, moved swiftly to sign him in 1968, and Ocaña repaid their faith by winning the Spanish national road race championship in Mungia. For Ocaña, the symbolism of the victory dwarfed even the privilege of wearing the yellow and blood-red jersey of the Spanish champion for the forthcoming 12 months; his father was dying, at just 49 years of age, ravaged by a prostate cancer for which he had refused any treatment. Luis had ridden the entire race in Mungia possessed by the idea of returning to his dad's bedside with the champion's jersey and laying it at his father's side 'as a testimony to my affection for him'. 'Bitterly, I kept telling myself that everything would have been wonderful if destiny had spared my father this illness,' Ocaña later wrote in his autobiography. 'In fact, my sister Amparo had just given birth to her second child. Life was being renewed all around us, bringing into our family new faces to love, to feed, to bring up, but, alas, there was also this dreadful ordeal that my father was enduring on his bed of suffering.'

While the writing was a little overwrought, it chimed with the tragic aura the cycling world would come to associate with Ocaña, as over the next two years, he alternated swashbuckling success with crashing failures like his early exits from both the 1968 Vuelta and the 1969 Tour de France. Like De Vlaeminck, he was mercurial, swarthy, enigmatic – and also, crucially, immune to the spirit of resignation which had infected much of the peloton since 1968. As of the start of 1970, he was also now backed by one of the strongest teams in international cycling, sponsored by biro makers Bic. At first, on signing with team and their manager Maurice de Muer, Ocaña had worried that the Dutchman Jan Janssen might be a cumbersome presence alongside him, but the pair had proved to each other and De Muer at Paris–Nice in March that their talents – Janssen's speed and cunning, and Ocaña's rapier accelerations in the hills – were perfectly matched. Ocaña finished second behind Merckx despite frittering energy with reckless and fruitless attacks. Janssen responded to his new teammate's claims that he would one day topple Merckx with a sceptical '*Ah bon?*', while De Muer told him to stop racing like 'some kind of cycling Don Quixote' – the only novel that Luis had ever read. A month later, Ocaña appeared to be learning fast as he triumphed in his national tour, the Vuelta a España, with a performance almost Merckx-like in its assurance.

'The sniper who played into his rivals' hands has now been replaced by a lucid, organised, top-class rider,' De Muer told him after the Vuelta, and Ocaña bore out his manager's commendation with a masterly win at the Dauphiné Libéré, the last major test before the Tour. While, in June, Merckx began an exhausting but lucrative, made-for-TV schlep around France to recce some of the key Tour stages, Ocaña returned to his now beloved Armagnac, the French wife he had married on Christmas Eve in 1966, and a new level of expectancy.

The Luxembourger Johny Schleck, his team- and roommate at the time, says that Bic's cosmopolitan, orange-clad army felt that they had no more, no less than a potential Tour winner in their number.

'Merckx was the king at the time, but we felt that Luis, with the ability he had in the mountains and the ability he had on the flat above all, was a possible Tour winner,' Schleck says. 'He wasn't explosive but he was enormously strong. When he accelerated, it took him a while to open up a gap, but he went so fast that he blew everyone off his wheel, one-by-one, until no one was left. He could climb in the saddle, with his hands on the drops, and just batter people. He had these big, rippling thighs and I think he must have produced about as much power as anyone in the peloton back then.'

Unfortunately, Schleck and everyone else knew that Ocaña's thighs were as thick as his skin was thin. 'You could practically see through it, Luis was so sensitive,' another ex-teammate, Philippe Crépel, confirms. Schleck agrees that this was the one, major doubt that Ocaña needed to banish in 1970, particularly after a 1969 race that had started promisingly then thudded to a halt with a crash on the Ballon D'Alsace and withdrawal two days later. 'He was a very fragile, very sensitive character. Sensitive to everything, even success,' Schleck says above the drum of raindrops on a hospitality gazebo at the 2011 Tour de France, where his sons Andy and Frank are among the star attractions. 'Luis used to get carried away. I personally think that he was very bad at dealing with pressure, right from the start. Sometimes he was on a cloud and sometimes he got out of bed and nothing was right with the world. Back then, going to the Tour de France with Luis as our leader was a big step into the unknown.'

If the press and other riders were all unanimous in considering Luis Ocaña the main and perhaps only threat to Eddy Merckx's designs on a second straight Tour de France win, after four days the defending champion himself wasn't convinced. Merckx was satisfied on two counts – one, a specialist from Brittany had been successfully treating the sciatica (that was now the diagnosis) in his left leg and, two, even on the plains of north-west France, Ocaña looked to Merckx like a man on the edge. This, says Marino Vigna, was yet another weapon in the Merckx panoply. 'Eddy was very good at judging his competitors. He would come to me at the start of races and say, "Watch so and so today. He'll be good. And they invariably were." In the stampede to the line and a bunch sprint won by Godefroot in Lisieux, Merckx had positioned himself within spying range of Ocaña and made this unflattering assessment: 'I got a good look at Luis. He looked washed out and had his mouth open like he was about to die. People are saying that he'll be my most dangerous rival in the mountains. I hope they're right, but he has to show a bit of resistance.'

Ocaña wasn't listening, but an attack in the first kilometre on that fifth stage towards Rouen in Normandy was a brave riposte. Needless to say, Merckx was alert to the danger, reacted quickly, and a second consecutive bunch sprint ended with another win for Godefroot.

Almost a week in, the Merckx mind was unusually unencumbered – except for one thing. His friend Italo Zilioli had taken the yellow jersey on Stage 2, after Merckx's victory in the prologue, and the circumstances of the 'handover' had sparked yet another row with Lomme Driessens. Zilioli and another Faemino rider, Georges Vandenberghe, had marked Godefroot when he attacked to join four other unfancied riders early on the stage to Angers, and initially refused to contribute to the pace-making until Driessens appeared at their side. 'OK, you can go!' Driessens told Zilioli. When the gap back to the main peloton grew to five minutes, Merckx loomed to offer viewers the unusual spectacle of the race leader chasing down a teammate and purportedly his 'best friend in cycling'. The time gap as Zilioli took the stage and 20 bonus seconds was 24 seconds – enough to dispossess Merckx of his yellow jersey by four seconds.

Merckx said that he was angry not because his friend had broken rank and followed through on his pre-Tour promise-cum-threat to 'see what I can do myself'. Nor was he upset, Merckx said, because he'd dreamed of keeping the yellow jersey all the way to Paris. His concern, he claimed, was that Zilioli would now burn himself out before the mountains, where Merckx needed his help. Although Marino Vigna admitted that it was he who had urged Zilioli to forge ahead, Merckx blamed Driessens.

Six days later, perhaps in an effort to atone or reingratiate himself, Driessens instructed Merckx and the Faemino Red Guard not to wait when Zilioli punctured close to the finish in Valenciennes. 'I'd told them to stay at the front to help Eddy, and Zilioli wasn't there when he punctured,' Driessens explained that night.

Looking back now – and partly because it wasn't the first or last time that Merckx's brand of sporting leadership lapsed into megalomania – it seems fair to doubt whether he was really more concerned with 'needing Zilioli in the mountains' or monopolising the Tour. Zilioli, for his part, is still sticking to his version and sticking by his friend: 'I was the kind of guy who, if he had good legs, would just go to the front and take off, without really thinking too much about the consequences. Eddy wasn't angry with me. He was just concerned about how much energy it would take to defend the jersey. That night, he said, "Italo, today you've done a lot of work, and it's a long Tour." You see, a lot of people thought Merckx only had an accelerator, but he had an accelerator and a calculator. Eddy used to say "Legs don't have a brain."'

In his first day back in yellow, as the race headed towards the Brussels suburb of Forest, just a few blocks from Woluwe-Saint-Pierre, Merckx again welded power to intelligence in a devastating attack with Lucien Van Impe. Any other rider might have gifted the stage-win to his fellow escapee in return for a 1'20" reinforcement of his race leadership, but Merckx only knew one kind of charity, the one that consisted of donating his prize money to good causes, as he would at the end of this Tour. Besides, he didn't like wheel-suckers – or '*profiteurs*' as he called them – and Van Impe had already shown that tendency in his first 18 months as a pro.

The surprise move and victory, plus a further strengthening of Merckx's position in the afternoon time trial, delighted the fans in Brussels but appalled the Tour director and *L'Equipe* journalist Jacques Goddet. 'Gentlemen, this is a catastrophe!' Goddet blurted in the newspaper's evening editorial meeting, brandishing a printout of the general classification, which Merckx already led by over two minutes.

Luis Ocaña's ninth place and 3'38" deficit were alarming but not a death sentence with four mountain ranges – the Vosges, Jura, Alps and Pyrenees – still jutting invitingly out of the road map. Unbeknown to Merckx, however, Johny Schleck's misgivings about his team leader's mental fortitude were proving sadly accurate, as Ocaña's stomach tied itself in knots more intricate and painful than the hairpins he was about to face on Stage 10. Merckx knew all about how and where stress could collect, germinate and tyrannise in the body, having suffered the same problems as an amateur, and now he hastened Ocaña's collapse by escaping with 13 other riders 170 kilometres from the finish line in Divonne les Bains. Earlier, just five kilometres into the stage, Merckx had chased the Portuguese Joaquim Agostinho only to be told that Agostinho had a score to settle after his contentious disqualification the previous day. More to the point Agostinho '[needed] a cow, and you, Merckx, have enough money to buy a hundred!' Later, though, Merckx was in no mood to compromise; standing behind the finish line outside Divonne's palatial casino, the journalist Gianpaolo Ormezzano waited with the Molteni team manager Giorgio Albani for what was now a three-man lead-group of Merckx, the Molteni rider Guerrino Tosello and the Belgian Georges Pintens to swing around the final bend. Ormezzano recalls: 'I said to Albani, "If he lets Tosello win here, he's got a friend for life," but of course then Merckx smokes him.' Ormezzano then walked over to where Merckx had stopped, already looking refreshed, and put the same point to Merckx as he had to Albani: 'If you'd let him win, you'd have had a friend for life.' Whereupon Merckx gestured towards the fans craning over the barriers and mumbled in his usual, bass montone, 'I owed it to them. They have the right to see the best man win.'

Four days later, following two further Merckx masterclasses in a time trial around Divonne and the big Alpine stage to Grenoble, Ormezzano would be the bearer of bad news which turned Stage 13 into a sorry one for both Merckx and Ocaña. Ormezzano had become as close as journalists could to Merckx over the previous three years, partly because the youngster had made him and his pre-race punditry look good by winning the 1966 Milan–San Remo, and more recently because, says Ormezzano, 'I'd defended Eddy when the Italian press started turning on him for ruining their vision of Felice Gimondi dominating international cycling.' In recent times, Merckx had come to know of Ormezzano's involvement in local politics and taken to addressing him as 'Il Senatore'.

Now, in Gap, Ormezzano waited for Merckx to come under the banner and into the mêlée, ready to relay some terrible news: their mutual friend, the Faemino team manager Vincenzo Giacotto, had lost his battle with throat cancer and died the previous night. For Ormezzano, Giacotto had been 'one of those people who was impossible to dislike, except for the fact that he supported Juventus, which for a Torino fan like me was the worst sin a man could commit'. Amid tears, Merckx now described him as a 'real friend'. Once or twice, after Savona, he had wondered whether Giacotto really believed that he was innocent of doping, and the mutual trust had briefly lapsed. In future, though, Merckx would cherish his memories of a man, he said now, 'whom I really liked as a human being'. A few metres away, Italo Zilioli sat propped against the trackside and wept into his hands. His association with Giacotto went back further than Merckx's, almost a decade.

At around the same time, another fragile bird, Luis Ocaña, was bringing to an end a terrible ordeal that reached new timbres of agony on the Col du Noyer. When his Bic teammate Charly Grosskost could take no more and climbed off his bike, Ocaña briefly wanted to follow him, but instead prolonged the martyrdom which would provide rich material for his memoirs two years later. 'I touched the depths of despair... In front of a fountain which my fever lent the appearance of an oasis, I was even tempted to abandon. I was ashamed, as I told myself that I had no right to finish the stage, with Charly having abandoned. I kept telling myself that I wasn't worthy of his sacrifice... My face was like Christ's on the cross, but the solicitations of my directeurs sportifs seeped into my being and had the effect of a cracking whip.'

The following day, once again, Merckx and Ocaña found themselves united in suffering but divided by minutes on the torrid slopes of the Mont Ventoux, the 'God of Evil demanding sacrifice' described by Roland Barthes. In the morning, Italo Zilioli was still so shaken by Giacotto's passing that, when the minute's silence in his former boss's honour ended, his head still hung and it was left to Merckx to cajole him with a hand on the shoulder and an '*Allez, camarade!*' The way the pair then channelled their grief on the road where Tom Simpson had perished three years earlier then bore out what Zilioli said about how they responded very differently in adversity; if, as *L'Equipe*'s Antoine Blondin had said, the Ventoux was 'a witch's cauldron', the rare brew of sadness and adrenalin spurred Merckx to yet another devastating solo win, while Zilioli floundered with Ocaña further down the mountain. Two kilometres from the summit, now flagging, Merckx had paid his respects to Simpson and the monument that marked the site of his collapse in 1967 by removing his cap, while Jacques Goddet jumped out of his race director's car to leave flowers. Moments later, having been too exhausted to even raise a hand from the bars as he reached the summit and the finish line, Merckx caused a brief but serious alarm by barging past reporters while complaining that he had 'fire in his belly'. For a few, nervous minutes, the spectre of Simpson and an unthinkable déjà vu hung in the heat haze, as the second-placed rider, Martin Van Den Bossche also felt unwell and was bundled into an ambulance. Van Den Bossche now found himself sitting next to the rider who the previous year had killed his dream on another legendary peak, the Tourmalet – Eddy Merckx.

'I can still hear the tour doctor, Pierre Dumas, saying that my heartbeat and circulation were good but that they'd give me a shot if

I didn't regain full consciousness in the next two minutes,' Van Den Bossche says. 'I heard him counting, "Sixty, fifty-nine..." then him telling his assistant to "Get it ready", meaning the shot. Fortunately within a minute I was awake, and then Merckx came in. They closed the door, and we were in there for an age, about half an hour. It turned out quite well because there were these two Citroëns waiting to take us down the mountain with a police escort. We went down at a hundred and twenty kilometres an hour with sirens wailing and fans still all over the road. It was absolutely terrifying, but the good thing was that we arrived at the hotel an hour before our teammates who had been blocked on the mountain.

'In the end it was much ado about nothing,' Van Den Bossche puffs. 'Both of us had been fine all the time. My directeur sportif Giorgio Albani had pinched my hand in the ambulance, and I'd pinched back. Meanwhile, our mechanic Ernesto Colnago was outside, sobbing and thinking that I was dead. Albani opened the door and told him to stop the cinema!'

If Merckx's victory wasn't assured before then, barring accident, it was now. In his hotel bed in Avignon, he had much to ponder besides what was now nearly a ten-minute lead over the second-placed rider on general classification, the Dutchman Joop Zoetemelk. As well as thoughts of Giacotto and Simpson, on the Ventoux's barren upper slopes, Merckx had been haunted by the old neurosis that ran straight down his spine and into his leg. As it did, as he had done on numerous other occasions during the Tour, he had reached into his back pocket for his allen key and began adjusting his saddle height as he rode. At the top of every pedal stroke, he braced himself, waiting for his leg to lock completely.

The panic was more frightening than any pain, and Merckx didn't intend to reacquaint himself with the feeling at any point in the

Tour's last nine days. He would limit himself to 'just' two more wins, in the time trials in Bordeaux and on the final day at La Cipale in Paris, scene of his second consecutive enthronement as the Tour de France winner.

It would be wrong to suggest that Eddy Merckx's battles were over, that he faced no more opposition after Stage 14 to the Mont Ventoux. Neither Ocaña's token, consolatory breakaway win at Saint-Gaudens, nor the young Frenchman Bernard Thévenet dropping and beating Merckx by over a minute on the Pyrenean stage to La Mongie, however, provided the champion elect with anything like the challenges which were increasingly coming from behind the barriers and inside the press enclosure.

Goddet's remark about Merckx's 'catastrophic' early lead betrayed the resentment which had again festered throughout the Tour, and which Merckx seemed powerless to assuage. Coming from him, the tiniest faux pas could be magnified to assume the proportions of a blasphemous insult. While Ocaña was winning at Saint-Gaudens, the Faemino soigneurs had arrived at the team's allotted sleeping quarters in a stuffy school hall, and immediately taken the executive decision to check the entire staff into a hotel up the road in Barbazan. Later that evening, while they were eating, the former rider turned Tour bigwig Albert Bouvet strode through the dining room towards Lomme Driessens, race regulations in hand; sleeping and eating in a location not selected and approved by the race organiser, Bouvet reminded Driessens, was forbidden. Merckx and company duly trudged upstairs, packed their things and, in Merckx's case, had barely slept when the alarm sounded for the next stage to La Mongie. Later that morning Merckx didn't help himself by adding the lunch-pack laid on by the race organisers to his list of grievances, tipping its contents on to the tarmac in front of a group of journalists and squashing an unripe peach under his feet. 'We anxiously await the day when the champion demands moules marinières in Sainte-Marie-de-Campan [the village at the foot of the Tourmalet], or maybe Lobster Thermidor,' Antoine Blondin wrote in *L'Equipe* the following day.

The subtext was that Merckx was abusing his power, perhaps without even realising it. Whether he meant it or not, he had been swept along in the slow, seamless transition from boy genius to super-star, with all its trappings and the added complication, in cycling, of the authority that the best rider could exercise over other competitors. The French rider Cyrille Guimard was one of a number complaining that Merckx was now so strong that he was able to play God; he could 'choose' who was allowed to win at his own convenience. Godefroot had been 'allowed' to win the green points jersey only because Merckx liked him, and as a result of an agreement with Driessens even before the race started in Limoges that Merckx would grant him this privilege in return for the odd favour along the road.

The real problem, though, was that there was no longer anything cute or coltish about Merckx to the outside world. He was 25, his face still fresh and unlined, but it had somehow transmuted out of its previous innocence into a colourless, frigid mask. The more the high-brow magazines searched, the more they sent their best and most intuitive interviewers to stare and forage deep inside his soul, the more mystified they became. The now defunct *L'Aurore* newspaper had taken the bold and unusual step of dispatching one of its top female writers, Odélie Grand, into what must have been – and remains – one of the more male-dominated and lecherous environments in professional sport. The interview requests rained down, not from Grand in the direction of the riders, but the other way around. When she met

Merckx, however, Grand was confronted with an opaqueness that she had only previously encountered, she said, in the film star Ryan O'Neal. 'Most of the time I did feel that the attitude of my subject was influenced by the fact that I was a female reporter,' Grand told Roger Bastide. 'I'm used to it, whether it's an actor, a politician, a finance magnate or a writer that I'm talking to. It's only ever a kind of mockery or scorn, at least a kind of humour that's not particularly charitable. But in front of Eddy Merckx...nothing! His gaze gets lost somewhere over your shoulder and erases you from the picture. It's a black-out. You no longer exist. He replies with a yes or a no, but he's thousands of kilometres away, on his own inaccessible planet.'

Grand could rest assured that she wasn't the only one. Another 'name' writer on the 1970 Tour, Lucien Bodard, had built his reputation on one of the toughest beats in journalism, reporting on the rise of Communism in China, but even he couldn't get to grips with Merckx. Of his stage win in Grenoble, Bodard remarked, 'Merckx, a super-winner in unprecedented fashion, scurries away looking a tiny bit bored, with nothing to say, not even a word of satisfaction... It comes as the biggest surprise to discover that Merckx isn't a robot constructed by engineers. He turned himself into a robot. With him there is no sense of aspiration, no sense of predestination, no flame. Just the realisation that he was unique, different from the rest, and he had to take advantage of that. And so he turned himself into a machine with extraordinary attention to detail and permanent application. He is the human bicycle.'

Bodard's portrait was well observed, but from Merckx's vantage point, on the inside looking out, it was pointless for these people to want or demand answers or a charisma as transcendental as his talent. The issue, indeed, was their expectations as much as his inarticulacy, the smile that his mother had told him 'wasn't commercial' all those years ago in Woluwe-Saint-Pierre, or his profound awareness of his own limitations. He told Marc Jeuniau, 'I spend a third of my life on the bike, another third on the massage table or at the wheel of my car, and I need another third to sleep. In five years, when I'm not racing any more, then I'll have time to read, to go to the cinema and the theatre, or go to conferences, and I imagine that I'll enjoy it very much.'

If former teammates recall that one of his pet hates was poring over tactics at the end of races, wouldn't it also hold true that he had little appetite for discussing them with journalists? On all other matters, one of the pressmen who perhaps genuinely understood and sympathised with Merckx, Gianpaolo Ormezzano, perhaps sums it up when he says, 'To me Merckx was just a superior person, in his head and his legs, but I mean by a sportsman's standards. Maybe if you had put him in charge of a nuclear physics laboratory he would have blown up planet Earth. I don't know... What I'm saying is that he was smart but his gift was for riding his bike.'

Merckx had demonstrated it again to win the Tour de France by nearly ten minutes. Thirty positions on general classification and one hour, six minutes and 59 seconds was the size of the abyss between him and Luis Ocaña.

12
deplumed

'For the first time, I was dictated to by a stronger rider than me.
Now I think it's all over.' EDDY MERCKX

For the second time in little over two years, Eddy Merckx lay in a foetal position on a hotel bed, his bottom lip quivering. The role fulfilled in turns in Savona by Vincenzo Giacotto, Italo Zilioli and Martin Van Den Bossche now fell to the Dutchman Rini Wagtmans.

'It's over. This Tour, me as a rider…it's all finished,' Merckx sobbed.

'Come on, don't be ridiculous,' Wagtmans told him, paraphrasing the words expressed in manifold ways, in manifold languages, in the thousand or so telegrams that the Tour postman had just delivered to Merckx's bedroom. 'Remember what I told you under the podium this afternoon. Remember what I saw. I tell you, it's not over…'

Almost a year to the day earlier, during the 1970 Tour, Merckx had sent Jean Van Buggenhout to meet Wagtmans in a hotel car park in Pau and offer him a ride with Merckx's new Molteni team the following year. Wagtmans had immediately given Van Bug his word and his signature – if he remembers correctly, 'on the back of *La Dépêche du Midi* newspaper'. The idea had been for Wagtmans to enter the fold of Merckx's disciples, but until a few days ago he felt that, alas, Merckx had given him a lot more help than the other way around. A fast-talking, even faster-descending livewire of a rider, Wagtmans was also something of a maverick. His nickname, the '*Witte Bles*' or 'White Blaze' referred both to the shock of white which struck his hairline like a lightning bolt and to his speed going downhill, but there was also something luminous and volatile about his whole approach to riding his bike. At a time when Merckx spent much of the winter competing in Six Days and racking up thousands of kilometres in training, Wagtmans consigned his bike to the garage in October then barely touched it again until March. Usually, within weeks, the sparks would be flying from his pedals, and Wagtmans would have fireworks prepared for the only race that mattered to him: the Tour. But not this year. Still desperately short of fitness in May, he had become so demoralised and downbeat about his prospects of making the Molteni Tour team, that it had taken a phone call and a stern pep talk from Merckx to bring him around. 'Rini, you can't train a thousand kilometres in three months and expect to be good. You wonder why I'm so good, but I ride more than two hundred kilometres most *days*...'

Previously, Wagtmans had thought that Merckx 'trained like a foolish man'. As the Tour approached and he finally discovered his sparkle, Wagtmans realised that there was logic in the lunacy.

Now, though, in Marseille, he watched Merckx writhe, listened to his moans and briefly reverted to his old assessment. If Merckx thought that he was finished, that the 1971 Tour de France was over and Luis Ocaña had won, 'foolish' really was the only word.

As for what had happened between Orcières Merlette and Marseille a few hours earlier, well, says Wagtmans today, that was simply 'the greatest Tour de France stage of all time'.

There had been signs, just a lot of little things and one or two big ones all spring. The previous season had ended not with a whimper but no real rousing finale, either, as the next phenomenon off the Belgian cycling production line, Jean-Pierre 'Jempi' Monseré,* over-shadowed Merckx by winning the World Championships in Leicester. The following week, Rik Van Looy headed out for a training ride, saw Vic Schil and Jos Huysmans on the road from Herentals to Grobbendonk, and told them no, he couldn't think of anything worse than riding with them all the way to Namur. The old 'Emperor' then turned around, pedalled back to his house and hung up his bike for good. Thirty years later, Van Looy would dedicate just three sentences to Eddy Merckx in his autobiography. After initially agree-ing to an interview for this book, one of the first he would have done for half a decade, Van Looy changed his mind midway through the first question about the 1965 Paris–Luxembourg, wished me well, and put down the phone.

If it had been goodbye and good riddance from Merckx in 1970 too, Merckx's farewell to the Valente brothers and Faema was tinged with regret both at Giacotto's passing and the way their relationship had deteriorated since the spring. Merckx's new team would be Molteni, the cold meat manufacturer, whose gold and navy-blue jerseys had previously been sported by Gianni Motta and Michele Dancelli. Merckx finally signed a two-year contract four days after a Tour of Lombardy in which Motta had stifled his every attack, and Franco 'Crazy Heart' Bitossi had won in a sprint. In their meeting at Molteni's headquarters in Arcore near Milan, team manager Giorgio Albani agreed that Merckx could bring 'with him' ten Belgians and one Dutchman, Wagtmans, but insisted that there was no room for

---

* Monseré's career and life would be tragically cut short in March 1971, when he was hit by a car which had strayed on to the course during a race in Reite in Belgium and died instantly. Felice Gimondi says today that, 'Along with Merckx, he was maybe the biggest talent I've seen.'

Marino Vigna as a third directeur sportif alongside Lomme Driessens and Molteni's current Italian coach Marino Fontana.

Two months later, in mid-December, Merckx and Claudine accepted Italo Zilioli's invitation to join him and his family at their alpine retreat in Limone Piemonte, close to the French border but hundreds of kilometres from the maelstrom of scrutiny and intrusion which life had become in Belgium.

In a matter of hours the Turin-based newspapers were getting tip-offs; not only was Merckx at Limone, but he had shouted some profanity, in Flemish, at a drunk female who had heckled him in a bar. The next day, a photographer was waiting when he stepped out with Zilioli for a walk in the woods. Merckx made angrily towards him and grabbed the camera. 'Now I'm going to break it,' he growled, this time in Italian. 'No photos, no interviews, not even a word,' he then muttered, before disappearing over a fence and into the forest with Zilioli.

One of the journalists sent to 'doorstep' him, *La Stampa*'s Maurizio Caravella, brought home what Merckx was now up against the following day. 'Merckx is now advertising [Molteni's] cold meats rather than [Faema's] coffee, but he still doesn't care about advertising himself. Is he really so strong that he can afford the risk of becoming unpopular? He's obviously sure of it.'

Merckx's foremost preoccupation, as always, was winning on his bike, and all seemed well on that score at the Molteni training camp in Tuscany in January. Where in previous years it had been Vittorio Adorni and Italo Zilioli, now the Italian neo-pro Giancarlo Bellini was blown away. Merckx was five kilos over his racing weight, but there was nothing particularly unusual or alarming about that at this time of the year; in the diaries or *Carnets de Route* which he was now keeping with the journalist Marc Jeuniau and would publish at the end of the year, Merckx archly claimed that Martin Van Den Bossche, with whom he had been reunited at Molteni, was carrying 15 kilos of excess baggage.

Paris–Nice in March was his first major encounter with Ocaña in 1971, and Merckx's first victory by a score of three stage wins to nil and just over a minute on general classification. The next week, Milan–San Remo saw a repeat of the shameless spoiling tactics or *catenaccio* Motta had employed at the previous autumn's Tour of Lombardy, but also an even stronger performance by Merckx and a victory – the best of his four to date in 'La Classicissima'. No worries, no scares there. On to Het Volk on 25 March. Another win, after a pulsating duel with Roger De Vlaeminck. The next weekend, the same cast at the E3 Harelbeke, and success for De Vlaeminck. The first false note sounds, and the first whistles from the crowd. Next a win for Georges Pintens in Gent–Wevelgem, then at the Tour of Flanders another lapse, if that's what you called being trapped in the peloton as your teammate Georges Van Coningsloo makes a hash of the finale to get smoked by Evert Dolman.

Paris–Roubaix is the next big one. Molteni have Merckx and Merckx-lite, Herman Van Springel, and both are poised in the key break when they hear Lomme Driessens's engine snarling. They turn around to see their directeur sportif trying to run Walter Godefroot off the road. Seconds later, Godefroot has Driessens by the scruff of his neck, hanging halfway out of the driver's seat window. Now it's Godefroot, the usually docile 'Flemish bulldog', snarling: 'Lomme, if you do that again, I'm going to pull you out of this car.' When Godefroot rejoins the leaders, Merckx's head is still shaking. 'That was bad,' he says, 'but the worst of it is that it wasn't even deliberate. He's just a dreadful driver.' That contretemps turns out to be the tip of the iceberg, or rather the sharp edge of one of the beastly cobblestones that cost Merckx five punctures and all chance of victory, which goes to the Belgian Roger Rosiers.

Next faux pas – Merckx is mobbed by fans at a trade fair in Milan, gets ill, and has to skip Flèche Wallonne. While the cat's away...the Gypsy plays. Merckx pays him this back-handed compliment in his *Carnets de Route*: 'So it was that [Roger] De Vlaeminck got his annual big win.'

Merckx could snipe, if indeed that was his intention, but going into his rematch with De Vlaeminck at Liège–Bastogne–Liège there was little to choose between their respective Classics campaigns. Merckx knew better than anyone that another failure in La Doyenne would cause hysteria among the Belgian media. The only solution was to pull out a win of the same *cru* as his 1969 Tour of Flanders or Liège processions. This meant resisting the temptation to turn and wait when he found himself alone 90 kilometres from the line, briefly joining Joseph Spruyt, the Luca Brasi to Merckx's Godfather, then ditching Spruyt and riding all the way to Liège in the freezing rain. This was the familiar script, but Merckx had forgotten his lines: as Pintens gave chase from behind, Merckx imploded on the Mont Theux and his advantage sank from five minutes to just over one minute. He was barely advancing. He thought first about abandoning, then hallucinated that Pintens was already upon and past him, before finally regaining his composure. Merckx decided to allow himself to be caught around four kilometres from the Rocourt velodrome, whereupon Pintens would counter-attack immediately and commit hara-kiri. His brain, clearly, was working just fine even if his legs were not. Plan B worked perfectly and Merckx duly took the sprint.

If ever, though, a victory had felt uncannily like a defeat, it was this one. Not to Merckx, who was delighted in spite of having suffered 'like never before', but to the journalists waiting for him to recover and explain himself under the podium. The following day, most at least found it in their heart to salute his bravery. In *Le Figaro*, for example, Louis Vincent invited readers to 'bless the errors [with or without inverted commas] of a champion who still reacts like an amateur, after five years as a pro and a star'.

Merckx himself knew that he had been too bold, that he hadn't fully recovered from the illness that had kept him out of Flèche Wallonne. He was also adamant that the troubles with his left leg were now behind him. That, however, would be a little presumptious, as would any notion that more who had watched Liège had been struck by his incredible resilience and lucidity than his collapse on the Mont Theux. Having opted for the Dauphiné Libéré rather than the Giro d'Italia in May, he was 'sickened' to discover that certain French journalists were trying to 'demolish him', seizing on and exaggerating the importance of his every mistake. On Stage 2 from Grenoble to Annecy, Ocaña was one of several riders to distance him on the Col du Granier. Merckx claimed that a problem with his gears had held him up; Ocaña countered that only the rain and the way that it had hardened his legs near the summit and on the descent had allowed Merckx to regain contact. The French journalists nodded. The pair were closely matched for the remainder of the race, but victory in the decisive final time trial and overall standings went to Merckx. The Spaniard was second. 'He's going very well. He's getting better every season,' Merckx granted – a resounding endorsement compared to what he had said at the Tour the previous year.

At his final warm-up race before the Tour, the Midi Libre, Merckx showed that his form and desire to silence the critics were tapering nicely by winning two stages and the overall classification. It was the first time that Claudine had travelled with him for the duration of a stage race. One French newspaper, preposterously, reported that she was now working for Molteni as a directeur sportif and masseuse.

So it was that the spring had ended, and the Tour began, with Merckx as confident as a two-time winner deserved to be and *Paris Match* asking on its front cover, 'MERCKX – Is he going to kill the Tour de France?' Jacques Anquetil, who had taken his critical faculties into retirement with him, appeared to answer that question on page 34. 'If [in Coppi's day, when everyone used to fight the best rider], Merckx had taken the risk of attacking 100 kilometres from the finish like he did in Divonne-Les-Bains last year or on the road to Mourenx in 1969, he would have finished outside the time limit. Last year he was vulnerable but his opponents lacked inspiration or audacity.'

Meanwhile, for a few days after the race set out from Mulhouse, Rini Wagtmans couldn't shake the feeling that he was getting in somebody's way. After Molteni's victory and Merckx's immediate confiscation of the yellow jersey in the 11-kilometre team prologue which opened proceedings, Wagtmans's sense of unease peaked at around lunchtime the following day, after the first of a mind-boggling trio of stages to be ridden in the space of 12 hours had been won in a bunch sprint by Eric Leman. Merckx saw race co-director Félix Lévitan arriving in the tribune overlooking the finish line with the yellow jersey over his arm, pointed to the chair next to him, and told Lévitan to 'just put it there'. Lévitan seemed to take great delight in raising and wagging a finger. '*Non non non*, monsieur Merckx,' he said. 'This isn't for you. It's for your teammate, monsieur Wagtmans. Your time on the overall standings is the same but he crossed the line ahead of you.'

'*What?!!! What???!*' Merckx fumed.

'He was really mad, although he also calmed down really quickly and was really nice to me about it,' Wagtmans recalls. 'But I wasn't comfortable. He was my boss; he should have the jersey. So I decided I'd get dropped on the next stage to Fribourg and give it straight back to him. I had great legs and would never have got dropped but I made up a story about my shoes being a size too small and rubbing, and I lost one minute. Of course, I posed no threat to Eddy for the Tour win, but Merckx wasn't happy if he wasn't winning.'

Merckx reacquainted himself with his favourite feeling the next day after a high-octane, high-risk sprint to pip De Vlaeminck in Strasbourg. Just three days in, with a 20-second advantage on general classification and the next week consisting entirely of flat terrain as the Tour looped anti-clockwise from east to west, north to south, Merckx afforded himself a rare luxury: he went a week without a single stage win.

Certain members of the French public clearly hoped that his barren run was destined to last. In amongst thousands of messages of support delivered by the Tour postie, and a sprinkling of hate mail, was this message sent from Paris on 2 July stapled to a photograph of Claudine and Sabrina:

Eddy Merckx,

You're nothing but a druggie and a good-for-nothing if you don't leave the Tour and leave your jersey to someone else unhappiness will strike you you are too pretentious and a bastard. If you win the Tour de France see this photo you must know them yes well they will both have their throats cut with razors and it will be your merit and your prize for the Tour.

You see what I mean?

Greetings

PS. This warning is no joke

*

Seen from Clermont Ferrand, the city at its base, the Puy de Dôme is not an impressive mountain, or rather, volcano. Television advertisements for the mineral water springing from this oasis of '*la France profonde*' creates the false expectation of soaring craters beneath a lush green moquette, but that is not the view from Clermont. Only when one rides out of the city by bike, through Chamalières and on to the road corkscrewing up and around the volcano for 14 kilometres do things get interesting. Jacques Anquetil and Raymond Poulidor's head-to-head, shoulder-to-shoulder battle on the Puy's slopes in 1964 provided the defining images of their rivalry, an age, and the Puy's mythos among cyclists.

Seven years later, in 1971, the Puy decided nothing but did throw up a few interesting pointers. Merckx had controlled the race throughout Stage 8, his men smothering every attack in readiness for what he hoped would be his booming explosion, but something on the spiral staircase up the Puy hadn't quite clicked. It wasn't one leg this time but both of them: Merckx felt somehow blocked, rusty. Four kilometres from the summit, Ocaña danced and quickly gained 40 seconds. Three kilometres later Joop Zoetemelk and Joaquim Agostinho also decided that Merckx was moving too slowly and left the yellow jersey behind. Summoning all of his guts and none of the style they preached in coaching manuals, Merckx clawed back 20 seconds in the last 500 metres but still trailed the stage winner, Ocaña, by 15 seconds at the finish line.

As it had been for Merckx on the Mont Ventoux 12 months earlier, Ocaña's next stop was an ambulance. Again just 'cinema'; Ocaña was fine and that night made an important announcement to his roommate Johny Schleck: 'I'm going to do it. I'm going to beat Merckx, Johny.'

Schleck nodded in acknowledgements not agreement. At least not yet.

'When Luis said that, I thought, OK, but there was a lot still to do because with Merckx you could never sleep easy,' Schleck says. 'Luis was also a bit obsessed with him. That wasn't always his fault. Merckx was the only rider anyone talked about, and Luis wanted to break that, but I also have to say that it was often the media who would come to the hotel and say, "Luis, no one's putting up any resistance to Merckx. Someone has to do something. Is it going to be you?"'

The anti-Merckx brigade had their answer and new hero in Grenoble. As they had in the Dauphiné, the Chartreuse mountains plagued Merckx. Ocaña's attack on the Col de Porte took him and three others clear and to a one-minute, 36-second advantage by the time the stage was over and Bernard Thévenet had won. Merckx didn't know whom or what to blame. 'It's maybe a mechanical thing. I'm going to try a new bike,' he mumbled. Above jeers from the crowd, Merckx then conceded, 'I haven't lost confidence at all, but I can see that something's amiss. I can't get into top gear.'

The unvarnished fact was that Merckx had lost the yellow jersey to a rider who wasn't his teammate for the first time in his career. Joop Zoetemelk led Ocaña by one second and Merckx by one minute. The next morning, in *L'Equipe*, the Tour's co-director and resident bard Jacques Goddet trilled that, 'Nothing will ever be the same again.' 'If the beautiful bird has been deplumed, he will probably still be eagle of this sport for some time. But he's no longer out of reach,' Goddet wrote. 'He will no longer be able to dictate the outcome of races and the way they are won on his own, at the command of his omnipotence.'

There was and is no really satisfying way to describe what happened next. Maybe in an era when Merckx hadn't already used up all the superlatives there may have been the odd adjective or metaphor still lying unclaimed. As it turned out, the day before what

Rini Waytmans maintains was the 'greatest Tour de France stage of all time', perhaps there is no higher accolade for what Luis Ocaña achieved between Grenoble and Orcières-Merlette than this praise from the writer Philippe Brunel: 'The one time when he's not sick and he doesn't fall, Ocaña produces an exploit which goes beyond Merckx's exploits, *against* Merckx at Orcières-Merlette.

'Luis lived his life at the extremes,' Brunel goes on, 'and that was why he became the only person to challenge Merckx, because you had to be extreme to take on Eddy Merckx.'

Whether it was or wasn't better than what Merckx had produced at Mourenx in 1969, we can be sure that Ocaña's ride was truly Merckx-esque and probably inspired by him. Just 13 kilometres from the stage start in Grenoble, on the Côte de Laffrey, which, says Merckx's mountain lieutenant Joseph Bruyère, 'wasn't really a "Côte" or hill but a "terribly hard and long mountain pass"', the Portuguese Agostinho bolted and Ocaña shot after him. Lucien Van Impe and Joop Zoetemelk, in his yellow jersey, followed. Merckx did not. By the time he and the rest of the peloton groaned over the summit, they trailed Ocaña by two minutes.

Ocaña claimed that it was all premeditated. He wanted the yellow jersey, of course, but also Merckx's scalp and revenge for traumas wreaked in 1970 by the next mountain, the Col du Noyer. Johny Schleck suspected it had been more impulsive than that. 'Luis wasn't Merckx,' he says. 'He never calculated or thought about the long-term consequences. If he felt good, he'd attack, simple as that.' Just how exceptional Ocaña felt on this particular day became clear when the four fugitives extended their lead in the long valley before the Col du Noyer, with Ocaña doing the majority of the work. Beneath that see-through skin described by his old teammate Philippe Crépel, muscles that perhaps even Ocaña had never seen before flexed and contorted like girders beneath the blow torch of the afternoon sun. If ever a man had looked in his element, it was Ocaña – specifically at the moment, between the two walls of a deserted canyon identified on maps as the crête des Baumes, when in a single smooth movement he leant forward again and pulled away from Agostinho, Van Impe and Zoetemelk.

The rocky gorge towering above them now took on the symbolism of a watershed. 'From that point, the feeling I had was one of a winner,' said Ocaña. 'This truly was a spectacle. For Ocaña it was the start of a new life,' Goddet wrote.

As he began the descent off the Col du Noyer, its ghosts all exorcised, Ocaña learned from a smiling Maurice De Muer in the Bic team car that Merckx was now over five minutes behind. What he couldn't know was his old nemesis was on the brink of giving up and had said as much to the Belgian in-race radio reporter Georges Malfait. He had towed the peloton almost single-handedly for nearly 100 kilometres. On the final climb to Orcières-Merlette, Ocaña extended his advantage by a further four minutes. He had already spent two minutes resting in an ambulance next to the finish line, completed his post-race TV interview and pulled on the yellow jersey when Merckx appeared around the final bend. Merckx turned around to see Zoetemelk hovering in his slipstream as he had been for the last two hours and resolved to at least outsprint the Dutchman. Third place, behind Van Impe who had stayed away for second, turned out to be scant consolation. 'For the first time, I was dictated to by a stronger rider than me. Now I think it's all over. Ocaña has been dominating for three days... I don't know what's wrong, but I'm incapable of attacking,' Merckx said.

Ocaña had beaten him by eight minutes and 42 seconds on the stage and now headed Zoetemelk by eight minutes and 43 seconds on general classification. Merckx was over a minute further back, in fifth place overall. 'I don't think he had recovered, after all the hot weather of the past few days. I had to hurt him while he was down,' Ocaña had said in his now familiar Franco-Spanish patois at the finish line, its tone still somehow pregnant with foreboding.

Johny Schleck confirms that 'ten minutes in those days wasn't the end of the world'. He and Ocaña also knew that 'Merckx would never accept defeat'. Disingenuously or diplomatically, Schleck calls Merckx 'Le Grand', when in 1971 for him and Ocaña it was 'Le Grand Con' or 'Big Idiot'. Le Grand's performance that day had been extraordinary. Everyone just sat on his wheel and let him chase all day. He just went on and on. Nonetheless, that night, Luis seemed confident. He said he'd take the yellow jersey all the way to Paris. We thought he would too.'

Merckx contemplated this eventuality from his bunk in the Club du Soleil, the resort resembling a prison where he and his shell-shocked Molteni tribe were due to spend the next two nights. He didn't know it yet but his efforts in defeat would be the subject of gushing tributes in the next day's papers. Jacques Goddet called it the most moving performance of his career. And yet, says Rini Wagtmans, Merckx was 'completely depressed, saying silly things, like that he'd never beat Luis Ocaña again. We all tried to gee him up but he was having none of it.'

At least Merckx was still in the race. Ocaña's blitz had cost Walter Godefroot his place in the Tour. Godefroot had finished outside the time limit. It had also cost Gaston Plaud, Godefroot's Burgundy-glugging, foie gras-guzzling team-manager, all hopes of keeping Godefroot at Peugeot in 1972. 'I punctured twice on the Col du Noyer, but Plaud had sent our second team car up ahead of me because he was obsessed with the team classification,' Godefroot remembers. 'After the second puncture, I'm standing at the side of the road and along comes the broomwagon. The door swings open and Roger De Vlaeminck is sitting there. "Walter, get in!" he says. But I want to carry on. I'm overtaking riders all the way up the final climb, they're telling me to slow down, and I end up missing the time limit by a few seconds. Plaud says that he'll pull some strings and get me back in the race but I'm furious with him. I say, "I did my job as a rider, you didn't do yours as a directeur sportif." The next day's a rest-day, and I spend it getting a lift back to Belgium with Jean Van Buggenhout, who's come to the Tour to see Eddy!'

Even if he hadn't wanted to admit it, perhaps not even to himself, Merckx had not given up entirely in Orcières. Before retiring to the dreary confines of the Club du Soleil, he had taken delivery of a new bike from one Belgian mechanic, Charles Terryn, and readied it for battle with another, Marcel Ryckaert. The next day was a rest-day, but unwinding was the last thing on Merckx's mind. Instead he summoned his teammates and descended the road where his agony had climaxed the previous afternoon, and which they would have to negotiate downhill the following day. Merckx watched Rini Wagtmans, the 'White Blaze', flashing though the bends and an idea began to flicker in his head. He mentioned it to Wagtmans, then they spoke again at the end of the ride. That night, the ten Molteni riders that formed Merckx's strongest Tour de France team to date went to bed knowing that the next day's supposedly 'flat' and 'routine' 251-kilometre stage to Marseille would be anything but.

Earlier, Ocaña had held an impromptu press conference in his room and invited the 15 or so attendees not to spare him 'trick questions' about the Tour being over. His teammate Bernard Labourdette agreed that, 'With a phenomenon like Merckx, you never know what to expect'. Prophetically, Labourdette added, 'Maybe he's plotted an attack somewhere where we think nothing will happen.'

The 10th of July dawned bright and, at first light and some 1,800 metres above the sea, already warm. Raymond Riotte of the Sonolor team was up with the cocks, like every day. The son of farmers from Burgundy, Riotte couldn't kick certain habits even if now there were no cows to milk or hay to bale. Often at first light, he would pad the hotel corridors or head outside for a stroll, savouring the last silence before the world stirred back into life. Now, though, as he made his way through the grotty bowels of the Club du Soleil, Riotte noticed a strange whirring noise coming from an adjacent room. He followed it to a doorway, poked his head around the corner and rubbed his eyes. It looked like...no, it *was* Merckx, churning away on the rollers.

'Eddy, Eddy, what are you doing?'

'Oh, you know, my legs didn't feel great so I was just trying to loosen up,' Merckx told him.

'But have you seen the length of the stage? We've got 250 kilometres to do, in this heat...'

When his teammates woke and assembled for breakfast, Riotte told them what he had seen. Clearly, no one had passed the message on to Luis Ocaña. The forecast '*canicule*' or heat wave had prompted Lévitan and Goddet to move the stage start from 8h10 to 8h00, but Ocaña was still dawdling with Spanish reporters when the appointed hour drew near and the riders began to gather on the start line. Merckx had seen him, and Johny Schleck had seen Merckx position himself in the front row of riders beneath the start-banner. 'I said, "Luis, look out. *Le Grand* is on the front line." Luis just said, "Come on, he's not going to attack on the descent."'

When Wagtmans also glanced over his shoulder and saw Ocaña still nattering, he knew that the heist was on. Félix Lévitan climbed into his race director's car, raised his flag and – if Ocaña's later complaint was to be believed – hadn't yet lowered it before, to use Wagtmans's sound effect, 'BOOM! Off I went. Like an atomic bomb.'

Within seconds, while Ocaña flapped, Merckx and two team-mates, Joseph Huysmans and Julien Stevens, were in Wagtmans's jet stream and divebombing towards the valley. Another ace descender, Lucien Aimar, had also joined them together with Ocaña's teammate Désiré Letort and four others. Behind, Barry Hoban was among the riders caught with Ocaña in the screeching mayhem. 'Everyone had had new tyres glued on the previous day, and they hadn't bedded down yet. People were falling off all over the place,' Hoban remembers. 'The other thing that made it so hard was that usually when you're descending it's after a climb when the size of the peloton has been dramatically reduced. There, over a hundred of us were trying to come down this little hair-pinned road together...'

By the time the ten kamikazes had reached the valley, their advantage was already around a minute. The stage was set – 'the greatest in Tour de France history' according to Rini Wagtmans. What followed could be summed up as a 240-kilometre, five-hour game of cat and mouse – but with the speed and suspense of the most gripping action thriller. Throughout those five hours, the gap between the peloton being pulled at least initially by Bic and Merckx's group was never greater than one minute 50 seconds and once or twice dropped as low as 40 seconds. Before long, the ten in front had shrunk to nine with just three Moltenis; Stevens hadn't trained on the rest-day, with Lomme Driessens's blessing but to Merckx's annoyance, and couldn't hold the wheels. Merckx and Driessens then disagreed again – Merckx protesting that they were getting nowhere and should give up, and Driessens overruling him. The other Molteni directeur sportif in the race, Giorgio Albani, then committed a costly error by sending four Molteni riders back to help Joseph Bruyère when he punctured after 45 kilometres. With the peloton barrelling towards the Med at 50 kilometres per hour, there was no hope of the quintet regaining contact and hence being able to lurk near the front of the peloton, infiltrating the Bic paceline and hindering their chase. These spoiling tactics were Josep Spruyt's speciality, but he was among the riders sent back to rescue Bruyère. Merckx was not the only one to suggest later that Spruyt's harrowing could and would have killed the chase and killed the Tour in his favour.

As the route headed out of the Southern Alps and towards the lavender fields of Provence, Ocaña was beginning to struggle, three or four positions from the front. He shouted to Schleck to slow the pace. 'We've got enough of an advantage…' Bic were now getting help from the riders of two other teams, the all-Spanish Werner line-up and Cyrille Guimard's Mercier.

Reaching Marseille, Merckx and his group had the feeling that they were entering a ghost-town. Some barriers were still being erected, and behind them the pavements were devoid of spectators until the final 200 metres. Common mythology and the first-hand accounts of most who were present that day have it that the race was 'two hours ahead of schedule'. In reality, it wasn't much more than half an hour, but that was still enough to catch hundreds of fans, a few TV crews, and one or two VIPs on the hop. The mayor of Marseille, Gaston Deferre, was furious. 'The Tour de France will never set foot in this city again, as long as I live,' he ranted, having seen the Italian Armani pip Merckx for the stage win. Sure enough, the Grande Boucle would not return to Marseille until 1989, after Deferre's death. Downhill stage starts would also be a thing of the past. No sooner had he crossed the line than Ocaña was moaning on live TV about Wagtmans's 'false start' back in Orcières-Merlette.

Merckx had regained two minutes and 12 seconds and was now second on general classification, just over seven and a half minutes behind Ocaña. His instinct told him that it had all been 'a lot of work for too little reward'. Before heading for the showers near the finish line, where his frustration would turn to anger on learning that four of his teammates had been sacrificed for Bruyère, Merckx made his way towards the podium. As he walked, Wagtmans accosted him. 'Eddy, I'm coming with you,' he said. 'I want to watch Ocaña.'

Wagtmans had first come across Ocaña a couple of years earlier at the Ruta del Sol. Like most who came into contact with the Spaniard, he had been struck by Ocaña's kindness and the way his heart seemed to throb from his sleeve, in success and failure. Wagtmans had also immediately picked up on another thing: 'He was obsessed with the colour yellow. Whenever he wasn't racing, he was always wearing something yellow.'

Yellow was still the hue of Ocaña's jersey on the podium in Marseille, but also, Wagtmans now remarked, of his complexion. 'All the colour had drained from his face. He had lost too much power that day. When Merckx came down off the podium, I stopped him and said, "Eddy, Ocaña has no future in this Tour de France. Trust me."'

Later that evening, Wagtmans reminded Merckx of what he had seen and what he had said. As had been the case two nights earlier in Orcières-Merlette, however, Merckx seemed consumed by pessimism. 'I'm finished. It was too much for too little,' he repeated.

'Usually,' says Wagtmans, 'after one hour, it was like he was waking up again – he was so fresh. But that day, he couldn't pick himself up for three hours. I knew, though, even if Eddy didn't, that Ocaña was worse.'

*

From the finish line in Marseille's old port, they had gone straight to the city's Marignane airport. A plane was waiting to deliver them to Albi, but before they boarded Raymond Riotte saw Merckx striding purposefully towards Cyrille Guimard. 'Why the hell were you chasing with Ocaña?' Merckx demanded. Guimard responded with a supercilious grin and by indicating that he had been riding to protect his own position in the points classification, and Mercier's in the team standings.

It was barely credible that this could be any team's priority so early in the Tour, and no one knew that better than Merckx.

'What do you take me for, a bloody idiot?' Merckx snapped with a dismissive flick of the hand. 'Anyway, why are you worried about those things? You're not even going to make it to Paris,' he added before turning and walking away.

Nerves were clearly fraying. The following afternoon in Albi, that became apparent when Merckx triumphed by 11 seconds over Ocaña in a hilly 16-kilometre time trial, then complained angrily to Félix Lévitan about television motorbikes sheltering the Spaniard on the course. Not for the first time in his career, Merckx felt that he was being victimised. Why, also, had seven Spanish climbers from the KAS team been granted a reprieve having finished outside the time limit the previous day in Marseille? They would surely now be Ocaña's allies in the Pyrenees. Lévitan made it clear to Merckx that he was wasting his time and breath.

The atmosphere was turning febrile, with some nasty undertones. Predictably, Driessens had stoked Merckx's ire and urged him to confront Lévitan, but he was far from the only agent provocateur. On live Belgian radio, seeing cars and motorbikes swarm around Ocaña, Luc Varenne had called upon the Belgian navy to bombard the French coastline. If that sounded like a joke in more ways than one, the French director responsible for the incriminated close-ups of Ocaña was quite serious when he accused Merckx and Driessens of 'flagrant bad faith'. He vowed to limit Merckx and Molteni's airtime should an apology not be forthcoming within 24 hours.

But the real reason for Merckx's angst was the general classification reminding him that Ocaña still led by seven minutes, 24 seconds. He was running out of stages. Just three big, back-to-back opportunities remained over three days in the Pyrenees. It was a good thing that he didn't generally believe in omens: the first instalment of the troika was to head from Revel to Luchon, over the Col du Portillon which Ocaña's father had crossed by foot on his way into France and a new future 20 years earlier. Not only that, but on the eve of the Tour, *L'Equipe* had published an unusual prediction from a mysterious correspondent-cum-soothsayer who had correctly predicted Rik Van Looy's abandonment near Pau the previous year.

'We gathered our most unusual snippet, just by chance, on our visit to Tour base camp [in Mulhouse]. We give it to you exactly as it was recorded, a whisper in our ear: "This Tour will be full of drama. Merckx won't win. Not only will he fail, but he will abandon. He won't even make it to Luchon. His defeat will be consumed on the descent off the Col de Menté, even before he climbs the Portillon."'

13
if

'All things being equal, he would have still beaten Merckx,
but, you always have to put something in brackets:
Merckx was Merckx.' JOHNY SCHLECK

One day early in May 1994, Philippe Brunel looked across a restaurant table at Luis Ocaña and for a few seconds allowed his thoughts to drift with his friend's. Ocaña's face was rounder than it once had been, his hairline had slightly receded, but the cheekbones still jutted and when Luis spoke of the Tour de France embers, if not exactly the old fire, still glowed in his eyes. 'You know what, Philippe?' he said. 'Nowhere else in life have I got back the feelings I used to have as a cyclist. If someone told me now that I could ride the Tour de France and die the second I crossed the finish line, I'd sign without a moment's hesitation.' Brunel smiled but there was still a lump in his throat and his eyes were damp. A few minutes earlier Ocaña had told him that he had an incurable, fatal form of hepatitis. Ten days later, Ocaña took destiny, and a pistol, into his own hands.

In 1971, the Tour de France wasn't yet finishing on the Champs Elysées, the cyclist's Elysium, as it does today. Even if this had been the case, however, Luis Ocaña couldn't end the Tour in Paris and access paradise – for he had been consigned to hell a week earlier on the Col de Menté.

That morning in Revel Eddy Merckx had warned or tipped off his friend from Belgian radio Luc Varenne: stick with me today, I'm going to batter Ocaña until one of us breaks, him or me. The first 140 kilometres passed off largely without incident before Merckx began his bombardment on the Col du Portet d'Aspet. One attack, two, both quashed by Ocaña. Merckx now settled calmly back into his saddle, ready to double the dose on the Col de Menté.

His legs felt good going uphill for the first time in the Tour. Ocaña's, by the look of things, did not. The Col de Menté rears steeply out of Ger de Boutx before settling into a steady 7 per cent gradient as it tacks from east to west across the Bois Epais or 'Thick Wood'. Halfway up the climb, Merckx resumed his assault and Ocaña again responded, but black clouds were now gathering like portents of disaster. 'I notice that Ocaña's progress isn't as smooth as it was and, above all, that he hasn't been able to eat. Could he be on the brink of collapse?' Merckx wondered in his *Carnets de Route*. As the storm began pummelling their backs, Rini Wagtmans glanced across at Merckx and at first mistook the rainwater for tears. Then he too turned to observe Ocaña and saw the premonition he'd had in Marseille materialising before his eyes. Thunder clapped and lightning flashed. The so-called 'White Blaze', Wagtmans, recalls that it was 'like World War II – or like the Devil was playing with us'.

Ocaña's own lieutenants, Johny Schleck and Bernard Labourdette, could see trouble not in the skies but in the way their captain insisted on answering every Merckx attack. 'Luis, calm down!' they told him.

Minutes later Merckx and Ocaña, in that order, were aquaplaning off the road on the other side of the pass within milliseconds of each other. In weather that has been variously described as 'cataclysmic' and 'apocalyptic', Ocaña overshot a left-hand hairpin and rag-dolled into a tiny brook. He was remounting within seconds when another rider also careered off the tarmac and into his midriff. Merckx was back on his bike immediately, while Ocaña made it momentarily to his feet before a second knock-down. He and his yellow jersey lay sodden in the flood, as the French author Pierre Carrey put it, like something painted by El Greco or sculpted by Rodin. This time he would not attempt to continue.

Joop Zoetemelk claimed the next day – and the annals have recorded ever since – that he was the rider who struck Ocaña. Oddly, however, what jerky footage exists of the crash suggests that Zoetemelk may have only glanced Ocaña and that it was the Portuguese rider Joaquim Agostinho who ploughed into him. This version has been confirmed in the past by Lucien Van Impe, who witnessed the accident from the inside of the bend. It is also backed up by Johny Schleck. Agostinho, alas like Ocaña, can now never have the final word: he also died tragically, almost ten years to the day before the Spaniard, when he hit a dog and crashed while leading the Tour of the Algarve.

Before the debates and conjecture could begin, Merckx pressed on, oblivious to the drama unfolding higher up the mountain. On one hairpin, he saw Wagtmans appear over his shoulder, fly off the road and 300 metres into a field in an 'unbelievable position – lying horizontally on his saddle, legs akimbo'. 'Both wheels of his bike were broken but he never fell! We were the puppets of a monstrous fury,' Merckx shuddered.

'I was trying to stop the back wheel with my feet! You have to think like a skier in those conditions,' Wagtmans cackles now. At the time, the Mercier directeur Louis Caput struggled to see the funny side. 'Wagtmans diced with death today,' Caput said that evening.

The result of the Tour, at least, was suddenly beyond doubt. Merckx had looked the strongest rider in the race ever since the Alps, and he took no further risks en route to second place in Luchon and what had turned from a seven-minute deficit on general classification to a two-minute lead over Zoetemelk. José Manuel Fuente, one of the KAS riders rescued from the wrong side of the time limit in Marseille, had escaped early in the stage and held on to win by over six minutes in Luchon.

While Merckx glumly allowed himself to be draped but not properly clothed in the yellow jersey, Ocaña was evacuated by helicopter to a clinic in Saint Gaudens. Initial reaction to his fall had been hysterical. Some of the first on the scene feared that he had broken his spine. After briefly losing consciousness in the helicopter, Ocaña was given painkillers, an X-ray and a much less serious diagnosis once he reached Saint Gaudens. 'The current diagnosis, providing there are no more complications, is thoracic contusions and a pronounced state of shock,' said a doctor's communiqué.

A question that at this point no one dared to ask, preoccupied as they were with another big 'if', would stalk Ocaña to and beyond the grave. Given that he was discharged from the clinic in Saint Gaudens at noon the next day, were his injuries so severe that he couldn't have soldiered on? Most at least respectfully let a decade or two pass before uttering the unspeakable. Thus Merckx's friend, the television journalist, Théo Mathy, left it until 1999 to confess that, in his opinion, Ocaña was physically capable of continuing but had been broken psychologically. The storm and the Tour doctor's panicked conclusions had done the rest. 'I ask myself whether Ocaña didn't abandon a bit quickly; it was his second abandonment in three Tours,' Mathy speculated. Another journalist, Walter Pauli, endorses and supplements the same view with another premise: 'I'm pretty sure that Merckx would have carried on, in Ocaña's shoes. Pretty sure. When you look at what pain Merckx endured in later Tours... Physically, there was no way that Merckx could beat him but you had to know Ocaña. The psychological destabilisation was enough.'

Whether they do or don't believe that Ocaña could have at least tried to ride on, most generally agree that the 'Merckx factor' played at least some part in his downfall. Lucien Van Impe says that Ocaña was 'the first rider who wasn't afraid of Merckx', but no one can know to what extent it was all bluster, and how much bravery genuinely remained now that Merckx was homing in. There were certainly signs that Johny Schleck had been right about his teammate's vulnerability to pressure. As much as Bernard Labourdette, for one, told Ocaña to forget about Merckx, he seemed determined to ape his former *bête noire*. That meant responding when Merckx attacked and even sending his teammates with Merckx's Molteni men whenever they broke clear. Hence, early on the stage, the Bic pair Désiré Letort and Alain Vasseur went to mark Roger Swerts and Herman Van Springel. 'He wanted to ride like Merckx and Merckx's team, but there was no need,' says Merckx's wing-man in the mountains, Joseph Bruyère. 'By doing so, he wore out men who could have been there with him and given him some security on the Col de Menté. Maybe he wouldn't have taken those risks then…'

Bruyère's next observation would make uncomfortable reading if Ocaña were still alive. 'It's too easy to say that Merckx would have won the Tour anyway…but Ocaña preferred to leave us guessing by abandoning.'

Thus Bruyère pre-empts the debate that has outlived Ocaña and will outlive Merckx, namely who would have won if fate hadn't intervened. In almost all other circumstances, in any other Tour, the arguments would all have been fatuous. Contrary to the widely held, nigh-on fundamentalist misconception that the Tour winner had to be the strongest man in the race, it was actually about negotiating the course, manoeuvring around fortune – and these were talents on a par with the ability to pedal. Merckx would win not '*à la pédale*' but fair and square nonetheless. In 1971, though, at stake was a bigger and more prestigious prize than just the *maillot jaune*: Merckx's scalp and by extension the title, like a boxer's gold belt, of world's strongest cyclist.

It is to Merckx's credit not only that he refused to don the yellow jersey on Stage 15, but also that he has largely refrained from hypothesising in the 40 years since. The closest he came at the time was admitting in his *Carnets de Route*, 'before the accident the conviction was growing in me that I was going to beat Ocaña'. That evening in the Lycée des Garçons de Bagnères where Molteni were staying, and even the following morning, Merckx was utterly demoralised and threatened to abandon. Jacques Anquetil pleaded with him to keep going, but even more compelling was Lomme Driessens's reminder that the wheel-sucking Zoetemelk or Van Impe stood to triumph if Merckx left. Merckx agreed but already sensed that his third Tour victory would be perceived as a hollow one. That hunch was corroborated by the French press after the next day's stage to Superbagnères. 'It's obvious that Merckx, dragging the ubiquitous Zoetemelk in his wheel, wouldn't have been able to make up even a fraction of his handicap on the radiant Luis,' wrote Jacques Goddet in *L'Equipe*. In the same paper, Pierre Chany decreed, 'without any danger of getting it wrong, and on the faith of the dramas we saw yesterday, that Luis Ocaña would have condemned everyone else to the role of bit-part players if he'd been in the race today'.

Zoetemelk is one of those who maintains today that Ocaña would have held on. Johny Schleck, as you might expect, is another. Seven stages remained between Luchon and Paris when the Tour was 'decapitated'. They included the bizarre 19.6-kilometre mini-stage straight out of Luchon and up to the ski resort of Superbagnères, a 145-kilometre leg-breaker taking in the cols of the Peyresourde, Aspin, Tourmalet and Aubisque the next day, four stages for opportunists then the traditional time trial, traditionally won by Merckx, to the Cipale velodrome on the final day. As it turned out, Merckx had also hurt himself on the Col de Menté, specifically his right knee, and ended up riding economically in the remaining two Pyrenean stages. Sure enough, he then finished two minutes ahead of everyone in the 53-kilometre time trial to La Cipale in Paris. Against Ocaña, he would no doubt have summoned even more strength, not to mention motivation.

'All things being equal, he would have still beaten Merckx, but, you always have to put something in brackets: Merckx was Merckx, and Luis had never beaten him before in a grand Tour. Merckx would have attacked him all the way to Paris,' Schleck says.

This, indeed, is everyone's doubt: to what extent was Merckx going to 'harass' Ocaña on the road from the Pyrenees to Paris as he had promised, and how much resilience did Ocaña have left? Raymond Riotte says that Merckx had not left Ocaña in peace for 'a single second since Orcières-Merlette' and would not until he had the jersey. Riotte is also one of those who considered Merckx, and not bad luck or bad weather, to be the architect of Ocaña's demise. 'It was only a matter of time before he exploded,' he says. 'Even on the Col de Menté, Eddy had attacked him and made him chase. I don't care what anyone says: Eddy provoked that crash. Eddy lit the bomb. OK, so there was the storm, but that wasn't what did for Luis. I was convinced, and still am, that Eddy was going to win that Tour. He would just have carried on bombarding Luis.'

In other words, if Ocaña's fragile body wasn't going to desert him, it somehow seemed inevitable that his nerve and ability to make lucid decisions eventually would. It was and is the hallmark of all great self-saboteurs – or, as they are now commonly known in sport, 'chokers'. For some, like Italo Zilioli before Ocaña, the pressure was never greater and the magnetism of failure never stronger than in the antechamber of glory. But did Ocaña deserve the label? Had he choked on the Col de Menté? The future would provide some indication. Awaiting that there was tragedy, not irony, in the notion that Ocaña had been obsessed with crossing the Portillon, where his father had entered France two decades earlier, ahead of Merckx if not at the front of the race.

'Luis wanted to lead the Tour into Spain after the Col de Menté – that's why he desperately wanted to follow Merckx. If it had been someone else besides Merckx, he would have done the same thing,' says Bernard Thévenet, who would finish fourth in the '71 Tour. 'It's certain, though, that the duel between Ocaña and Merckx was top-notch stuff. Luis was someone who was really hyper-motivated with an opponent in front of him. Maybe, in front of Merckx, his motivation was even greater and became excessive. He really wanted to beat Merckx, but then Luis wanted to beat everyone in the mountains. That warm blood perhaps just boiled a bit hotter against Merckx...'

Luis Ocaña and Eddy Merckx were both 26 at the time of their 1971 showdown. Merckx's orchestrated visit to Ocaña's newly built, 'tastefully decorated' (Merckx's words) villa in Bretagne-de-Marsan on the morning of Stage 17, the champagne Ocaña gave to him, Merckx's invitation to 'come back and win next year', and their handshake at the end carried with them the promise of further, more bellicose encounters. Battles which, alas, would never materialise, as Ocaña failed to ever reproduce the heroics of 1971, except when Merckx was absent from the Tour in 1973. That year, liberated from his nemesis, Ocaña rode and dominated in a manner worthy and reminiscent of Merckx. Then the ogre returned in 1974, the hex resumed, and Ocaña scuttled for cover.

In other races, for a short time, he seemed unaffected by what had happened. The pair squared up again a few weeks after the Tour at the 1971 World Championships in Mendrisio. Ocaña looked in imperious form before committing a mistake that was too easy to dismiss as bad luck – drifting backwards to get a drink in Merckx's line of sight. Merckx's attack was instantaneous, a second professional rainbow jersey was on its way, and Ocaña was furious. 'I'll never forgive myself,' he said.

He still won big races, notably the Dauphiné in 1972 and of course the 1973 Tour, but also went out on a low note with a positive dope test at the 1977 Tour. The last few years of his career had been a regret-tinged diminuendo. In 1973, he had already begun planning for the future, buying an old Armagnac distillery and its 20 hectares of vines. The Armagnac trade, though, was an expensive and volatile one to enter – certainly a dangerous environment for someone with moods as fickle as Ocaña's. 'I don't think 1971 ruined his career – he still went on to win the Tour in 1973,' says Johny Schleck. 'Anyway, Luis wasn't going to carry on racing for the rest of his life. He wanted to put away enough money to get the vineyard up and running. That was his big passion, his land. But Armagnac's not an easy product. I think he'd maybe invested too much and got a bit short of cash. He could have sold his land, but he was very emotive about the whole thing and what someone else would do with it. He'd say, "My land's for making Armagnac, and making it the way I want it made." That's how Luis was. He'd made a big investment, emotional and financial… I don't know if it was because of that, but he became very stressed, then ill, and what happened happened. In any case, stress was in his life every day.'

Philippe Brunel's eyes and voice still mist with nostalgia when he talks about Ocaña. Over the course of a long career reporting and poeticising on cycling for *L'Equipe*, Brunel has met and become close to many now departed cyclists, but has cried only for Ocaña. In 2002, he wrote a fine biography of Merckx and today often wishes 'that when I see Merckx, it could be just as another human being and not Eddy Merckx, because he's a wonderful person to spend time with'. Of Ocaña, though, Brunel says just, 'We were brothers.'

'I would never say that Luis died on the Col de Menté, but when he falls there's this sense that his family history has given him, of his father who flees Spain and Francoism, over the Portillon, carrying all his worldly possessions. There's this sense not of malediction but at least melancholia about Luis and his life, and that increases with the fall. There are people who say that he could have got up but that's false. Two riders smashed into him. I also think there was a third thing – this idea, somewhere, that happiness wasn't for him. I think that like all Spaniards, he had a relationship with fatality that unconsciously made it impossible for him to get over that thing. To him, there was a sense of "I fall, it's fatal, it couldn't have gone any other way."

'In any case,' Brunel continues, 'Luis died a bit every day when things didn't go as he wished on a bike. What he told me that day in 1994 about wishing he could ride the Tour again and die on the finish line...that showed that he had a visceral, almost mystical relationship with his profession, which is perhaps why he had problems after he retired. Merckx is the greatest champion in the history of cycling, but there are other riders who are the very expression of the sport, who left a very deep impression, who expressed what cycling should be. It's like in life – occasionally you do things that you shouldn't do, but you do them anyway, and you're right, because you can't always be calculating or rational. Cycling's not a sport for accountants. The mark that Luis left on cycling wasn't much more than one performance, his ride to Orcières-Merlette, but that mark was indelible, like the essence of cycling distilled in a perfume bottle. That's why I loved Ocaña and also why he and Merckx would have become great friends in other circumstances. I'm sure of that. Ocaña, Merckx and Jacques Anquetil were kindred spirits. They had this relationship with life, this attitude of, "We'll grab life by the scruff of the neck. We won't conform. We'll take it head on." Yes, if Luis was still alive, he and Eddy would get on famously now.'

14
hour of need

'You're a real gherkin!' JACQUES ANQUETIL

Merckx ended up winning the 1971 Tour – the one that he said he and Ocaña both 'lost' when the Spaniard crashed – by a shade under ten minutes. If he was the villain before, the emergence, then downfall of a tragic hero, had eroded his popularity still further. Again, Merckx didn't or couldn't help himself. On the Pyrenean blockbuster to Gourette, he chased then berated Lucien Van Impe, guilty of wheel-sucking for 12 kilometres on the Tourmalet then 'jumping away under my nose'. He then sought retribution on Cyrille Guimard for his earlier 'conspiracy' with Ocaña by attacking in the pine forests of the Landes. The ambush gave Merckx his fourth stage win in the Tour and the green points jersey formerly held by Guimard. 'I think Guimard's green jersey is still hanging from a pine tree somewhere in the Landes!' he tittered years later.

If he didn't know to what extent the French public had turned on him before, even after those threatening letters early in the Tour, he did when a fan pelted him with stones in Angoulême. Or when the choruses of 'Eddy, Eddy' he remembered from La Cipale in 1969 had turned to jeers two years later. 'It was particularly bad that year,' says Rini Wagtmans. 'I can remember the stones in Angoulême. The

French just couldn't understand Eddy. They had Thévenet and Poulidor, and to them he'd just ruined the party.'

Even away from the Tour, in the criteriums, it seemed that age
and money were doing nothing to curb Merckx's cannibalism. Losing
was still that 'big drama in his life' that so mystified Dino Zandegù.
One afternoon in 2011 – for the record at around two o'clock –
Zandegù's memories of a circuit race in Modigliana four weeks after
the '71 Tour come cascading back.

*Dino, Dino, what's this: Zandegù first, Merckx second?! Amazing!
How did you do it?*

'Oh yes, I don't know what it was – my dinner the previous night
had gone down well, or I'd slept well – but I was on one of those
days, a day with a capital "D"! It was a hard race, circuits six kilometres long with a climb called the "Calla". Three laps from the end,
Merckx starts stirring the pot then puts in this vicious attack.
Suddenly there are only six of us left. On the penultimate lap we're
all still there, then we get to the hill, this "Calla" for the last time.
Merckx thinks he'll put on a show...but I go away with him! Six
hundred metres from the top of the climb, I'm dropped, but not by
so much that I can't catch him on the descent. He knows I'm on his
wheel, but I'm too tired to come through. "Pull! Pull, you good-for-
nothing...!" he's shouting. He's calling me all the names under the
sun in this half-Flemish, half-Italian, half-French, half-invented patois
– "*Verdomme* this, *bastardo* that!" – then he tells me that he'll see to
it that I never race again if I do the sprint. I say nothing – part of the
prize is a golden hen that's worth quite a lot of money, and I want to
win it. So, anyway, we come under the kilometre-to-go kite and I go
like a rocket and do the sprint of my life to win. Five metres beyond
the finish line, I spot a gap in the crowd, turn off the road and down
this little gravel path. At the end of the path is a house. I jump off

my bike, sling it over my shoulder, burst through the open door of the house and run upstairs into one of the bedrooms. An old woman is there in her bed. I wake her and she starts shrieking. I say "Granny, granny, be quiet! I won't hurt you, but Eddy Merckx is coming after me and he wants to rip my face off!" She says that she's going to call the police, but eventually she calms down, and I end up staying in there for half an hour. I finally poke my head outside, check he's not waiting, then ride off to get my prize. When I get to the podium it's just me and the organiser because everyone else has gone home. It was worth it, though – I still treasure that golden hen!'

At around the same time, while Merckx was preparing for the World Championship road race that was another nail in Ocaña's coffin, Lomme Driessens was getting ready for a change of scenery in 1972 in a team other than Molteni. Driessens informed Merckx that he would be leaving Molteni at the end of the season in a letter in August. The writing, though, had been on the wall for weeks if not months. His policy of allowing some riders' wives to stay with them at stage races and banning others was just one of many things that irritated Merckx. Over the summer a bad relationship had slowly turned into an unsustainable one. Merckx didn't ride Paris–Tours in September, but even from afar he could tell what to expect from Driessens when he took up his new role with Van Cauter-Magniflex the following year. If Magniflex's Rik Van Linden was able to win in Tours, Molteni's Marino Basso reported back to Merckx, it had been in large part thanks to Driessens. Had he not known it before, Merckx would soon discover that, as journalist Walter Pauli reminds us, 'Driessens was obsessed with revenge.'

Perhaps the biggest indictment of him, though, was that Merckx never needed any of the attributes that Driessens had employed to great effect before and would in future against Merckx. His brag-gadocio, his mind games and even his knack for spotting talent had all become redundant. Rini Wagtmans, who was also leaving Molteni at the end of 1971, but only because Merckx had urged him to accept Goudsmit-Hoff's astronomical offer, agrees. 'Driessens was also a special coach,' Wagtmans says. 'There was no Internet, so team managers relied on their nose, and Lomme's was brilliant. He would come up to you at the start of a race, put his right hand out to shake your hand, then put his left hand on your back and squeeze the flesh, then he'd go back to Merckx and say, "Eddy, don't worry about Wagtmans. He's three kilos overweight."

'He loved to play these psychological games. Sometimes, in the race, he'd tell someone to attack, and they would, then you'd get back to the hotel that night and he'd berate them for attacking. "When I say 'Attack!' that means you do nothing!" he would say. "When I want you to attack, I'll say 'Wait!'" He was always trying to trick the opposition.

'I think Eddy got to the point where he didn't need those games,' Wagtmans concludes. 'Cycling was simple to him. It was just a race. We weren't animals in a circus. We were racers. Eddy knew that.'

Merckx's order of priorities is well illustrated in his 1971 *Carnets de Route*. For most in his position, a published autobiography would be the obvious outlet for the grievances about Driessens that had been piling up since 1969. Again, though, even in the printed word, Merckx's dislike for conflict is apparent when he stresses that the story about Driessens's conniving at Paris–Tours was only Basso's version. Merckx himself devotes barely a single anodyne sentence to the end of their collaboration. Most likely, he and his ghost-writer Marc Jeuniau assumed that the audience was far more interested in how he had closed the season with victory in the only major Classic or 'monument' which still eluded him, the Tour of Lombardy in Italy. That, though, was a story told before almost *ad infinitum* – of Merckx riding everyone including Ocaña off his wheel, in this case 50 kilometres from the finish line close to Argegno on the western shore of Lake Como. Of his 54 victories in 1971 – his highest tally to date, with his highest win-ratio of 45 per cent – Merckx claimed that only the Tour de France and the Tour of Lombardy had been 'premeditated'. The rest, all 52 of them, had presumably come about just because Merckx felt a rumble in his stomach.

Merckx had erected the tightrope on which he would spend the 1972 season. He had condemned himself to win just as much, under penalty of critics announcing his terminal decline. Meanwhile those critics, and other forces trying to knock him, continued to multiply – the catcallers in the crowd, Ocaña, De Vlaeminck, old adversaries like Gimondi and Bitossi, new ones like Driessens, the sciatica that returned intermittently, fame, expectation, plus a Tour de France organisation which looked to have joined the Merckx refuseniks by plotting the most mountainous route for years in 1972. As well as all of this, Merckx had to find time to be a husband and a father. In August 1972, Claudine would give birth to a son, Axel. The couple's first child, Sabrina, had caused Merckx one of his biggest disappointments of 1971 by failing to recognise him on his return from a training camp in Italy early in the year. Seeing her husband's crestfallen face, Claudine had tried to reassure him. 'It's understandable that she wouldn't recognise you after a few weeks apart.'

As ever, Merckx could see only one solution to the dilemma he had outlined, rather poignantly, to Marc Jeuniau in 1971: 'Because I'm very successful, people imagine that I have no problems, when it's really the opposite that's true.' He would just have to work even harder. He started at Molteni's training camp in Laigueglia in January, then at Paris–Nice in March he realised to what extent his antagonists had redoubled their efforts and their vitriol over the winter. A terrible fall on the finishing straight in Saint Etienne at the end of Stage 3 hurt Merckx's hip and back to the point where doctors advised him to abandon, but even more painful was the backstabbing that followed. First, Ocaña's directeur sportif Maurice de Muer and Lomme Driessens lobbied hard for the rule waiving any time losses incurred due to crashes in the last kilometre to be disregarded for Merckx, who had got up and struggled over the line 42 seconds after the winner Eric Leman. Fortunately, every other directeur sportif opposed the motion, and Merckx retained his race leadership. The following morning in Saint Etienne, Ocaña scoffed that there was 'nothing wrong with Merckx'. He then proceeded to attack him, in vain, three times on the Col de la République leaving the city. This prompted a rare outburst by Merckx in his 1972 *Carnets de Route*.

'I find Ocaña's behaviour deeply unpleasant,' he wrote. 'First of all because he's quite aggressive about me when he speaks to journalists, and then also because he takes himself for the boss of the peloton. He tells all the riders what they should be doing, he gives orders, he calls anyone who goes off the front back into the group, he looks daggers at anyone who's shaping to attack. Who does he think he is? Prince Juan Carlos, or Franco?'

Merckx's superiority over Ocaña in the remaining six stages set the pattern for their duels throughout 1972 and indeed the rest of their careers. Unfortunately for Merckx, at Paris–Nice, one man had been faster than both of them: the 35-year-old Frenchman Raymond Poulidor.

Order was restored at Milan–San Remo, where Merckx won for the fifth time in seven participations. No one except those immediately behind him saw his attack because, as Merckx put it, the descent off the Poggio is 'like the dark side of the Moon'. Stated with less modesty, he was too quick there for the TV cameras.

The first half of his Classics campaign was beset by a recurrence of the pain resulting from his crash at Paris–Nice. A new round of tests revealed that Merckx had a torn muscle in his back and a cracked lumbar vertebra. In the circumstances, he had every right to feel as 'happy as a king' after his seventh place in the Tour of Flanders. A week later, he was less pleased with the same finishing position in Paris–Roubaix. Without a tyre blow-out in Arenberg Forest Merckx 'had the feeling that I would have prevailed without too much difficulty'. The 'ease' with which Roger De Vlaeminck was able to win his first Roubaix title, said Merckx, 'demonstrated that the opposition was relatively weak'.

Merckx didn't yet know it, but this would turn into a key theme throughout 1972, for all that it had promised to be his hardest season. More than in 1968, year zero of Merckx's first mandate as the absolute ruler of professional cycling, as 1972 wore on, a belief started to take hold that a second generation was failing in its 'duty' to furnish worthy challengers. At the time it sounded condescending, but Merckx had been right about De Vlaeminck and his 'one big win a year'. The Gypsy skipped Liège–Bastogne–Liège to ride a lucrative circuit race in Italy, leaving Merckx to romp to his third victory in La Doyenne. When Merckx won even more impressively at Flèche Wallonne three days later, De Vlaeminck was in a football stadium watching Club Bruges play Antwerp. Merckx had found out at the 1971 Tour how much an opponent's absence could devalue his success. It was no surprise that he 'would have preferred it if De Vlaeminck had been racing at Flèche'.

De Vlaeminck and Ocaña's pluck had set them immediately apart from the rest, but even between them and Merckx the discrepancy was huge, in the head more than the legs. The '72 Giro d'Italia would be by some distance De Vlaeminck's best performance in a major tour to date – yet he was still 'only' seventh. 'Three weeks was a long time for me,' De Vlaeminck puffs in his kitchen in Kaprijke. 'Physically I was good enough to win a major tour, but I didn't have the right mentality or support. I only realised after ten days of the 1971 Tour that maybe you couldn't sprint for every bonus, follow Merckx every time he attacked and get the green jersey. By the time we got to Orcières-Merlette, I was stick-thin. I couldn't go on. Even when I wasn't physically tired, mentally I found it exhausting. Drinking still water every day, watching everything you ate for three weeks? After ten days I was gagging for a Coca-Cola.'

Another would-be scourge rocked Merckx at the Giro, but he combined every vulnerability of the other contenders with not all of their strengths. José Manuel Fuente was shoulder-high to Merckx, a brilliant climber and the only true winner in the stage to Luchon, which had been fatal to his compatriot Ocaña in the 1971 Tour. Fuente had also just won the latest edition of his national Tour, the Vuelta a España. As the Spaniards who had ridden the Vuelta often were, Fuente was in superlative form for the Giro and intended to prove it on Stage 17 finishing atop the highest road pass in Italy, the Passo dello Stelvio. On the Stelvio, Fuente declared, he would not only beat Merckx but put him outside the time limit.

If only Fuente's tactics or professionalism equalled his chutzpah. Walter Godefroot says that by this point in his career, Merckx had come across three riders with potential to trouble him in major tours, 'but in all of them there's something missing'. 'One is Pingeon who is a big talent but is a bit crazy, or at least not very professional,' Godefroot explains. 'Then you have Ocaña who must have a great physical gift to do what he does but is always in the disco after criteriums. The third is Fuente, who is brilliant at climbing but also at smoking heavy cigarettes and drinking cognac.'

Franco 'Crazy Heart' Bitossi was even less impressed with Fuente. 'He rode very badly,' Bitossi says. 'He used to get to a climb, put his head down and bolt off the front whether it was the right place to go or not.'

This was fine on stages consisting of just a single ascent like the one to Superbagnères in the 1971 Tour, or the one up the Blockhaus climb on day four of the '72 Giro. Merckx hated this kind of exercise. He therefore wasn't surprised that Fuente had taken the pink jersey, or to have trailed him by 2'30" at the summit. Dino Zandegù, incidentally, still blamed Merckx's ferocious pace at the foot of the climb, not Fuente, for dumping him outside the time limit and out of what turned out to be his last ever Giro. 'The saddest thing that ever happened to me, and all Merckx's fault! The saddest day of my life!' Zandegaù says.

Four more stages, though, were all it took for Fuente to show his limitations and for Merckx to reclaim the race lead. Fuente had speculated after a blisteringly hot sixth stage that 'if there had been a big climb today, Merckx would have lost five minutes'. The next morning in Cosenza, though, he had his KAS teammates slurp ice-cream while Merckx assembled his teammates for 40 breathless uphill kilometres to warm-up. At the top of the first climb of the day, the Valico di Monte Scuro, the difference in their methods of preparation equated to a few metres of asphalt. By the time they reached Catanzaro 125 kilometres later, after a Merckx masterclass in descending and riding on the flat, Fuente was over four minutes back and Merckx had reclaimed the pink jersey.

Fuente threatened for a second time a week later on the Alpine stage finishing up the Monte Jafferau, but was again undone by his naivety. His attack on the penultimate Sestriere climb came much too early, and he was almost at a standstill when Merckx arrived like the grim reaper to scythe him down a kilometre from the finish line. Fuente consoled himself with a stage win on the Stelvio, although Merckx was well inside the time cut and now three days away from his third Giro title. His final winning margin would be five and a half minutes. Fuente had at least earned second place and a compliment which perhaps said more about Merckx's antipathy for Ocaña than his admiration for Fuente: 'Fuente is a great champion – there's an abyss between him and Ocaña, no comparison.'

This, ventured the detractors, was but the insecure voice of a man who had kept close tabs on Ocaña during the Giro, and who knew to what extent the Spaniard had dominated the Dauphiné Libéré. Jacques Goddet concluded ahead of the Tour whose route he called the most mountainous in history that, 'Ocaña should be clearly superior to Merckx over the climbs.' Another Jacques, Jacques Anquetil, supported that view by noting, completely erroneously, that Merckx hadn't dropped an important rider on a climb for two years.

Alas, they were all dupes to their desperate longing for variations on a theme that had been playing on repeat since the 1968 Giro. The greatest tribute to Merckx and the worst slight on his competitors was that his victories were now losing their identity in an uninterrupted blur of brilliance. His Molteni team manager Girogio Albani had summed it up at Milan–San Remo in the spring, when Merckx had crossed the line alone then asked Albani, 'Were you surprised to see me?' 'With you, nothing surprises me any more,' Albani replied. The bigwigs at Italian state broadcaster RAI felt the same. They announced that they would drop live coverage of the Giro in 1973 – akin to the BBC doing the same to Wimbledon – and show only half an hour of daily highlights.

If the Giro win had provoked yawns, similarly, Merckx produced a fourth Tour win which differed from the previous three only in that the attacks came later in stages, with slightly less zing, a bit more calculator and a bit less accelerator. The first seven stages were at least enlivened by his tug-of-war for the yellow jersey with Cyrille Guimard. After that, Merckx won the first stage in the Pyrenees, regained the lead and proceeded to outride Luis Ocaña on every mountain stage. Ocaña's excuse, at least in the first instance, was that his puncture on the Col du Soulor on Stage 8 had prompted an unsporting acceleration by Merckx. This was followed minutes later by Ocaña's second crash on a rain-sodden Pyrenean descent in two years. A week later, he fell ill in the Alps and had to abandon.

Merckx, meanwhile, won consecutive stages ascending two of the Tour's hallowed Alpine summits, the Galibier and Izoard, as well the final-day time trial. His final margin of victory was a little under 11 minutes over Felice Gimondi.

Merckx's commentary on Ocaña's race was so telling and accurate that it requires nothing further.

'What do I think of Luis Ocaña? He's a good rider. He made a big impression on me in the first week of the Tour, but he doesn't cope well with repeated efforts… It's not my place to cast judgement on Ocaña's qualities and his future but I'm convinced that by basing their route and their publicity on the state of grace that he was in last year, exactly when I was in poor form, the organisers have done him a disservice. And to end this debate once and for all, I'll ask all those who maintain that the war of supremacy between Ocaña and Merckx isn't over to examine our palmarès, and to remember that he's started four Tours and abandoned in three of them.'

As the 1972 Tour ended, that – Merckx's palmarès – now appeared to be the sole source of interest. Every adversary, two generations of

them, had been devoured. All that was left were hypothetical comparisons with past luminaries and their achievements. In the spring, an
Italian newspaper had already postulated that Merckx's victories
eclipsed the combined record of Fausto Coppi and Gino Bartali.
Alfredo Binda had won five Giri d'Italia, two more than Merckx, but
at 27 Merckx still had ample time to reach and surpass him. In the
Tour, Merckx could draw level with Jacques Anquetil with five wins
as early as 1973. That, though, looked unlikely, as the Giro and
Vuelta a España bosses were lobbying much harder to have Merckx
at their race in 1973 than their counterparts from the Tour. The
hostility he now encountered from the fans in France, plus the fact
that he now considered his duel with Ocaña over, were further
reasons to give the Tour the break from him that it seemed to crave.

What was Merckx to do in other races except keep winning?
There was no danger of boredom affecting him. His great secret, as
well as his deadpan enthusiasm, was his anxiety, which proved the
perfect antidote to complacency. Merckx once spoke of the 'scream-
ing uncertainty within me' which came from 'never [being] totally
sure what I was capable of'. Even in his total domination at the Tour,
he had agonised endlessly over his equipment, his health and his position on the bike. 'He was constantly calling Bruyère,' says Raymond
Poulidor. 'It'd be "Joseph, where's my allen key? Do I look too low?
Or too high?" At first you thought he must be suffering but, then,
from the way he rode, you realised that it was all in his head.'

Where fame could take most minds off the job, in Merckx's case
it seemed only to sharpen his concentration. 'Merckx is never alone
but he is always solitary,' wrote the *Het Nieuwsblad* journalist Willem
Van Wijnendaele. Such was his celebrity in Belgium that he now
found it impossible to isolate himself. One day, a journalist had
turned up unannounced at his house in Tervuren, and Guillaume

Michiels had to smuggle Merckx and his bike out of the house in the boot of his car. When they were out of eyeshot and a safe distance away, Merckx hopped out and set off for training. Early in 1972, he and Claudine had moved a few kilometres to an unostentatious, new-build villa on the secluded Snippenlaan in Kraainem, another eastern suburb of Brussels. Die-hard fans quickly cottoned on. Claudine would occasionally catch them peering through windows, creeping through the back garden or even trying to pinch Merckx's jerseys off the washing line. At the Giro in May, the Italians had perhaps grown weary of his victories, but they were still mesmerised in his presence. In Sicily, fans had blockaded Merckx inside his hotel, and it had taken all of Giorgio Albani's negotiating skills and decoy tactics worthy of the secret service to smuggle him out. Before that, the 1971 Tour of Lombardy had been the first ever cycle race (excluding the Olympics) broadcast on live TV in the United States and Canada. Merckx was now a global star – a fact reflected again by the presence at the Classics of a journalist from *Sports Illustrated*. The resulting piece served up curious titbits on Merckx's taste in music (Claudine: 'He likes Louis Armstrong and Fats Domino') his substandard garden maintenance ('the millionaire's grass was badly in need of cutting – a comforting sign of decay?') and the guesstimate that his basic salary from Molteni was $60,000. It also heavily quoted Jean Van Buggenhout on Merckx's relationship with Claudine. Was Merckx romantic? 'Oh, no, not at all. He was romantic only with his bicycle. Claudine was the first girl. Claudine is very good for Eddy. Eddy has to worry only about the bicycles,' said Van Bug.

There were endless, multiplying challenges off the bike, but a diminishing number that hadn't already been met on it. He hadn't yet won (or indeed ridden) the Vuelta a España, Amstel Gold or Paris–Tours, but otherwise little remained except records. One in particular fascinated him: the one people in cycling referred to just as 'The Hour'.

With doubts persisting about whether Merckx was merely the best of a bad bunch, a generation of riders weaker than those faced by Anquetil and Coppi, here was one way to prove his value in its purest terms. The prize was so prestigious because the exercise was so simple: ride as far as possible, on a track, in an hour. Merckx called it the 'the supreme test of cycling'. In 1876 Frank Dodds had set the first mark of 26.508 kilometres, and since then some of cycling's most illustrious names, including Coppi and Anquetil, had clambered over each other to raise the bar. The record had last been broken in 1968 by the Dane Ole Ritter. It now stood at 48.653 kilometres. To maximise his chances, and minimise his drag through the air, Ritter had made his attempt at altitude, in the velodrome built for the '68 Olympics in Mexico City. Having also considered the tracks in Munich, Milan and Rome, Merckx finally decided that he too would head to the Agustin Melgar velodrome in Mexico.

He was fortunate in that not since Blois had he felt as powerful, as agile and free of pain as in the autumn of 1972. The World Championships in Gap in France had been a failure due more to a flat course and the usual competing interests in the Belgian team than the winner Marino Basso's brilliance or Merckx's own mistakes. Over the following five weeks, Merckx had embarked on a winning spree that rekindled memories of 1969: in 33 starts, he won 22 times, very often with spectacular solo gallops like the one that brought him his second Tour of Lombardy.

Lombardy took place on 7 October. Exactly a fortnight later, Merckx was due to fly to Mexico. What his preparation lacked in time, he made up for in diligence and input from experts. The rarefied air at the velodrome, 2,285 metres above sea level, would be the main problem, as well as a potential advantage over everyone who had attempted or broken the record before Ritter. That, at least, was the opinion of Paolo Ceretelli of the Physiological Institute of Milan, who irritated Merckx by revealing several 'secrets' of the tests they had conducted on 12 October. 'Eddy Merckx has a special gift for long, marathon-type efforts,' Ceretelli said. 'He's in the top five out of the hundred elite athletes we've examined here. He can consume seventy-three cubic centimetres of oxygen per kilo per minute. Only a few Nordic skiers have gone as high as seventy-six cubic centimetres. His heart-rate is very slow, so his oxygen debt shouldn't be too great in Mexico. He'll lose five per cent in terms of physiological output because of the altitude, but he'll gain around twenty-five per cent in terms of aerodynamic drag, so his average gain on what he could do at sea level will be between 12 and 15 per cent.'

The most striking stat of all pertained to how many doctors Merckx was consulting. It was at least eight, including Ceretelli; Merckx's Molteni team doctor, Cavalli; his personal doctor Lemage and five others more or less connected with the University of Liège – Messers Petit, Pirnay, Noret, Maréchal and Deroanne. They had turned Merckx's garage in Kraainem into an enclave of Mexico on the outskirts of Brussels. Six times a day, Merckx would ride for half an hour on his rollers while the doctors pumped rarefied air into an adapted miner's mask covering his face to simulate the effects of altitude. If in the Agustin Melgar velodrome, Merckx would be pedalling 2,285 metres above the sea, in his garage the doctors had him riding at the equivalent of 3,600. Within four days, at the end of the sessions, his heart-rate was descending from over 150 beats per minute to under 100 within 60 seconds. Ceretelli said that Merckx's powers of recovery were 'exceptional' and reckoned that 'Nine hundred and ninety-nine times out of a thousand, he would break the record.'

Merckx, of course, was leaving nothing to chance. He knew that he had much to lose and little to gain. As Claudine said, 'Beat the record and he'd stay exactly where he was; fail and he'd come home a lesser rider in the public's eyes.' It didn't bear thinking about. On the Boeing 707 departing Brussels for Mexico at 4 p.m. on 21 October, he tried to distract himself by discussing his favourite football team, Racing White, with some of the 20 or so journalists on board. He also snaffled 'an enormous chicken', drank 'two or three whiskies', and polished off a police novel.

Over the next four days, some anxieties faded while others grew and multiplied. One major concern had been the Italian former rider enlisted to liaise with the Mexican authorities and prepare the track. During his racing career, Luigi Casola had been better known for japes like feeding cats amphetamine tablets than his exploits on the road. To Merckx and Van Buggenhout's relief, though, Casola had excelled himself. The same applied to the mechanic Ernesto Colnago, who had built what some were calling the most expensive bike ever made (estimated cost: one million lire) and also the lightest (5.75kg) using high-grade duralumin, aluminium and titanium tubes.

Merckx was less enamoured with the pollution in Mexico, which he called 'suffocating', and the weather, which was either too wet or too windy for training on the track or the attempt itself. He had wanted to visit Acapulco before the trip home but cancelled that plan when he heard that it was tacky and overdeveloped. He was beginning to sense that the whole expedition might be cursed. 'When I think of all the journalists who have come all the way from Europe at great expense to see me in action, and of what this adventure means to Molteni, after all they've invested, I'm terrified. My morale isn't good at all. Doing ten thousand kilometres and finding the same weather here as in Belgium...' he wrote in his *Carnets de Route*.

On the fourth day, finally, dawn sunlight flooded his bedroom in the Parc des Princes hotel. Doctor Cavalli did some quick checks: Merckx's heart-rate was 48 beats per minute, his weight 75 kilograms and his blood pressure 50-125. He was good to go. After a light breakfast of toast, ham and cheese, they went straight to the velodrome and were on the track by 6.45 a.m.

At around eight o'clock, Merckx completes part one of his warm-up. The weather will hold and the record is on. Where are the official time-keepers? Merckx is edgy. He asks Guillaume Michiels for a change of underwear, and snaps when it doesn't arrive immediately. The journalists with whom four days ago he was sharing drams and banter, he now ignores or just grunts at when they ask questions.

At 8.49, the officials have arrived. Around 1,000 non-paying spectators are banked around the trackside. The former king of Belgium Leopold and his wife Lillian are among the coaches, doctors and journalists gathered on the football pitch in the middle. The sun is now blazing. Merckx adjusts the collar of his silk skinsuit, mumbles one last unintelligible word to Michiels, then gets on his bike. There is applause, followed by a few seconds' silence, then the snap of the starter's pistol.

One hour and just over 149 laps later, the gun sounds again and Merckx pulls off the track. 'Ritter 48.653.92 KMs; Merckx 49.408.68 KMs' says the scoreboard. 'Eddy, Eddy!' go the crowd. 'New world record!' rasps the Mexican speaker.

Some had suggested that the figure in Merckx's mind before leaving for Mexico was 52 kilometres. He had flatly dismissed this. The schedule drawn up for him by journalist and Hour-aficionado René Jacobs would have seen him beat Ritter by just 103 metres. Merckx had bettered that with a technically imperfect, aerodynamically unrefined exhibition of brawn and determination. He didn't say it, but he appeared to have been inspired by Jacques Anquetil's prediction after his second record attempt in 1967 that, 'One day, someone will attack the Hour record as if it were a five-kilometre pursuit, then they'll just carry on without dropping their speed.'

In Mexico as a pundit for the Europe 1 radio station, Anquetil was among the first to congratulate Merckx as he dropped his bike and staggered across the grass. Encircled by elation, Merckx's face and body were still braided in pain. It took minutes before relief, not joy, finally overcame him. It was the reaction of a man who later encapsulated his attitude to the record, his amazing '72 season and his work in general in the following sentences: 'My conscience is clear [...] There are a few more races that I still have to add to my palmarès, but I've completed the lion's share [...] My success in Mexico allows me to look serenely to the future.'

For now, Merckx sat slumped in a chair, behind a locked door in the changing room to which only Michiels, Giorgio Albani and other members of his inner circle had access. Anquetil and his co-commentator, the ex-rider Robert Chapatte, were the only members of the media to have snuck past the police guard. There was pandemonium on one side of the door, nothing except Merckx's groans on the other.

'Oh, it hurts. It hurts so much…!'

Anquetil took a step closer, with Chapatte close behind him holding the microphone.

'Where does it hurt, Eddy?'

Still grimacing, Merckx held the underside of his thighs.

'Why? Did you not train over a full hour beforehand?' asked Anquetil disapprovingly. Merckx responded that, no, he hadn't.

'You're a real gherkin!' Anquetil now told him. 'I can't believe that you managed to pull off such an exploit in these conditions!

Imagine what you would have done if you'd taken the precaution of preparing properly! Imagine you'd have been ready, and how far you would have gone. It's quite simple – you would easily have broken 50 kilometres!'

Almost as soon as he stepped off the track, Merckx had indicated that his hour in the Agustin Melgar velodrome had been the most excruciating of his career and an experience he did not intend to repeat. Initially at least, the exploit had the desired effect of strengthening Merckx's claims as the finest athlete the sport of cycling had ever seen, before bike and in some cases medical technology blurred the historical hierarchy over the following two-and-a-half decades. Thus, the Italian Francesco Moser used blood transfusions and a space-aged 'time machine' to overhaul Merckx and smash through the 50-kilometre barrier in 1984. The Scot Graeme Obree, the Englishman Chris Boardman and the Tour de France stars Tony Rominger and Miguel Indurain then waged a four-way arms race in the mid-1990s, culminating in Boardman's 56.375-kilometre ride in the elongated 'superman' position in Manchester in 1996. Uneasy about what now seemed more like a mad scientists' symposium than a benchmark of sporting excellence, the International Cycling Union announced in 2000 that the Hour Record would revert to Merckx's 1972 mark and that all future attempts must be carried out on equipment procuring no great advantage over what he had used in Mexico. Boardman immediately returned to Manchester, added 110 metres to the new-old record, and promptly retired. Five years later, the Czech rider Ondřej Sosenka rode 49.7 kilometres to oust Boardman.

A supreme technician and hugely experienced pursuit rider on the track, Boardman now says that the contrast between his performance and Merckx's merely underlines the Belgian's talent.

'I didn't pay a huge amount of attention to what Merckx had done before my attempt, but I saw some footage afterwards and I was pretty impressed with the oxygen work he was doing in training. It was quite advanced,' Boardman says. 'Where he was ragged was when he got on the bike. His first kilometre was one minute and nine seconds, which was almost the same as what I rode when I broke the world four-kilometre record. It was just suicide. I spoke to him about it later and he just said, "Oh, I wanted to go off fast." You go off at that speed there's no way back. I mean, from a technical point of view, if you look at his graphs, it was appalling. That's not a criticism – if anything, it just shows how talented he was. It's actually a bit of a shame that he went off so fast because I think he could have gone further.'

In terms of equipment, Boardman says, Merckx was at a slight advantage, having ridden with just a leather skullcap, while the UCI insisted in 2000 that Boardman wore a full-size protective helmet. The debate about venue and altitude, however, is more complicated.

'I'm guessing that it would have been worse at altitude, where he was,' is Boardman's hunch. 'I mean, I was an hour from home and I knew exactly what the conditions were going to be. Temperature is a massive thing. Anyone who has ridden a bike will know how much it can affect your performance, if you go out and it turns suddenly hotter or colder. Then there was the wind. We looked at doing it at altitude and decided that sea level was the better way. As for equipment, if you look at the video, I'd say his pedals were roughly the same volume and the rest is pretty similar. The thing about the UCI insisting on a modern helmet did aggrieve me slightly. That cost me five hundred metres, in aerodynamics. Merckx's position actually wasn't too bad for a big guy. He got into quite a good crouch, maybe by accident. I think in those days the fact that they didn't have specific time trial bikes with different bars maybe helped; he was that much more used to doing that kind of effort in that kind of position.

'I had two very different experiences. 1996 didn't really hurt at all – I couldn't go any faster but I didn't hurt. I had such fantastic form. It was just foot to the floor all the way through,' Boardman continues. 'But the 2000 one was just horrendous. I knew after ten minutes that it was going to be one big grovel with a sprint at the end, which is not a nice prospect. The difference compared to time trials or big efforts is that there's just no letting up for an hour. You can't freewheel at any point, there are no corners, no time for letting up. I couldn't walk for four days afterwards. It was just horrible.'

In Merckx's case, by the reckoning of Felice Gimondi's long-time directeur sportif Alfredo Martini, it was 'even greater than what he had done at the Tre Cime di Lavaredo'. Mexico was also, says journalist Walter Pauli, where Merckx and his career met 'the end of perfection'.

15
sign of the times

'I'd never seen Merckx like that before. The truth is that he was already slowing down.' RAYMOND POULIDOR

Eddy Merckx was at least a year out when, at the end of his career, he claimed that by 1974 the press and public were fed up with his reign and pining for new faces. When a precocious, sandy-haired 21-year-old from the North Sea coast began winning sprints and contending in Classics in the spring of 1973, for some the future couldn't come soon enough. They had been here before, of course, with Roger De Vlaeminck and Luis Ocaña, but Merckx was now inching ever closer to his thirties. Meanwhile, Freddy Maertens had the air of a young Dick Whittington setting out for a land where the streets were paved with cobbles of gold.

For those who don't already know how Merckx and Maertens's careers continued and ended, there might be some clue on the morning of a Tour of Flanders 38 years after Maertens's breakthrough in the same race. While Merckx strides imperiously through the crowds in Bruges's Grote Markt, a few hundred metres away, Maertens joins the queue of journalists behind the espresso machine in the press room. Merckx wears a suit; Maertens sports a jumper. Merckx can't walk a yard without someone yelling 'Eddy! Eddy!', taking a picture or chivvying a son or a nephew to ask for an autograph. Perhaps if Maertens was out there among the crowds it would be similar for him. But that's just the point: Merckx would never be in the press room waiting for coffee. And if he was, there is absolutely no way he could stand there in his golf sweater, acknowledged only by the odd Flemish reporter who nods or says 'Hey', then moves swiftly on.

A day later in a café overlooking another handsome square, this one in Oudenaarde, a dozen or so women sip hot chocolate amid heated debate. Names like 'Devolder', 'Nuyens' and 'Gilbert' – all protagonists in the previous day's *Ronde* – waft through the room with the steam coming from their cups. If this doesn't erase all doubts about how much cycling impregnates the psyche in these parts, a 50-metre walk to the Tour of Flanders museum just might. Of all the artefacts stored here, one national treasure attracts more attention and curiosity than the rest, and it, or rather he, generally lurks in the café at the back of the building. The museum's curator, Freddy Maertens is also its star, and here no one ever makes him queue for coffee.

Merckx knew all about Maertens even before the youngster finished second in the Flanders of 1973, and Merckx was only third. That day Lomme Driessens, now in charge at Rokado, shamelessly assigned the journeyman Willy De Geest to stick like superglue to Merckx's rear wheel for almost the entire race. Merckx went back to Kraainem that night and vented his spleen to Claudine about opponents being more interested in hindering him than winning themselves. Maertens's performance, though, was hardly a shock. 'I heard that Merckx had been keeping tabs on me when I was still riding as an amateur,' Maertens says now. 'I think he already knew or imagined then that I'd become a rival for him.'

'When I turned pro, it was both easy and difficult. All you had to do in races was follow Eddy or get as close to him as possible, which of course wasn't easy. That was the problem. The other one was that, while it was the smartest thing to do most of the time, by focusing on him and trying to stop him winning, you could also lose races. I saw that a lot with riders at the start of my career.'

Including, presumably, De Geest in that Tour of Flanders…

'Eddy wasn't the kind to be jealous, though,' Maertens continues. 'He didn't need to be. There's no room for jealousy. Just for battle. It was like a big cake – when I turned pro, Eddy had a huge portion of the cake, a few others had their own slice, and the rest fed off scraps. When I came along, I just took another slice and Eddy's got maybe a tiny bit smaller. That said, our rivalry was starting to build in the spring of 1973. We were talking to each other outside of the races, but in them it was starting to heat up nicely.'

Maertens says that, contrary to what Merckx has always maintained and history seems to affirm, it was Merckx who 'practically picked the Belgian team' ahead of the 1973 World Championships in Barcelona. That wasn't the case but logic suggested that it almost should have been; Merckx had, after all, enjoyed possibly his best ever Classics campaign and won two major tours before the end of the '73 spring. Forced by illness to skip Milan–San Remo and still rusty at the Tour of Flanders, he tore through what was left of the Classics to win Gent–Wevelgem for the third time, Amstel Gold in Holland for the first, Paris–Roubaix for the third and Liège–Bastogne–Liège for the fourth. Four days after Liège, he started his first Vuelta a España. A 17-stage race, whose highest mountain was the 1,145-metre Coll Formic, proved easy pickings against Luis Ocaña, and he duly prevailed over the Spaniard by just under four minutes. A four-day breather, then it was on to the Giro d'Italia and another first: Merckx wore the pink jersey of the race leader from the start of the race in Belgium to the final podium in Trieste. Five days in, he had already snaffled three stage wins and sent this ominous missive for anyone awaiting his decline: 'To use an Italian expression, "*L'appetito vien mangiando*" – appetite comes with eating. I'd be lying if I said that mine was sated.'

On the road to a seven-minute, 42-second overall victory ahead of Felice Gimondi, there was just one unexpected twist: for the first time in five years, at Forte dei Marmi, Gimondi had beaten Merckx in a time trial. 'Five years! Five long years!' Gimondi moans today. 'Five years!' Gimondi's directeur sportif at the time, Giancarlo Ferretti, echoes him. 'And Gimondi wasn't a pantomime horse! But he couldn't beat this monster,' Ferretti adds.

It wouldn't be Merckx and Gimondi's last battle of the 1973 season. Whether it was Merckx or the Belgian cycling federation, Royale Ligue Vélocipédique Belge, who really picked the national team, results in 1973 made Merckx an automatic choice for the Worlds in September – and that also applied to Maertens. Along with Roger De Vlaeminck and the former milkman (nickname: 'The Flying Milkman') Frans Verbeeck, and together with his Flandria teammate Walter Godefroot, Maertens had already pulled up a chair at the top table of Belgian cycling. 'Maertens is fast, he's good on the flat, on the climbs…we're all a bit scared of Maertens in 1973,' says Roger De Vlaeminck.

In Spain, Merckx could at least count on three of his most trusted and able teammates, the three Josephs: Huysmans, De Schoenmaecker and Bruyère. That and a course weaving up and around the Montjuïc park that Merckx had discovered at Catalan week in March and left him licking his lips. Having sat out the Tour de France, he was also in brilliant form. So brilliant that a time of six minutes and ten seconds in a one-off five-kilometre pursuit match against Joop Zoetemelk on the track in Amsterdam, in cruise control, had him briefly contemplating a tilt at the world track championships.

Belgium had the perfect captain on the perfect route in the perfect form. Nothing, though, was ever straightforward when riders who for the other 364 days of the year defended the interests of their trade teams were bundled together in the sky-blue, yellow, black and red Belgian national colours. One morning before the road race, the Belgian team at least put up a united front on a group-training ride on the Montjuïc circuit. In their Flandria trade team, Walter Godefroot had taken Maertens under his wing at the start of the season, and now the two rode side-by-side. When Godefroot saw and recognised Tullio Campagnolo in the Italian national team vehicle, he called out a jovial greeting.

The founder and owner of the biggest component manufacturer in cycling, Campagnolo was a powerful man. It hadn't escaped his notice, either, that Godefroot rode for a team which, at the start of the year, had broken Campagnolo's hegemony over the European peloton by signing a deal with the upstart Japanese Shimano. Godefroot's win on a bike equipped with Shimano Dura Ace components at the Ruta del Sol in February had been the company's first ever in a major European race.

Campagnolo could have borne a grudge, but he had always liked Godefroot.

'*Ciao*, Walter! So, who's going to win on Sunday?' he shouted out of the car.

Godefroot pointed to Martens. 'Him.'

'Oh no, not him,' Campagnolo replied. 'He rides for Shimano.'

The car sped off with Godefroot smirking, and Maertens letting his teammate know that he hadn't much appreciated Campagnolo's 'joke'. 'What if he's serious? What did he mean?' Godefroot reassured him that it was nothing, just an off-the-cuff remark. Sure, maybe Campagnolo had put up a win bonus for riders using his firm's gears and brakes on Sunday, but so what? Maertens frowned. That night, he would lie awake in bed replaying in his head what he believed had been a threat.

The Belgian team's stars and water-carriers assembled again, off the bike, in their pre-race base camp at the Hotel El Rancho in Lloret de Mar the night before the race. These meetings were a ritual for most of the major nations, and served mainly to determine how financial gains would be divided in the event of success. The national federation would put up a substantial bonus, the winner's trade team too, and there were factors to consider like the appearance fees a world champion could command in criteriums, and also the fact that in most cases the winner would have relied to some extent on the help or at least non-opposition of riders who were usually his rivals.

As every year in the Belgian camp, the discussion was loud and lively.

Roger De Vlaeminck remembers: 'There are eleven or twelve of us in the room and we start talking about *tactics*. "*Tactics*". I mean, how can you talk about "*tactics*"?' Otherwise stated, one rule usually applied in Belgian national teams – the law of the jungle. 'Anyway,' De Vlaeminck continues, 'Merckx is saying that he'll give us a certain amount of money if we work for him [Maertens claimed that it was 100,000 Belgian francs], and Freddy and I say that, no, we'd rather work for ourselves. The only agreement we have is that if one of us attacks, none of the other Belgian riders can go after him unless he's sure that he's not dragging a rider from another national team with him. We all agree on that.'

This all became highly relevant when, the following afternoon, having already pruned the lead group to just six riders, Merckx launched his second big attack on the Castillo climb two laps from the end. What happened next was to be dissected and debated endlessly in the Hotel El Rancho that night and in the Belgian press for years to come, but the television pictures are irrefutable: Maertens is the first to chase Merckx from a starting position *behind* Felice Gimondi and Luis Ocaña and what *should* have been the best seat in the house. Had he stuck, Maertens, and certainly Belgium, couldn't lose: either Gimondi and Ocaña would have tried to catch Merckx and frazzled in the heat, leaving a fresher Maertens to counter-attack alone later, or they would have succeeded and Maertens would have been both the best-rested and the fastest rider in the four-man group. In a third eventuality, Merckx would have ridden away to a third world title alone. But instead Maertens decided to twist. Within seconds Ocaña and Gimondi were snug in his slipstream and the trio joined Merckx.

All was not yet lost. Far from it. Merckx had never been beaten by either Gimondi or Ocaña in a meaningful sprint, not since the 1966 Tour of Lombardy where Gimondi had outfoxed rather than outkicked him. Maertens was even faster than Merckx. They both also looked across at Gimondi and Ocaña and saw signs that both men were tiring. Gimondi had few illusions about a sprint finish but even fewer alternatives. 'I knew that I was going to lose the sprint, but I couldn't not do it because the Italian national coach, Nino Defilippis, had left Gianni Motta at home to stake everything on me. I was obliged,' Gimondi says. 'It was a question of saving my balls.'

If Gimondi was flagging then so, it seemed, was Maertens. Merckx claimed later that Maertens had continually asked him to refrain from attacking on the last two laps in return for the promise of help should the race end in a sprint. Merckx had hesitated for a second, then accepted the quid pro quo.

Maertens was already leading when the quartet rounded the final bend, and Ocaña was already struggling. But as Maertens engaged his turbo with 200 metres to go, something very odd happened: Merckx's legs turned to lead. It took Gimondi a few seconds to realise, during which time Maertens slowed to see where he had left his teammate. As Merckx's thighs chopped, his shoulders rocked and his momentum drained, Gimondi glimpsed the chance of a lifetime, and Maertens had no choice but to forget about his compatriot. In the final 100 metres Gimondi swung right across Maertens, their shoulders met, then Gimondi veered back to his left and over the line centimetres ahead of Maertens. Now Maertens turned again. 'Coward!' he spat as Merckx passed on his left-hand side. Some also claimed to have heard him immediately accusing Merckx of selling the race to Gimondi, either because he was a friend or because that pair both used Campagnolo components.

More recriminations would come later, but for now Merckx was inconsolable. The 'real drama in his life' was playing out before the eyes and cameras of the world. In 1974, the French documentary *La Course en Tête* would capture the full asphyxiating anguish of these moments, as Merckx sat speechless in the Belgian pit area then in the passenger seat of a team vehicle. At one point an autograph hunter appears at the car window. Merckx's instinct is to oblige him or at least apologise that he can't. He tries to open his mouth but nothing comes out. He then does his best to hide his face. It is a brief but telling snapshot from the inside of the Merckx goldfish bowl.

An hour or two later, back at the El Rancho hotel, the arguments had begun and would rage into the night. At first Merckx didn't want to see Maertens, but after dinner with Maertens at a nearby restaurant, Herman Van Springel and Rik Van Linden brought the pair together. Merckx's main bugbear was the Maertens counter-attack, which had raised Gimondi and Ocaña from the dead and was a flagrant breach of their pre-race agreement. Maertens, in turn, was furious with Merckx for insisting on the last two laps that he would win the sprint as long as Maertens performed lead-out duties; one man had kept his half of the bargain, the other had not. Maertens believed that Merckx had been cooked, knackered, but too proud to admit it, as well as too happy for his friend Gimondi to become world champion at Maertens's expense.

The single thing they both agreed on, not that it mattered, was that Gimondi should have been disqualified for changing his line in the final sprint. 'We complained to the commissaires after the race but were told, "Disqualify Gimondi? We can't do that to our friends at the Italian Federation,"' Maertens says now, repeating the allegation he made at the time.

Both men went to bed still seething, and would have fooled not even the most inexperienced, incompetent body language expert when they appeared on a TV chat show together back in Belgium the following day.

'There was a moment in the race when I didn't feel very good, and Eddy came and said he was riding fantastically, and it was my duty to lead him out,' Maertens told the host in a barely audible mumble.

'I don't think we'll be enemies from now on, and I think that everyone will ride their own race. We should stay sporting, and I don't think there's any reason to ride against a certain rider,' Merckx added, with equal lack of conviction.

Who had been right, who had been wrong, and what did it matter in the context of Merckx's career?

Proceeding in order, there is little doubt that it had been a mistake for Maertens to follow Merckx when he attacked on the Castillo. Not only that, but, having denied it at the time, Maertens acknowledges now what others including Merckx, Godefroot and De Vlaeminck have all said about the way he blazed Merckx's trail in the final 300 metres. 'I started to lead out the sprint two kilometres from the finish,' he concedes. 'The problem was that it's not easy to lead out a sprint when you're a sprinter yourself. I perhaps didn't do the best job. You can see that when I accelerate, I go too fast and put two bike lengths between Eddy and me.'

De Vlaeminck, incidentally, agrees but thinks the real issue lies elsewhere. 'Why was Maertens leading out Merckx? I would never have done that. *Never*,' he says.

Another impartial observer – at least we assume – Gimondi, believes that Maertens's error wasn't so much the speed of his acceleration as its timing. 'He started winding it up with two kilometres to go, but if Merckx or Maertens had done a short sprint, they would have beaten me hands down, because I had no jump, I was screwed.'

Having accused Merckx, Gimondi and the race referees who hadn't disqualified him, Maertens focused next on his great Campagnolo conspiracy. Nearly four decades later, the theory that Gimondi, Merckx and Tullio Campagnolo somehow connived to guarantee a winner from the Italian manufacturer's stable has been roundly discredited...except by Maertens. 'We'll never know what happened with Campagnolo and Shimano,' he says sombrely. 'I think only they'll ever know. It was Shimano's first year and, while they didn't have the history or prestige of Campagnolo, their equipment was already good. I just know that Campagnolo did three-quarters of their advertising in Spain, and that Shimano wasn't nearly on the same scale.'

Perhaps better than Merckx, Walter Godefroot came to understand Maertens and the ill-feeling that would grow between him and not just Merckx, but a number of riders in the mid-1970s. From his vast, open-plan living room in Nazareth near Gent, Godefroot speaks with such authority and insight on almost anyone and anything from his era that it is easy to see why he later became a highly successful team manager, albeit one whose record was severely tarnished by doping scandals before his retirement in 2006. He wasn't always so lucid, he admits, and on the night of the Barcelona Worlds, he sided with his Flandria protégé. Within months, in 1974, their relationship had begun to deteriorate.

'First of all, the Campagnolo thing,' Godefroot says. 'I might have put the idea in Freddy's head. I might have said something about Campagnolo maybe giving their riders a bonus if one of them won. That's possible. We were just talking like that. But Freddy immediately told other people who maybe got the wrong end of the stick or blew the thing out of all proportion.

'The story's not feasible, not reasonable. At first Maertens and I got on well. It was already my eighth year as a pro, so I could teach him a few tricks of the trade, what to look out for and so on,' Godefroot continues. 'But there were people who took advantage of certain situations, people who weren't trustworthy, and Freddy was vulnerable. On the other hand, he didn't trust us. He didn't trust my generation, Merckx's generation, yet Merckx always keeps his word. It comes down to personality.'

Maertens's feuding with Merckx, says Godefroot, had just begun and would go on for decades, still with Barcelona at its source. For Merckx, the '73 Worlds represented maybe his bitterest defeat to date and also one of his most unexpected. In one sense, Maertens's machinations had done him the favour of obscuring his collapse on a course and finishing straight that could scarcely have suited him better. He had failed to win the Worlds before, but always on courses or with teammates who brought more hindrance than assistance. The bottom line in Barcelona was that whatever Maertens had or hadn't done shouldn't have mattered. That it did may just have been a sign. Because that was the new face the people were really yearning for – the one belonging to a declining Merckx. He only had to look at Raymond Poulidor for proof that turning 30 needn't be a death knell, but the Frenchman was the exception; cyclists in general didn't last as long as they do today, and Merckx fully expected to burn out sooner than most. Had he not told Marc Jeuniau in 1971 that he would not ride on beyond 30, and that in any case his aggressive riding style was incompatible with any kind of longevity? He was now 28. Already in that 1971 season he had said that his bruising duel with Ocaña made him 'feel like I've aged terribly'. In *Coureur Cycliste Un Homme et Son Métier*, released in 1974, he would then address this message to his fans: 'Don't fear for one second that you'll see me on the decline, served up on a plate to a vengeful peloton, like some shipwrecked, stranded sailor clinging to the buoy of his former glory. At the first signs that I'm weakening, and maybe a bit before, I'll bid farewell... There have been one or two who haven't known when their time had come, having succumbed to the nostalgia of a glorious past... I know that I'm strong enough to use my head not my heart at the right time.'

To suggest that he was already slipping in the final weeks of the '73 season, already flouting that self-imposed deadline, would have been premature. Of course it would. He proved it with a consummate ride in Paris–Bruxelles, his 'home' race which returned to the calendar after a seven-year absence, and another one at the GP des Nations. He then obliterated Roger De Vlaeminck, Frans Verbeeck, Franco Bitossi and the rest of the Italian '*gruppo*' to win a third Tour of Lombardy on 13 October. That, at least, is what it said in his *Carnets de Route* for the 1973 season. Evidently the book went to press before 8 November, when it emerged that Merckx's urine sample after Lombardy had contained traces of the banned drug norephedrine. On this occasion it didn't take Merckx long to solve the mystery: the Molteni doctor Angelo Cavalli, the erstwhile Italian federation doctor who had tested his urine samples in Savona, soon remembered and publicly admitted that he had prescribed Merckx the cough medicine Mucantil, which contained the offending substance. Not that the alibi cut any ice with the authorities; Merckx was stripped of his Lombardy win and left furiously lamenting another anti-doping injustice.

Was this another indicator, the faintest portent like Barcelona that, even if his opponents weren't yet encroaching, maybe the sporting gods were closing in? The unbroken winning run in major tours dating from the 1968 Giro coincided with a six-year period during which Merckx's longest lay-off due to injury had been the 12 days after his crash in Blois. There had been punctures, illnesses and crashes, some at crucial times, but nothing that had compromised an entire major tour or Classics campaign. History had shown that the best riders possessed an uncanny knack of avoiding such 'imponderables', and indeed this was one of the reasons why they took their place among the elite. What passed for luck was also, actually, often nothing of the sort. Merckx was 'luckier' than Ocaña, for example, because he happened to be a better bike handler in wet weather, because Mother Nature had blessed him with a more robust constitution and immune

A packed circuit in Leicester, England played host to the 1970 World Championship road race. For once, Merckx was overshadowed and beaten by another precocious Belgian, Jean-Pierre 'Jempi' Monseré.

Merckx often revelled in the very worst weather conditions, as was the case here in Paris–Roubaix in 1970. Though Roger de Vlaeminck claimed that only his puncture allowed Merckx to drop him and win.

The drama of Luis Ocaña's crash on the Col de Menté in the 1971 Tour de France. Race director Jacques Goddet, far left, is a beleaguered spectator.

Merckx winning his first Tour of Lombardy in the Sinigaglia velodrome in Como in 1971. The race was the first major cycling event outside the Olympics to be broadcast live in the United States.

Merckx marauds to the Hour record on the Agustín Melgar velodrome in Mexico City in October 1972.

Joseph Bruyère, followed here by Merckx and Raymond Poulidor, became Molteni and Merckx's irreplaceable mountain enforcer.

With Théo Mathy. Merckx had a difficult relationship with the press throughout his career, who became increasingly frustrated with their failure to get under his skin.

'I'm only truly happy when I'm on my bike,' Merckx once said. Or, it seemed, when making endless, infinitesimal adjustments to the three dozen or so machines he kept in his garage.

Balancing daughter Sabrina on his handlebars as he arrives home in Kraainem after a training ride in 1973.

Merckx shares a joke with Jos Huysmans, one of his longest-serving domestiques, over dinner at the 1973 Giro d'Italia.

From the left, Messers Parecchini, Mintjens, Merckx, Swerts, Spruyt, Huysmans, Van Schil, Bruyère, De Schoenmaecker, Janssens – Molteni's formidable team at the 1973 Giro.

Merckx leads Roger De Vlaeminck, Walter Godefroot and, only just in shot on the left, Freddy Maertens, on his way to the last of his seven Milan–San Remo victories.

Still in the yellow jersey, but is Merckx praying for a miracle in the 1975 Tour?

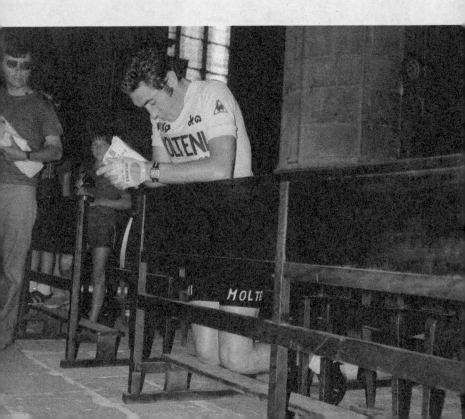

Did Merckx's hopes of a sixth Tour win in 1975 disappear when a spectator punched him on the Puy de Dôme? Is that already his fear here, within minutes of the fateful blow?

Moments before Bernard Thévenet passes and leaves Merckx for dead on the climb to Pra-Loup in the 1975 Tour de France. He would be the first man to defeat the Cannibal in the Tour.

The anguish of Merckx's capitulation en route to Alpe d'Huez in the 1977 Tour de France is vividly captured in this picture taken seconds after he has crossed the line.

system, and in all sorts of other regards that owed more to genetic or nurtured merit than random forces. The day when Merckx's 'luck' took a turn for the worse would in fact be the day when he no longer had a sufficient margin of superiority to master his rivals, the weather, the politics of the peloton, media pressure and anything else that professional cycling could throw at him. Barcelona and the positive test at Lombardy had been isolated blips, but they were harbingers of the kind of adversities that would one day overwhelm and outnumber his coping mechanisms. And on that day, if not before, Merckx knew that there would be no shortage of volunteers to dig and then dance upon his grave.

Plenty were already toting their spades early in 1974, for Merckx's spring was by general consensus a 'disaster'. The first symptoms of a chest infection appeared at Paris–Nice, then kept him out of Milan–San Remo. Soon he was diagnosed with viral pneumonia. He did admirably to come back and finish fourth at the Tour of Flanders, then second behind Barry Hoban at Gent–Wevelgem. He then lined up at the 1974 Paris–Roubaix believing that he was nearly back on song, only to be eclipsed by an irresistible Roger De Vlaeminck. The next day, Merckx was told by his doctor that his lungs were not yet clear and that he must rest for another two weeks. He therefore missed Liège–Bastogne–Liège and Flèche Wallonne. Not since 1965, his first season, had Merckx finished the spring without a single Classic win.

It was little wonder, then, that the press in Italy was already utter-ing that unspeakable word – 'decline' – when he returned to action there at the end of April. A report in *La Stampa* said that he was 'agitated and insecure' and 'no longer himself'. The evidence? Merckx had said himself before the Coppa Placci that he was only racing to train. And Merckx never, *ever* raced just to train.

In May, Maertens riled him at the Four Days of Dunkirk, where a series of on- and off-the-bike spats confirmed that their made-for-TV reconciliation the night after the Barcelona Worlds had been a PR charade. The trend of other riders troubling if not beating Merckx then continued at the Giro, which he had only decided to ride when his illness in the spring left him short of racing. Again, the main thorn was José Manuel Fuente, although it was the Italian pair of Gianbattista Baronchelli and Felice Gimondi who both came heart-stoppingly close to beating him. As in 1972, Fuente took the pink jersey at the first mountainous opportunity, on Stage 3 to Sorrento. He then won two further stages to lead Merckx by over two minutes by the halfway mark. Fuente's fate, though, was already sealed according to Franco Bitossi; having been critical of his tactics in 1972, Bitossi now says that, maybe like Ocaña in the 1971 Tour, the Spaniard had been lured into trying to beat Merckx at his own game. 'He'd had the pink jersey for over a week and during that time had tried to ride like Merckx and make his team ride like Merckx's. In doing so, he had worn himself and them out completely. He then paid the price and collapsed,' Bitossi says.

Fuente hinted at the same thing when, in a documentary about the 1974 Giro fittingly entitled *The Greatest Show on Earth*, he said the rest of the peloton lost its bearings when Merckx wasn't leading. He, clearly, had not known quite what approach to take and duly buckled on Stage 14 to San Remo.

He won one more stage, to the Monte Generoso, but that day Merckx didn't care about the result. Fifteen kilometres into the stage, Giorgio Albani had pulled alongside him in his Molteni team car and announced that Jean Van Buggenhout, Merckx's long-serving manager, was 'in great pain and has had to be hospitalised'. Merckx worked out instantly, from the look in Albani's eyes and what he knew about Van Bug's recent heart problems, that his old friend and business brain had died.

Having initially wanted to abandon, Merckx struggled on, grief-stricken. If Maertens had at least contributed to his undoing in Barcelona, another member of the new generation, the 20-year-old Baronchelli, now assumed the same role. We know that Merckx was not superstitious, but there was a real risk of him crash-landing precisely where his Giro career had taken off, beneath the Tre Cime di Lavaredo on the final mountain stage in the Dolomites. Only a courageous last kilometre in pursuit of Baronchelli and Fuente under the three majestic Lavaredo spires saved him. Two days later the Giro was his...by 12 seconds from Baronchelli, the second smallest margin of victory in the Giro's history, and 33 from Gimondi.

Merckx's edginess had been apparent throughout the race, not least in his constant fussing over his equipment. Faced with Merckx's demands and incessant tinkering with the 15 bikes he had brought to the race, one of the Molteni mechanics had left the Giro 'on the verge of a nervous breakdown and swearing that he would never work with me again' – Merckx's words in his *Carnets de Route*.

The race had ended, incidentally, with Merckx claiming that another of his old mechanics, Ernesto Colnago, had offered him a substantial fee to gift the pink jersey to Baronchelli, something that Colnago denied. Baronchelli too naturally rebuffs the allegation, while also offering some interesting insight into how a new wave of riders was slowly dismantling the Merckx mystique.

'The Colnago story is an old folk tale,' Baronchelli says. 'Why on earth would Merckx be selling a Giro to a twenty-year-old? Because he needed the money? Come on... As for his aura and whether I was intimidated by him in that race, I'd say you're not scared of anyone at twenty years of age. The generation who had been riding with Merckx for years revered him and were terrified of him. I certainly wasn't. I don't think it was a coincidence that Gimondi and I ended up closest to Merckx in that Giro: on the one hand, you had a young and fearless guy like me and on the other you had probably the only guy from Merckx's generation who had worked out that you couldn't try to beat him at his own game. You had to feed off scraps. All those guys who went in thumping their chests, trying to challenge him head on, had been chewed up and spat out. It had happened to Motta, to Ocaña and to Fuente. If Fuente had waited for the last climbs in the mountains, he would have taken a Giro off Merckx, but instead he wanted to kill him by going on the first climb all the time. Merckx was maybe there for the taking but Fuente couldn't take advantage.'

If Baronchelli wasn't blinded, if he could see signs of mortality, that didn't necessarily mean that everyone would, particularly not those riders who had been tortured for years. Maertens and Baronchelli were still juniors in 1969, when Merckx created a memory that his old directeur sportif Marino Vigna said 'terrorised' the peloton for years thereafter. At around the same time Gimondi had learned through painful experience that trying to wrest control of a race from Merckx was akin to waking a sleeping giant. The consequences were often humiliating. Thus a pattern of resignation or submission had gradually taken root. That or just a way of racing which was hardwired for defence and, as Fuente said, left many disoriented or ill-equipped when Merckx was either absent or below his best. Maertens, Gimondi and many others had said that racing against Merckx was easy because, instead of monitoring 100 or more potential opponents, you only really had to watch him. Thus, the peloton's rhythms became adapted to Merckx.

Even when he did weaken, he would surely therefore have a year or two's grace while those whom he had battered into anaesthesia processed what was happening. Or if not grace, at least a time when all of the savoir faire he had acquired since Blois would make up for the fact that he was no longer quite as strong. Was this what was already happening in 1973 and 1974? Hard to tell. Certainly, though, there seemed to be a lot of truth and an element of denial in the long passage he devoted in his 1974 *Carnets de Route* to explaining why he was no longer wreaking such carnage in the mountains.

'It's mainly a psychological thing,' he wrote. 'A young rider taking on the mountains for the first time goes about it with a ferocious appetite. In the 1967 Giro d'Italia I was climbing big mountains for the first time in my life. What I did on the Blockhaus that year was the performance of a new champion who was getting to know not just the mountains but top-level cycling. The most unlikely challenges appealed to me... In 1969, my irrational exploit on the stage to Mourenx was the performance of a man riding his first Tour and needing, for the reasons you know about, to leave a fabulous mark.

'If I found myself alone 100 kilometres from the finish in a Tour de France, now I would ease up,' he continued. 'I'd think about what lay ahead, the efforts I'd still have to make before the finish line. Five or six years ago, I'd have put my head down and plied on without thinking.'

The problem that maybe Merckx did or didn't acknowledge was that his 'irrational exploits' were central to what had made him Merckx. As Walter Godefroot remarks, what had demoralised his competitors early in his career were not his victories but the manner in which they were achieved. 'Merckx wasn't just winning, he was winning with panache, attacking from a long way out, dropping everyone. He was the only one who could do that. It made him seem like a different species.' As time went on, however, his wins were looking more and more like those of a mere mortal – a superior man to the others but a man nonetheless. Previously they hadn't been just triumphs but traumas for those on the receiving end.

Make no mistake, it was going to be a slow process. The old tyrant still stirred. He could still dole out gifts and punishments like the cycling Almighty he remained. At the Tour of Switzerland a few weeks after the Giro, Franco Bitossi seemed doomed for an agonising near-miss when his old friend caught him 400 metres from the line in Lausanne, only for Merckx to wink in his direction and let him win.

Alas, there was no such charity for Barry Hoban in the first week of the 1974 Tour de France.

'I'd done well in the prologue, which Eddy had won, and that put me in a good position to get the yellow jersey because there were eight stages before the mountains and lots of bonus seconds on offer,' Hoban recalls. 'There were three hot-spot sprints on every stage with thirty seconds going to the winner of each one. So, yes, being a fast sprinter, I thought I had a good chance of getting yellow. Anyway, on the first stage in Brittany, we're going though this village, round a corner and towards this hot-spot sprint when who should appear under my arm and beat me but Merckx. I say "Eddy, what are you doing? You're going to win the Tour by fifteen minutes. You can give the yellow jersey away for a day or two." He just looked across and said, in that low voice, "Yes, Barry, but it's *my* yellow jersey…"'

So Merckx was still Merckx…for the moment. Hoban and his mates still feared the worst when he was quiet in the morning before stage starts. 'You could tell when he was on a good day. You picked up on the nuances after a while,' the Englishman says. 'Some mornings you'd see him at the start and say, "All right, Eddy?" and he'd be happy to chit chat. "Good ride yesterday, Barry" – stuff like that. But on another day, you'd say "All right, Eddy?" and get a grunt at most. That's when you'd say to yourself, "Uh oh, it's going to hurt today."'

They would still, also, tell and laugh at the same jokes.

'We'd always say, "Let's hope there are no roadworks today." In France there used to be these little robots waving flags to warn you before you got to roadworks. The joke being that Eddy would attack as soon as any flag went down.'

Hoban, though, knew that Merckx wasn't kidding when, with the mountains behind them and victory already assured, he rode straight out of the peloton 12 kilometres from Orléans and the end of Stage 21a. 'I'd never seen anything like it. He went right up the middle of the road. I said to my mate Gerben Karstens, "He's not playing around." He just rode away from the whole peloton and won by a minute and a half.'

The same attack gave the journalist Walter Pauli one of his abiding childhood memories. 'My dad and I always used to eat French fries for lunch on Saturday, and I can remember eating my fries and calling to my dad in the kitchen, "Merckx has won the stage!" He said, "What? How? In a sprint?" No one could believe it. But all that had happened was that someone had said he'd won the Tour with no panache, and he'd got angry. That was the real Merckx.'

As much as his lack of panache, the critics accused Merckx of equalling Anquetil's record of five Tour wins against a threadbare field. Ocaña, Gimondi, Fuente and Zoetemelk were all absent for assorted reasons. This left the 36-year-old Raymond Poulidor to provide the stiffest resistance and even drop Merckx by nearly two minutes on the summit finish at Pla D'Adet in the Pyrenees. 'I dropped him every day in the mountains in that Tour,' Poulidor says. 'I'd never seen Merckx like that before. The truth is that he was already slowing down. On the Mont du Chat in the Alps, I left him for dead. Or so I thought. But he was still a fantastic descender, and he came back and beat us. That year he was already relying more on his head than his legs.'

In fairness to Merckx, if at the Giro he had started short of racing, at the Tour he was hampered throughout by the leftover wound from an operation to remove a cyst in his groin four days before the start. Most riders wouldn't even have started the Tour. Merckx finished it and won, often enduring agony. His phenomenal resistance to pain would be one of the last pillars of excellence, maybe the last, to crumble.

The bottom line at the end of 1974 was that he was still number one. He proved it by winning a third World Championship road race on a brutally difficult circuit in Montreal, Canada. His celebration was as effusive as any in his career. Claudine watched on TV back home and told her husband on the phone that it had been the best day of her life. Even if, to others, Merckx winning still seemed routine, 'the heaps of problems' he had faced in 1974 meant that to him the taste of victory had never felt sweeter or more ephemeral.

16
knockout!

'I mean, besides the fact that it was the shittiest podium presentation I've ever seen, it was such a shock, such an earthquake for cycling.' BERNARD THÉVENET

Joseph Bruyère was the kind of domestique who was worth his weight in gold, all 82 kilos of him. In the 1974 Tour a few people had questioned Merckx's team, but no one was in any doubt about the value of the rider Merckx called simply '*mon Joseph*'. Self-effacing to a fault now like he was then, even Bruyère admits: 'In 1974, I did a great Tour de France.'

It wasn't just the fact that he had worn the yellow jersey on the Tour's first ever trip across the English Channel, on the stage leaving and finishing in Plymouth. With Merckx's limitations in the mountains becoming ever more apparent, it was vital that his teammates kept the racing in the Alps and Pyrenees under control, at a cruising pace safe for Merckx's ageing diesel engine. Merckx had outlined the problem in his 1974 *Carnets de Route*: 'I've never been a true climber... Counter-attacking or even responding to a real climber's attack is impossible for me. My strength in the mountains consists of keeping a very high pace to make it very difficult if not impossible for the real climbers to attack... My tactic is simple and known by everyone: I try to keep the pace very high going uphill to suffocate my rivals.'

Bruyère notwithstanding, if Merckx had struggled in the mountains in 1974, it was partly because his team was ageing with him. He had been challenged on this topic in an interview with *Miroir du Cyclisme* early in the season, and conceded, 'It's true that I've had a few disappointments with young riders and so I prefer to surround myself with experienced men.' The question that some were asking when July and the Tour came around was whether, in the same way as Merckx, riders like Vic Van Schil, Jos Huysmans and Joseph Spruyt weren't compensating for their waning strength with other 'attributes'. Bullying and intimidation, for example. After days of complaints that Merckx and Molteni had installed a sporting dictatorship, refusing even the most innocuous rider any freedom of movement, Joseph Spruyt overstepped the mark on Stage 16 to Pla D'Adet. Unspoken ceasefires at certain points in certain stages of the Tour were nothing new; neither, as Merckx pointed out, was it unusual for a rider who broke them to feel the wrath of the peloton. What wasn't acceptable was the venom in Spruyt's tirade at Cyrille Guimard after the Frenchman's early attack, and even less so Spruyt's punches after Guimard's second breakaway attempt. In the ensuing controversy, Guimard wasn't blameless himself, but still received most if not all of the public's sympathy. He, too, saw Spruyt as a Luca Brasi-type figure, the chief heavy in a team of mobsters. 'Mafia' was the word that Guimard actually used. Merckx was naturally cast as its boss. While condemning Spruyt's assault, Merckx wanted people to understand that 'Spruyt has rarely frequented the salons of Madame de Pompadour and his vocabulary isn't quite as refined as [the famous Belgian journalist] Luc Beyer's.' In other words, yes, he had behaved like a thug but that was just Spruyt. Guimard was the real villain, said

Merckx. Why had he gone telling tales to Jacques Goddet and then repeated his accusations on TV?

Even Bruyère had been whistled the next day, but then he was used to it. The difference this time was that the abuse was coming from the fans and not members of the peloton. Everyone in the bunch knew that when Bruyère loped to the front to begin his demolition derby, pain in ample doses would follow close behind. They made their displeasure heard accordingly. Thus Bruyère became the unlikeliest, most unassuming of public enemies. Had he learned to be nastier, a bit more thick-skinned, he might have been another Merckx. 'But Bruyère could never have been a leader,' says Walter Godefroot, 'because when Bruyère starts to hurt he drops back immediately, whereas Merckx attacks.' It didn't seem to matter, either, whether the distress was physical or psychological; at the 1974 Giro, Bruyère's performances had supposedly suffered terribly because he missed his wife.

His lack of personal ambition made him the ideal lieutenant – albeit one with a porcelain morale. Merckx was naturally drawn to sensitive, quiet types, and Bruyère was also fiercely loyal. The man who had acted as middleman in his signing for Faemino in 1970, Jean Crahay, said that if you asked him the time, Bruyère would reply 'Merckx!'

Some tough love from Merckx after the Giro seemed to have transformed Bruyère in the 1974 Tour, and he confirmed his new standing with a magnificent ride at the Worlds in Montreal. Even by his own modest admission, he and his team captain then made a 'thunderous start' to the 1975 season. Bruyère was in the form of his life and, against all odds, Merckx was about to put together his best ever Classics campaign in his 30th year.

Having claimed some rare slices of glory for himself at Het Volk and the Tour of the Med, Bruyère catapulted his leader to a sixth

Milan–San Remo win on the Poggio. Ten days later, in the Amstel Gold Race in Holland, it was the same story. Merckx first, Bruyère third.

Merckx was just getting started. He would go on to win his third Tour of Flanders, having shaken off the last of the opposition five kilometres from the line. He then took his fifth Liège–Bastogne–Liège with a narrow victory over Bernard Thévenet.

But it was the Setmana Catalana, which had taken place in the last week of March, a few days before Flanders, that of all the spring races would have the biggest impact on Merckx's summer. Joseph Bruyère had again underlined his supreme, early-season form by romping away to take Stage 1 ahead of Merckx, Gimondi, Zoetemelk, Thévenet and Ocaña. He had bequeathed his leader's jersey to Merckx by Stage 4, when a civil war between the Spanish teams broke out on the road to San Bartolomé del Grau. Close to Campdevànol in the foothills of the Pyrenees, Vicente López Carril of the KAS team drew alongside him.

'We used to have the little pieces of paper with route maps stuffed into our pocket, and López Carril asked to see mine,' Bruyère says. 'I reached into my back pocket, handed it over, then somehow lost concentration and hit the wheel in front. I crashed and knew straight away that it was bad. It turned out that I'd broken my femur.'

Bruyère knew that his participation in the 1975 Tour de France was in jeopardy. At the 1974 Tour de France, particularly on the Col du Télégraphe in the Alps, even Merckx had struggled to hold his wheel. He was irreplaceable – and indeed would not be replaced.

Bruyère's injury apart, Merckx couldn't have hoped for a better spring to mute the mounting uncertainty – his own and other people's. But it ended badly, with another of those setbacks that were becoming increasingly frequent, when he fell ill with tonsilitis four days before the start of the Giro and was bed-ridden for several days. Merckx pulling out created a dilema not only for the Giro organiser Vincenzo Torriani but also for himself: only once had he started the Tour de France having not previously completed the Giro, and that was in the 1971 race where Luis Ocaña battered him for the first week-and-a-half while Merckx groped for his best form.

The best, indeed the only available alternative to the Giro, was combining the Dauphiné Libéré with the Tour of Switzerland – 18 days of racing in the high Alps. The Dauphiné proved a sobering measure of how much ground Merckx had to recoup; if Freddy Maertens winning the first six stages was hard to stomach, losing nearly 11 minutes to Bernard Thévenet in the Massif de la Chartreuse mountains that he seemed to despise represented the worst experience in the mountains of Merckx's career. Matters improved at the Tour of Switzerland, but that too was dominated by a Belgian rival, Roger De Vlaeminck. Merckx still wasn't himself in more ways than one: one day, he even asked De Vlaeminck if he would let him win a stage.

Everything felt somehow different as he set off for the Tour de France, and not only because the race was starting in Charleroi in Belgium, and he could ride there from his home in Kraainem. There were many familiar faces among his teammates – notably Spruyt, De Schoenmaecker, Huysmans, Mintjens and Marc Lievens – but something slightly odd about not starting the first stage proper in the yellow jersey, having narrowly missed out to the young Italian Francesco Moser in the prologue. Not since 1969 had Merckx failed to win at the first bite of the cherry.

The next day there was much to reassure him. On the first climb of the Tour, the côte d'Alsemberg, scene of a boyhood defeat to Felice Gimondi in 1963, a Merckx attack cost Gimondi and Thévenet a minute. That day there were two stages, and in the afternoon it was another of the riders tipped to trouble Merckx, Zoetemelk, who lost over a minute due to a puncture. Merckx would soon have mechanical problems of his own; on Stage 2 to Amiens, he stopped four times to make adjustments to his bike. There were no serious consequences, just the suspicion again that nothing was going quite as smoothly as it once had.

The difficulty for his rivals and everyone else who wanted to see him fail was that the alternation of hope and despair was a motif as old and repetitive as his supremacy: no sooner had optimism flickered than Merckx had doused it with a splash of his old brilliance. In the first time trial of the Tour, 16 kilometres on the Atlantic coast, typically, he put everyone back in their place with a 27-second win which gave him the yellow jersey. Another time trial four days later at Auch saw him win again, but this time by only nine seconds from Thévenet. The Frenchman was now third overall, two minutes and 20 seconds behind Merckx on general classification. Merckx predicted that the Peugeot rider would be his most dangerous rival in the mountains. 'I have to keep improving,' he said of his own form.

As much as his own fitness or Thévenet, as the Pyrenees approached, Merckx's team threatened to be his biggest source of concern. Stage 10 was but a taster with Gimondi taking a close-run victory in Pau and Merckx maintaining his lead. The course the next day and particularly the final ascent to the Pla D'Adet ski resort, brought back bad memories of 1974, when Raymond Poulidor, a recurrence of the sciatica in his left leg, and Bruyère's only 'jour sans' of the Tour had conspired to inflict one of Merckx's heaviest losses in the mountains of the Tour. On every other stage featuring multiple mountains in 1974, Bruyère says, 'I had been able to set the pace over every climb until the last one. There was only so much damage anyone could do to Eddy on one mountain.'

Merckx had decided that another of his Josephs, De Schoen-maecker, was the best equipped to act as Bruyère's stand-in a year later. De Schoenmaecker, though, had one big weakness: he was a dreadful descender. Consequently, in previous Tours, he had been deployed mainly on the first climb of the day and excused for the remainder of mountain stages. Even if he didn't come unstuck, the mental stress of a 100-kilometre-per-hour white-knuckle slalom off a Pyrenean or Alpine pass could often end up taking its toll on a rider's physical resources for whatever obstacles lay ahead. Even Merckx admitted that De Schoenmaecker was 'limited'. 'He descends the mountains with his buttocks and brakes clenched. Whatever he's done going up the climb is therefore cancelled out, and on the second climb of the day he languishes in anonymity.'

This less-than-sparkling reference seemed unmerited when he led Merckx and the peloton over the Tourmalet and the Aspin, but a little more accurate when he vanished to leave Merckx alone and exposed at the bottom of Pla D'Adet. Merckx should have been grateful that he had already eliminated Fuente – literally ridden him outside the time limit – on the stage to Roubaix. Unfortunately, Zoetemelk and Thévenet were still in the race, and in that order they both crossed the line just under a minute faster than the race leader. Merckx's advantage over Thévenet was down to a minute and a half.

Never had the mountains been so closely crammed together in a Tour de France. Eight mountain stages and the ranges of the Pyre-nees, the Massif Central and the Alps were to be covered in nine days. Pla D'Adet represented the last action in the Pyrenees, and two days later the first of two summit finishes in the Massif Central saw the Belgian Michel Pollentier win at Super Lioran. Again, on the final climb, Merckx received no help from his teammates. His legs, fortu-nately, were spinning more sweetly than they had in 1974, even if the same could not be said of the other men in Molteni jerseys.

'If you were really a champion, you could do it without your teammates,' Rik Van Looy used to tease him. Increasingly, if Merckx wanted to win a sixth Tour de France, it looked as though he might have to do just that.

The start of one Tour de France stage seems the perfect place to reminisce about another. Unfortunately, in the hospitality village tucked beneath the old city walls in Dinan, Bernard Thévenet keeps getting interrupted. First by so many one-off acquaintances and well-wishers that, having smiled or politely obliged their requests, he turns his seat to hide his face, then by around half-a-dozen calls in the space of 15 minutes from his wife. 'Is the water leaking directly out of the pipe? Have you checked the boiler...?' After the second or third call, he is embarrassed and feels compelled to explain. 'We've got a problem with our plumbing. Bit of an emergency...'

Thévenet has kept his thick Burgundian accent, a souvenir from the cycling backwater and vinicultural mecca where he grew up. If you didn't know their ages, based on their appearance now, you would guess that Thévenet was more than three years younger than Merckx, but only because he looks exceptionally sprightly for a 63-year-old. You would also guess from his affable nature that he was one of those whose preferred antidotes to Merckx, like Gimondi's, had been patience and pragmatism rather than bombast and bluster. And you would be right.

He started cycling only in 1962, on a bike with mudguards but also proper 'drop' racing handlebars. As far as Thévenet was concerned it was 'wonderful'. It was also highly fitting – he had spent part of his childhood in a hamlet called 'Le Guidon' or 'The Handlebar'. In July 1964 a criterium took place in La Clayette, up the road from his parents' farm. A few days or weeks later, friends who owned a nearby restaurant told him, 'Ah, we had a young Belgian lad in here on the day of the criterium. Good rider apparently. Can't remember his name...' Thévenet twigged immediately that it must have been Merckx, who was about to become the amateur world champion. When Thévenet himself turned pro six years later, he won his first race on the Mont Faron above Toulon, ahead of Eddy Merckx who had crashed.

Thévenet had been just one of the more resilient and prominent victims in the Merckx massacre which had continued ever since, but recently he had been inching almost to within striking distance. At the '74 Worlds in Montreal and the '75 Liège–Bastogne–Liège, he had been caught and passed only by a last, despairing Merckx charge. Then had come the Dauphiné.

'I can remember the day in the Dauphiné when he cracked,' Thévenet recalls. 'We were climbing the Col du Granier, the Cucheron and the Porte, what we called the Chartreuse trilogy. It just made him seem human again. Before that he'd seemed like a Martian. He was out of our reach, beyond our imagination even. He was head and shoulders above the rest of us physically and mentally. With hindsight, that Dauphiné and him losing eleven minutes that day was maybe a watershed, the moment when the mask started to fall, but at the time people just said to themselves, "Well, he was ill, now he's getting ready for the Tour." For me, mentally, it was very useful later when we got to the Tour. It was the first time that we thought, reasonably, that we could beat him in the Tour de France as well. You could suddenly see how you could nibble away and take a little bit of time every day in the mountains. He also didn't have Bruyère...'

And yet, Thévenet's challenge in 1975 had almost ended before it began. The man who had nearly masterminded Merckx's dethrone-ment with Luis Ocaña, the former Bic directeur sportif Maurice De

Muer, had moved to Peugeot at the start of 1975 and had a plan for Merckx's assassination. 'A guy who loses that much time in the Dauphiné can't be a hundred per cent for the Tour. There are these summit finishes. You have to get to the Pyrenees less than three minutes down on Merckx. If you're less than three minutes down, it's on,' De Muer had told Thévenet in Charleroi. But those best-laid plans threatened to go awry when his teammate Patrick Béon crashed and took Thévenet with him on his way to the prologue, leaving Thévenet with a golf ball-sized swelling on his knee. He then lost 53 seconds on Stage 1A to Molenbeek. 'The Tour de France wasn't even in France yet and I'd already blown half the budget, in terms of time,' he says. 'I said to myself then that it didn't look good. In the next few stages, though, I was very vigilant. Merckx won the first time trial very easily, but I'd punctured, then I almost beat him in the second one in Auch. We were about to enter the Pyrenees, and I was less than two and a half minutes down. We were back on schedule.'

Thévenet's confidence took a jolt when, on Merckx's command, De Schoenmaecker set a savage pace on the Tourmalet, but by doing so cannibalised his team. Thévenet duly attacked with Zoetemelk on the climb to Pla D'Adet and bit off 49 seconds of Merckx's overall advantage, despite a puncture 300 metres from the line. Zoetemelk now told the press that Thévenet would win the Tour. Thévenet wasn't so sure. 'We hadn't cracked Merckx, but it was just like we said before the Tour: if we nicked a bit of time from him on every summit finish, we could perhaps do it. But it was Merckx. We were all afraid of him. Still, you dared to dream,' he says.

Thévenet was less impressive at Super Lioran but knew that the next day's mountain-top finish on the Puy de Dôme promised to be much more significant. At the start in Aurillac, he peered through the crowds and drizzle at Merckx and tried to detect some outward sign of nerves or weakness. When they rolled out for the start and towards the Auvergne volcanoes he glanced across at his legs and wondered what secrets they held within. Theories did the rounds – that Merckx twiddling his allen key and adjusting his saddle was a good sign, or an ominous one, or Barry Hoban's that when he didn't talk he meant business – but Thévenet didn't subscribe to any of them. On the bike, in the mountains, there were no clues as both were as ragged as each other.

It was about substance, not style, and on the spiral staircase up the Puy Thévenet seemed to have more of the former than Merckx. Close to where Ocaña had dropped Merckx four years earlier, Thévenet darted clear with Lucien Van Impe. Van Impe, in turn, then pulled away from him 1,200 metres from home. Thévenet crossed the line 15 seconds behind Van Impe and waited. Merckx had one minute and 32 seconds to save his yellow jersey.

Like he had on the Puy in 1971, Merckx pounded harder as he passed the 200-metre-to-go banner on his right-hand side. He could also sense if not see the finish line or Thévenet being swamped by journalists beyond it. A gentleman in a blue jumper and white racing cap now flashed into his eyeline. The man tried to give him a friendly push, but Merckx was moving too fast and the hand just grazed his back. Before he could blink, he saw another body leaning into the road, this one in a beige coat, another arm and this time a clenched fist. The vision was accompanied by a thud under his ribcage, roughly over his right kidney. He placed his hand instinctively over the point of impact for a few seconds, then grabbed the bottom part of his handlebars and sprinted to save his yellow jersey by 58 seconds.

The pictures taken in the changing room close to the finish line of a bare-chested Merckx clutching his midriff, his face crumpled in pain like at Savona, would go around the world. He still had a hand on his stomach when he emerged minutes later in his Molteni tracksuit and went down the mountain with police to identify his aggressor. Outraged fans had already barricaded 55-year-old Nello Breton close to the spot where he had landed the most famous punch of 1975 outside of October's 'Thrilla in Manila' between Muhammad Ali and Joe Frazier. Breton told Merckx and the police that he had been pushed; from the replays, the alibi looked dubious. Months later, Merckx would make a point of attending the court hearing at which Breton was made to pay a one-franc fine and ordered to stay away from cycle races for the next two years.

How badly he had hurt Merckx was tricky to tell. The next day, a rest-day on the Côte d'Azur, the Tour doctor Philippe Miserez examined the race leader and confirmed that his stomach was only bruised, there was no need for an X-ray, but that 'a rider with a less robust constitution might have abandoned'. Thévenet didn't know what to think. It seemed to him, and plenty of others, that there was always something wrong with Merckx.

'I had a lot of time for Eddy,' he says. 'Contrary to what people sometimes said, he wasn't arrogant. He was also very straight: every time I punctured in 1975, he waited. The only issue I had with him was the way he was always complaining about some injury or ailment. It got tiresome, because he'd say that then win anyway. So it became like the boy who cried wolf. We just used to roll our eyes. "I'm hurting here. I'm hurting there..." "Yeah, sure you are, Eddy..."'

Perhaps the best indication to date of Merckx's vulnerability was that for once he kept his suffering to himself. No, in fact, for a second time, because he had done the same with the cyst that had handicapped him in 1974. Could it just be that, for two years now, Merckx had feared his margin of superiority was no longer such that he could publicise his weaknesses and not get punished?

*

Both men began Stage 15 from Nice to Pra Loup with the firm conviction that this would be '*le jour J*' – *the* day. The course featured five climbs – the Col de Saint-Martin, the Col de la Couillole, the Col des Champs, the Col d'Allos and the 6.5-kilometre climb to Pra Loup. The 2087-metre Col des Champs had never been climbed by the Tour and had immediately grabbed Maurice De Muer's attention when the race route was unveiled, so much so that De Muer had sent one of his old Bic riders, Francis Ducreux, on a recce. Ducreux's message to De Muer, says Thévenet, was 'Oooh la la, it's hard, it's narrow, the surface doesn't roll – it's the ideal place to attack.'

That, then, was precisely what they would do.

Merckx, meanwhile, had been eyeing up the descent of the Allos. By his own admission, Thévenet was a poor descender. The Allos, therefore, would be the perfect place for Merckx to show him who was boss.

Neither man, it was true, felt at his best as the peloton headed out along the Promenade des Anglais in Nice. Thévenet's legs ached but he tried to reassure himself: Pra Loup was 217 kilometres away. Merckx, meanwhile, changed bikes three times as the race now pointed north from the Med and into the Mercantour Alps, huge grey lumps of mountain which today smouldered like coals in an oven. By the time they reached the Col des Champs, Thévenet's legs felt reinvigorated and he began implementing the plan. One, two, three attacks; Merckx responded every time but felt spasms in his stomach as he did. Rather than alert Thévenet, he sent teammate Edouard Janssens back to race doctor Miserez's car for some painkillers. Thévenet tried three more times and three more times Merckx followed. Janssens and De Schoenmaecker – as well as Van Impe, Zoetemelk and Gimondi – strained to ensure their front-row seats for the next act on the Col d'Allos.

To take full advantage of the Allos descent, Merckx knew that the best policy would be to attack shortly before the summit. This was classic Merckx – a tactic he had used time and again since ironing out the kinks in his descending technique under Vittorio Adorni's tutelage in 1968. His surge, a kilometre from the top, was too quick for Thévenet. The Frenchman, though, couldn't have picked a better time to feel the dreaded hunger knock, '*la fringale*', and all power drained from his legs. Forced to eat, he also composed himself in readiness for the next 17 kilometres of twisting, turning, downhill horror, which Felice Gimondi's directeur sportif Giancarlo Ferretti, for one, would not forget; having plunged 50 metres into a ravine in his Bianchi team vehicle, Ferretti was lucky that the car landed and stopped on a small patch of scrub, and lucky to be alive.

'Plan B was to attack on the Col d'Allos, but I just didn't feel good enough,' Thévenet picks up. 'Then when Merckx attacked he got a hundred metres and I just stayed there, dangling, a hundred metres away. I could feel this *fringale* coming and I said to myself that I wouldn't make it to the finish if I didn't eat and take my foot off the gas. The way down was horrible, though. The Allos might be the nastiest, most dangerous descent in France. I got to the bottom of Pra Loup one minute, maybe one minute ten down. At that moment, I thought I was stuffed. After all the effort I'd made, everything I'd tried that day, I was still going to lose a minute to Merckx.'

For a few months now, you could have represented the balance of power in professional cycling with two converging lines on a graph. Descending, not as steeply as the Allos, but losing altitude nonetheless, was the line corresponding to Merckx. Rising in the other direction, slowly but surely gaining height like the 6.5-kilometre climb to Pra Loup, was the progress curve of Bernard Thévenet and the rest of the peloton.

The two lines had not yet intersected. They would do so, then begin to diverge again, just above the floor of the Ubaye valley.

After a kilometre-and-a-half of climbing, Merckx still led by well over a minute. His head bobbed as it always had, the earth and not just his bike seemed to jar when he bludgeoned the pedals, and his jersey was of a familiar hue. More than just an era, the sport's first and only ideology – Merckxism – was droning to an end as suddenly as it had begun in 1968 on the Tre Cime di Lavaredo.

When Felice Gimondi, oblivious to what had befallen Ferretti, caught then edged in front of Merckx, cycling had come full circle. Ten years earlier Gimondi had won the Tour. Now the man responsible for a decade-long eclipse in his career begged Gimondi to slow down. 'He told me to keep the pace steady because he was struggling. Well, he'd never said that before. There, already, something very different was happening,' Gimondi remembers.

Behind, Thévenet rode clear of the parasitical partners, Van Impe and Zoetemelk, but had no idea what was happening further up the climb. If he could just claw back 10 seconds, maybe half a minute, in 24 hours he would go for broke on the Col d'Izoard. There were no time checks coming from the official race vehicles and none from De Muer, so he relied on the crowd. 'I kept hearing the spectators who were giving me the time gaps, and from what they were saying, it seemed as though I was coming back to Merckx. I was right on my limit, but my morale was soaring every time someone shouted that I'd gained more seconds. I started thinking I was going to finish with him. Then, the next thing I started hearing was, "*Il est là, il est l`a!* He's there!*" but I could neither see him nor believe what they were saying. It was unthinkable that Merckx could have a collapse. Unthinkable that I could have gained a minute on him in less than five kilometres.'

The next day, in *L'Equipe*, Pierre Chany would write that by this point Merckx was travelling 'at the speed of a countryside postman'. Thévenet, by contrast, was rampant, as he is when he relives a moment which the TV cameras missed but is engraved in his memory and cycling folklore.

'Suddenly,' he says switching to the present tense, 'I see the Molteni car in front. But it doesn't really register. I'm going so hard that I can't really think straight. A moment later I'm with the car. Somehow, though, I'm still scared that he'll see me coming, counter-attack and that'll be the end of it. I get within striking distance on a bend with a strip of melted tarmac in the middle of the road, which he's taken right on the inside, along the line of spectators. I tell myself that he'll never dare to cross the melting tarmac – he'll get stuck in it – so I go all the way to the other side, where I'm almost hidden in the spectators on the right side of the road. I try to pass and get clear of him as quickly as possible, so that he can't respond. I see that he's not following and somehow I'm not surprised. The euphoria drowns out every other feeling…'

Moments later, Thévenet passed Gimondi. 'But ooohlalalala, it was hard,' he says. 'The last 500 metres were really steep. It just wouldn't end. It seemed so, so long. I crossed the line, collapsed over my handlebars, and it was the mechanic who told me, "You've got the jersey! You've got the jersey!" I said, "Don't mess around. I can't have taken a minute back."'

For a while it seemed that no one could quite comprehend. Amid chaotic scenes, two riders, Thévenet and Merckx, clambered on to the podium in their yellow jerseys. As though, having longed for revolution, the Tour was now dragging its feet out of the *ancien régime*.

The general classification was unambiguous: Thévenet first and Merckx second, 58 seconds behind.

'I mean, besides the fact that it was the shittiest podium presentation I've ever seen, it was such a shock, such an earthquake for cycling,' Thévenet says. 'I think most of the journalists that day had already written their story. But then everything had changed in those last few kilometres, and there was this hysterical stampede at the finish line. The podium was teeming, teeming with journalists. It was absolute pandemonium. I did the protocol, the interviews, then – there were no buses in those days – so I went back down the mountain and to the hotel on my bike. The hotel was almost exactly where I'd passed Merckx, about two kilometres from the finish line. It was crazy. The mountain was still full of people. Fortunately, everyone was going down by then, so they didn't see me coming, and by the time I'd passed them it was too late for them to grab me. But it was complicated.

'Maurice De Muer always used to buy champagne when we won, but we were only allowed a drop in the bottom of the glass. That night it was also a bit tiresome when the photographers started arriving and asking for pictures of me in the yellow jersey in every conceivable pose. It all felt a bit presumptuous to me. Everyone in the peloton knew that you were never safe with Merckx.'

Apparently, not even in your sleep. The following morning, Thévenet woke with a start and was relieved to see his yellow jersey draped over the chair where he had left it the previous night. In his dream, he and it had spent the night in Eddy Merckx's bedroom.

Why had Merckx buckled so spectacularly, so suddenly? A hunger knock of his own seemed the most logical explanation, but Merckx ruled it out. Had that been the case, he would have been ravenous on arriving at his hotel shortly after the finish, and that had not been the case. He thought it more likely that the painkillers he had taken on the Col des Champs had worn off somewhere on the descent of the Allos, which might explain his fainting feeling on the climb to Pra Loup.

Later it would emerge and Merckx would confirm that he had also taken an anticoagulant medicine before the start in Nice. This puzzles Professor Michel Audran of the University of Montpellier's Faculty of Medicine and the International Cycling Union's biological passport review panel. 'If you'd been punched, and were getting spasms in the lumbar muscles (as Merckx reportedly was), to my knowledge a doctor wouldn't prescribe an anticoagulant. You'd give the patient muscle relaxants, painkillers or maybe an anti-inflammatory. There might be bleeding and bruising and prescribing an anticoagulant would be dangerous to my mind,' Audran says.

Most likely, in addition to other factors, Merckx had over-estimated his stamina, rather like at Liège–Bastogne–Liège in 1971. Would it have been different with Bruyère in the Molteni team? Merckx's friend, the Belgian TV journalist Théo Mathy, for one, thought so. Bruyère feels inclined to agree with him. It is certainly hard to imagine that Thévenet would have been allowed or able to attack six times on the Col des Champs had Bruyère been setting the pace. The old Merckx could have soaked up this and probably what-ever effects still lingered from the punch on Puy de Dôme. Felice Gimondi overtaking Merckx, however, was the equivalent of Ali finally overwhelming Smokin' Joe Frazier in Manila.

The next day, the fight was effectively over, even though Merckx would keep on swinging. His attack on the descent of the Col de Vars took him a minute clear of Thévenet, but again Zoetemelk wouldn't help him, and the Guil gorge leading to the foot of the Izoard was too long for Merckx on his own. Merckx was reabsorbed, Thévenet counter-attacked and the Bastille Day crowds rejoiced. 'The best memory of my career,' Thévenet calls it. He carried on to win by over two minutes in Serre Chevalier and extend his overall lead to three minutes and 20 seconds.

Perpetual harassment had worked against Ocaña in 1971 and was Merckx's only option now. This, at least, was until what looked at first like a banal tangle with Ole Ritter in the roll-out of Valloire at the start of Stage 17 sent him sprawling. X-rays after the Tour would confirm that he had broken his upper jawbone in two places and trapped a nerve. After consulting the Tour doctor Miserez and ignoring his advice to abandon, Merckx immediately attacked Thévenet, first on the descent of the Col de la Madeleine then on the way down the Col de la Colombière. Both times, he opened up significant daylight but both times he was also caught.

An hour after the next afternoon's mountain time trial to Châtel in which Merckx had finished third and recouped 16 seconds on Thévenet, Théo Mathy found him curled up in his hotel bed, as he had been in Savona and in Marseille in 1971. It took Merckx an hour to get up and stumble to the bathroom. 'Today I found out what real pain is,' he said.

Merckx was still telling the press that he was the stronger man, and Thévenet the luckier one. In their face-to-face exchanges, he was more magnanimous. Not that losing gracefully was already a priority or even a possibility he entertained, but by staying in the race he also did his rival the immense favour of honouring his victory. Dr Miserez said that carrying on was 'crazy' and exposed Merckx to the 'risk of a serious sinus infection'. A telegram from the Belgian prime minister Leo Tindemans, however, urged him to press on and reclaim yellow in or before Paris.

Alas, Merckx's attacks on the Champs-Élysées turned out to be the desperate last lunges of a beaten, faded slugger. Gimondi reckoned that his aggression had cost him the Tour. But Merckx knew no other way; he had lived by the sword, died by the sword at Pra Loup, and now went down wielding it in Paris. His margin of defeat was two minutes and 27 seconds. 'I'll come back next year,' he vowed. Thévenet, he admitted, had built his victory in the mountains despite being a 'disaster going downhill'.

The backhanded compliments or criticisms made no odds to Thévenet. He had realised a dream. More important than that, as far as everyone else was concerned, he had written his name into cycling legend as the '*tombeur* de Merckx' – the man who brought down Merckx, Merckxism and the curtain on an era.

'I hadn't let him out of my sight for the last four days and, oddly enough, that meant we ended up chatting more than we ever had,' Thévenet recalls. 'He was definitely in pain – one of the things we spoke about was how he could only eat liquid food, and in fact I gave him a bottle one day. Even then, though, I thought for a second that he might be bluffing. I still think that he was trying to win the Tour with those attacks on the Champs-Élysées.

'He shook my hand at the end of the race and was very gracious. We went to the Hôtel de Ville, then the Elysée palace together. I think he was already plotting how he was going to beat me the next year. I realise now that I owe him a lot, for not having abandoned, because the image that I now have in France is "*Le tombeur de Merckx*". Winning the Tour was more important to me, but I think what marked the French public was that a little Frenchman had beaten this monster who had had this hegemony over cycling. He could have had more Tours de France if he'd been more selective about his goals but that wasn't his mindset. He was like a robot: "Race, win, race, win, race, win". His life boiled down to that. We were all there to ride and win races...but him a bit more than everyone else.'

17
cannibalised

'I think we all have a certain pool of energy and resilience,
but there's only so much ball-breaking you can tolerate.
You explode.' FELICE GIMONDI

'Don't fear for one second that you'll see me on the decline, served up on a plate to a vengeful peloton, like some shipwrecked, stranded sailor clinging to the buoy of his former glory. At the first signs that I'm weakening, and maybe a bit before, I'll bid farewell...'

These were the words that Merckx had written in 1974. He knew that sportsmen always pledged to go out at the top and rarely did, but was adamant that he would be the exception. Théo Mathy told him that he had known a lot of cyclists, many who had made the same promise, and none who had kept it. 'I'll be different,' Merckx assured him.

Merckx, it proved, wasn't always as good as his word, contrary to what Walter Godefroot says today. He turned 30 a month before the 1975 Tour de France and, according to the timetable that he had outlined in multiple interviews, ought to have been riding the Grande Boucle for the final time. Instead he left Paris with revenge and not retirement at the top of his 1976 agenda.

It was hard for Merckx to acknowledge the start of his decline, partly because no one else would. Like Thévenet in the last week of the Tour, everyone feared a bluff or at least a backlash. He had been written off before. Illness and injury had also, undeniably, constrained him at the Tour. As Thévenet says, 'Some of his aura had gone, and that was half of the battle, but he had still been the second best rider in the Tour, better than Van Impe and Zoetemelk and a lot of other riders who were supposedly among the best in the world.'

More of the Merckx mystique, however, would dissolve a month after the Tour at the World Championships in Yvoir. Perhaps conscious that more was at stake than just the rainbow jersey he had won a year earlier in Montreal, Merckx was determined to pre-empt the in-fighting that had previously dogged Belgian teams, and so took the bold step of inviting the entire national squad to his house the week before the race. Only Freddy Maertens and his Flandria team-mate Michel Pollentier declined. Their excuse? Kraainem was too far to travel from their homes near the North Sea coast. Maertens did, admittedly, give a different explanation in his autobiography years later: 'There was no point [in going]... Whenever Merckx, who was always given enough personal helpers by the Federation, spoke, it was always for his own benefit.' Roger De Vlaeminck, meanwhile, not only attended but was said to have slept over. Cynics in the press later speculated that the highlight of the evening might have been not Claudine's hospitality or culinary skills – but the point at which Merckx started writing cheques to ensure the collaboration of his guests in Yvoir. As usual, the pre-Worlds hype was matched only by the wild speculation.

The final, ritual meeting to determine tactics and incentives then took place on the night before the race. A fee of 50,000 Belgian francs, to be paid by the winner to his teammates in case of victory, was agreed. When the president of the national federation, the Royale Ligue Vélocipédique Belge, then interrupted dinner to open discussions about how their bonus would be divided among the 11 men, De Vlaeminck raised an arm and his voice.

'He was talking about the eleven men, and I piped up, "You mean ten and a half?" and pointed at Van Impe. It was a joke about his height, but Van Impe didn't think it was funny. He told me later that it cost me his help in the race and maybe the World Championships.'

If 'The Gypsy' couldn't count on Van Impe, he was shocked and thrilled when Merckx volunteered his assistance early in the race. On the sixth lap, Merckx had crashed into an overzealous fan who had spilled on to the course, hurting his left hip. Having rejoined the peloton, he immediately found De Vlaeminck and announced that he would now be his domestique for a day. His commitment was so whole-hearted, Merckx claimed later, and the sight of him helping his old foe so incongruous, that the Dutchman Gerrie Knetemann seemed unnerved on his behalf. 'How can you, Eddy Merckx, be helping another rider at the World Championships? Have you gone mad?' Knetemann asked him. Merckx later admitted that it had been a mistake; old habits died hard for De Vlaeminck, and when the Dutchman Hennie Kuiper attacked on the last lap, De Vlaeminck seemed suddenly to doubt Merckx's motives and was more preoccupied with following his teammate than their Dutch opponent. Had De Vlaeminck lurked in the chase group, Kuiper might well have desisted under pressure from Merckx. De Vlaeminck would then have been left to take the sprint. Instead he had to settle for second.

Kuiper's teammate Joop Zoetemelk had been taunted throughout the race by Belgian fans wielding giant lollipops – a snarky reference to his 'wheel-sucking' during the Tour de France – but that pair and Knetemann had had the last laugh. None of this trio was a superman yet their combined might had been easily enough to overcome Merckx, De Vlaeminck and Van Impe in the lead group on the final lap. As had been the case in July, on the hills, Merckx looked powerful but also uncharacteristically one-paced. As he crossed the line, Kuiper appeared almost to be beckoning with his right arm as he turned to look back down the finishing straight, as if to say, 'Come on! What's keeping you?' Over the next two years, Kuiper's Dutch Ti Raleigh team would be at the forefront of a generation that began to make Merckx and his teammates look like yesterday's men. Ti Raleigh's manager, Peter Post, jettisoned the all-for-one Italian model of which both Rik Van Looy and Merckx had been benefactors in teams sponsored by Faema in favour of a modern, multi-pronged and highly dynamic approach which over the next four years would bring Ti Raleigh a staggering 28 Tour de France stage victories. 'The tactical meetings would go on for hours,' says one Ti Raleigh rider from that era, the Briton David Lloyd. 'Post had been forced to come up with something new, because when the team started Merckx was so strong. He was like ten men on his own, plus he had another ten brilliant riders to help him!'

Thus, necessity had been the mother of invention, giving rise to teams, individuals and a peloton which, when the moment came, had prepared and knew exactly how to seize on and perhaps hasten his decline. As the formerly oppressed scented blood, they also sharpened their fangs and their performances. It was hard to know whether De Vlaeminck and Maertens had won nearly 60 races between them in 1975 more because they had improved or because Merckx had decayed. 'He was perhaps deteriorating, but not much in 1975,' reckons De Vlaeminck. 'It was easy to say that he wasn't as strong any more, but he was still finishing second if not first. It also coincided with my best year. I won over fifty races that season and was first or second in eighty. A bit later, Merckx became like a wounded lion: it was normal that everyone gathered around to tear off their strip of flesh.'

As far as Maertens is concerned, 'he didn't really weaken in one-day races until 1977' and indeed even Maertens at his best couldn't prevent Merckx from winning his seventh Milan–San Remo in March 1976. 'It was Maertens who was strong that day, but he somehow contrived to get everyone riding against him, for various reasons, whether it was stuff that he'd said in the press or that Driessens had said,' recalls Walter Godefroot. 'We are all looking at each other, De Vlaeminck's there, and just before the Poggio, Merckx attacks, but we can see it's not the best Merckx. We certainly don't think that he's going to win.'

Usually, it was Godefroot warning people not to discount Merckx. But having been joined on the Poggio by a 20-year-old compatriot, Jean-Luc Vandenbroucke, Merckx proceeded to wriggle clear on the descent and solo to his seventh victory in 'La Classicissma', one more than Costante Girardengo. 'It was the beginning of the end,' Merckx admitted later. It was also to be his last major victory.

The win in San Remo fooled everyone for a while. At the Setmana Catalana a week later, there were even glimpses of a vintage Merckx until a empty lunch-bag got caught in his wheel and caused a crash with consequences nearly as grave for Merckx's season as Joseph Bruyère's in the same race a year earlier. Merckx's 'luck' was definitely, revealingly, running out. Despite the resulting injury to his left arm, copious amounts of painkillers and sleepless nights that lasted almost throughout the Classics, he continued to threaten and scored top ten finishes at Gent–Wevelgem, Paris–Roubaix, Flèche Wallonne and in Liège–Bastogne–Liège. It was enough to convince some that he was still the favourite to win a sixth Giro d'Italia, and their faith was intact after ten days of racing. A cyst like the one that had hampered him at the 1974 Tour de France, however, now combined with more ordinary physical degeneration to send him plunging down the general classification.

What he was losing in power, agility and reputation, Merckx at least maintained in resilience and dignity. While he toiled at the Giro, another Belgian, Johan De Muynck, looked to be closing in on victory, but De Muynck's teammate Roger De Vlaeminck was preparing for an ignominious, ignoble exit. After one stage in Italy, Merckx saw De Vlaeminck walking past his door in the hotel that their teams were sharing and called him inside. 'My God, I had even more respect for him after that,' De Vlaeminck says. 'He showed me this wound that he had in his groin. It was as thick and deep as a finger. I couldn't understand why he was carrying on.'

Soon, indeed, De Vlaeminck would be leaving, apparently for no other reason than he couldn't bear to see De Muynck win the Giro, and certainly wouldn't contemplate helping him. According to another teammate, Ercole Gualazzini, somewhere near Calamento, halfway up the Passo Manghen, De Vlaeminck climbed off his bike then, inexplicably, ran straight into the dense forest lining the road and hid from his directeurs sportifs. They, De Muynck and Merckx were disgusted. On the penultimate day of the race, whether out of sympathy, patriotism or just plain decency, Merckx waited for and effectively saved De Muynck by pacing him back to the bunch after a fall on the descent from Zambla Alta into Bergamo. Sadly for De Muynck, it proved to be in vain as the 33-year-old Felice Gimondi narrowly overhauled him in the time trial deciding the outcome of the Giro the following morning.

Merckx's eighth place represented his worst finish in a grand tour since the 1967 race but was a testament to his courage. True, Molteni had offered him financial incentives to stay in the race, but as at the Tour a year earlier it was Merckx's stoicism that had kept him going. Whether riding though the pain had been sensible or not was another matter. When, a year or two earlier, his father Jules had suffered a heart attack, Merckx pleaded with him to heed the warning and scale back his hours in the family grocery store in Woluwe-Saint-Pierre. Jules had responded with a shrug; the urge to work was more powerful than he was. Merckx tried to protest but knew deep down that he felt exactly the same.

When he was in his twenties and his body's ability to repair and regenerate was still miraculous, his appetite for racing and winning had been his greatest strength. Now the coin had flipped and it became a weakness, as the pressures remained the same or even increased while his resources diminished. His least favourite parts of the job had always been the ones demanding his attention off the bike, and since Jean Van Buggenhout's death during the 1974 Giro Merckx had sometimes felt overwhelmed. Claudine took up some of the slack, but even she admitted that Van Bug's passing 'left a void'. Her husband may no longer have been the pedalling deity he once was, but he remained, for example, the man that journalists turned to for a reaction and teammates for a new home when Molteni left cycling in disgrace at the end of 1976. It would perhaps be too harsh to say the company owners' arrests were in keeping with Merckx's declining fortunes, but their exit certainly left a putrid taste. It wasn't the first time that the Molteni brothers had been in trouble with the law; never before, though, had they been accused of exporting 'sausages' which were actually just plastic wrappers pumped with manure and dumped at sea in an elaborate smuggling ruse.

What Merckx was supposed to know about any of this, nobody stopped to ask. The fact was that the Molteni brothers' fraudulent gains had been paying Merckx and his domestiques' salary, and there was now no Van Bug to find a replacement. Merckx would end up signing for Raphaël Géminiani's new FIAT-France team and taking old faithfuls like Joseph Bruyère, Jos Huysmans, Roger Swerts and Frans Mintjens with him. 'He was still as motivated as ever,' Bruyère affirms. 'That was one thing that never changed. Even in 1977, he thought he could win every race he entered. Unfortunately he was like a car that had been pushed to breaking point, driven over the speed limit for more than ten years. The engine was completely worn out.'

Before the end of 1976, he had done another patriotic good turn by helping Maertens to win the world road race championship in Ostuni, Italy, despite their feud still festering. Merckx himself was fifth, and sporadic flashes like this added to his conviction that another Tour de France or at least 'one more big one' was within his grasp. Always the most straight-talking member of his entourage, Van Buggenhout might have nipped his self-deception in the bud. As it was there were plenty, like his father-in-law Lucien Acou, who would assure anyone prepared to listen that Merckx the Cannibal was on temporary not permanent leave. 'Just you wait...' Acou would say, and wait everyone including Merckx did, or at least tried to. Patience had never been his forte in races, and at times now he turned himself into a sad caricature of the rider he had been, precisely the 'ship-wrecked, stranded sailor clinging to the buoy of his former glory' that he had vowed never to become.

At the '77 Tour of Flanders, he seemed to want to teleport himself and his fans back to the summer of '69, but instead all he did was make them wince. His slow suicide began the moment when he creaked clear of the peloton 140 kilometres from the finish and ended about an hour later when he was passed and left for dead by young tyros like Maertens and even older yet more successfully aged veterans like Godefroot. Friends in the peloton watched him and grimaced. 'I would try to talk to him whenever I saw him in those last couple of years,' says Franco Bitossi. 'I'd say, "Eddy, you know, you were so much better than us before that maybe you didn't have to make the same sacrifices as us. Perhaps you have to change some things. Race a bit differently. I don't know…" He'd just blankly nod his head, but I never got the impression that he was really taking much notice.'

Another old friend, Christian Raymond, says that the nickname that his daughter Brigitte had coined years earlier now 'caught up with Merckx'. 'Even if he always rejected the nickname, he wanted to be the Cannibal right to the very end,' Raymond says. 'He was convinced that the 1975 Tour was just a mishap, a blip, but it wasn't: it was a sure sign that he was on the decline. I always got on great with Eddy, both during and after his career, but I have to say that he was stupid to carry on after 1975. He'd always told me before that he would give up at age 30, so why didn't he?'

Hennie Kuiper is no doubt right when he confirms that Merckx's 'problem' had once been the very cornerstone of his success: his pure love of the sport and of winning.

'He seemed OK from the outside but I think on the inside it was tough for him,' Kuiper says. 'Years later I was a directeur sportif for a team which used Eddy Merckx bikes, and I can remember asking him, "Eddy, why did you do so many races?" He said that he just loved riding his bike so much. Which of course was fantastic for the sport. These days the Tour de France is so huge that a rider's season is judged on that and maybe a couple of Classics. Back then Eddy felt as big a responsibility to perform in a little criterium as he did in the Tour, because people were paying to go and watch him. He was angry when Greg LeMond came along later and only started focusing on the Tour. It wasn't the riders' fault, it was just the way sport had turned into a business. If you look at Eddy's palmarès, I don't think it's a coincidence that he won Milan–San Remo, which comes at the start of the season, seven times, and the Tour of Lombardy, which comes at the end, only twice. He probably would have won Lombardy seven times if he wasn't so exhausted by his racing when he got to October. If he'd maybe given himself a couple of months' break in the middle of the season, like riders do now, he perhaps could have won two more Tours de France.'

As far as Merckx was concerned, all hope of extending his and Jacques Anquetil's record of Tour de France wins to six still wasn't lost when he set off for the 1977 Grande Boucle. At the start of the Tour, even *People* magazine in the United States was ladelling his 'comeback Tour' with hype, and quoted Merckx vowing once again that, 'When I abdicate my throne, it will be in full glory – I'm not made to be second best.'

A bout of glandular fever had in part mitigated a wretched spring, and he seemed convinced, or at least tried to convince everyone else, that he was starting to rekindle his old sparkle. Aided by a route that barely skimmed the Pyrenees, remarkably, he maintained the illusion for 15 stages and was 25 seconds from Bernard Thévenet's yellow jersey on the cusp of the only two, truly difficult Alpine stages on the route. But on Stage 16 the next day, under the imposing silhouette of Mont Blanc, Merckx's limitations were brought abruptly into focus on the Col de la Forclaz. Having sunk out of the top ten of general classification, he then drowned completely on the Col du Glandon 24 hours later. His ascent of Alpe d'Huez was among the fastest in the field, a rally in some ways as gutsy as his ride to Marseille the day after Orcières-Merlette. But it was less the rise of a phoenix than the final, desperate flap of a bird whose wings had been clipped by age and his ceaseless determination to rule the skies.

On returning to their hotel room on the Alpe that afternoon, having himself finished outside the time limit, Merckx's teammate Patrick Sercu says that, 'I looked in the mirror, saw my sunken face and decided then and there that it was time to call it a day on the road.' Sercu, though, had won three stages and in some ways, at 32, was riding as well as at any time in his career. A year his junior, Merckx was really the rider with nothing left to give. His performance in the Alps had been affected by food poisoning, but surely that wasn't the only excuse for him finishing 13 minutes behind the leaders on the Alpe. Merckx didn't care. Sercu remembers, 'The next morning, while I was packing my bags, Eddy was already saying "Just you wait and see, next year…"'

Sure enough, having claimed all year that this would be his last season, his last Tour, he now called Claudine to inform her that, no, he wanted to come back and leave the Tour with a bang in 1978. 'Everyone at the Tour thinks that Eddy Merckx has suddenly gone crazy,' wrote Cesare Diaz, not mincing his words in *La Stampa* in Italy. Nothing of the sort, said the accused: 'I can't leave the people, my fans, with a memory as ugly as my Tour this year. Once again, I've lost the Tour because of an illness, not through my own fault, against riders who I still believe that I can beat.'

If his sixth place overall in Paris, over 12 minutes behind Thévenet, didn't pull the wool from his eyes, finishing dead last in the 1977 World Championships in Venezuela perhaps should have. Again, it was admirable that he had kept going, just as there had been lessons about his respect for himself and his audience in an unblemished record of starting and concluding 15 major tours (excluding his disqualification from the '69 Giro). Nevertheless, it can't have escaped Merckx that riders born before him, but subjected to different self-inflicted and external pressures, were still competing and winning.

Felice Gimondi was the oldest swinger in town at 36, yet still had kept pace with the youngsters to finish 11th in Venezuela.

'I lasted a couple more years than him at the highest level, but I never had the workload, either physical or psychological, that he had,'

Gimondi says. 'As far as racing was concerned, it was more the *way* he raced than the amount. Whether he was in Belgium, France, Germany or Italy, he took his aura with him, but also the immense pressure on his shoulders. That must have taken its toll. Sometimes I was in awe of that, as well. He had that for ten years. And I think it got him down in a similar way to the effect that he had on me. I think we all have a certain pool of energy and resilience, but there's only so much ball-breaking you can tolerate. You explode.'

From his first-floor lounge in Izegem in West Flanders, Patrick Sercu can look back today and say that in the end his old friend, teammate and Six-Day partner Eddy Merckx 'exploded psychologically and not physically'. Merckx signed contracts for no fewer than 14 Six-Day meetings in the winter of 1977 to 1978, perhaps because without Van Bug his arm was too easily twisted. He certainly hadn't considered that FIAT fully expected him to retire at the end of 1977 and wouldn't be interested in accommodating Merckx and his teammates in 1978. That, though, was what they told him, and what FIAT president Lorenzo Cesari announced at the Grand Prix des Nations at the start of October. This left Merckx with the monumental task of finding an existing team prepared to absorb him and his entourage or a new backer, all while honouring his track commitments. Within a few weeks, he had lined up the razor manufacturer Wilkinson, the team's new jerseys had been designed and everything including the riders were in place. Patrick Sercu was with Merckx when the deal was signed at the Six Days of Zürich at the end of November – and vividly remembers hearing the news that Wilkinson had changed their minds on 12 December. Perhaps it would have been better for Merckx at this point if everyone went their separate ways, but the loyalty of men like Bruyère and De Schoenmaecker left him under the moral obligation to come up with an alternative. Christmas came and went, Merckx was still searching and racing frantically, and the outlook was still bleak until he attended a Standard Liège–Anderlecht football match in January 1978, then went to dinner with a director of the clothing firm C&A the same evening. Twelve days later, his new C&A-sponsored team was unveiled to the press in Brussels. Merckx's big objective, he said, was the Tour de France.

Instead of relief, Merckx being Merckx, he now felt a daunting responsibility to repay C&A's faith. It didn't matter what anyone said, there was always a reason to keep on training, keep on racing and, in Merckx's deluded imagination, to keep on winning. He fell ill, again, at the team's training camp in the south of France, but was soon back on the bike and finishing fifth in the Tour du Haut Var in the hills behind Nice. Merckx was relieved and delighted with the result; suddenly, losing wasn't a drama but cause for quiet celebration. And if that wasn't evidence that the Cannibal was nearing or had already sat down to his last supper, the world wouldn't have to wait much longer.

18
a spoonful of sugar

'Did he have some product that others didn't have access to?
That's the eternal question.' CHRISTIAN RAYMOND

With the bells about to toll for the greatest career that professional
cycling had ever seen, it was natural that in 1977 and early 1978
thoughts were already turning to Merckx's legacy. At first glance,
there appeared to be nothing to debate, only to admire. The statistics said, and had been saying for years, that Merckx was just that:
the greatest.

Sadly, however, a Classics campaign unbefitting his name and
palmarès wasn't the only stain added to Merckx's gilded endowment
in the spring of 1977. For the third time in his career, at Flèche
Wallonne, he had tested positive for a banned substance.

If twice was a coincidence, three times was starting to look like a
pattern. Yes, as on the previous two occasions, at Savona in '69 and
Lombardy in '73, there were caveats and conspiracy theories; no, as
had been the case on those two occasions, the advantage procured
cannot have been significant. But the blemishes remained – three
asterisks that were part of the Merckx patrimony, like his 500 victories, plus the questions that would now legitimately outlive him about
how many of those had been achieved with artificial aid.

On this occasion there at least seemed to be little doubt that Merckx was guilty, as were Freddy Maertens, Walter Godefroot, Michel Pollentier, Willy Tierlinck, Karel Rottiers or Walter Planckaert, all other illustrious victims of what was immediately dubbed the 'Stimul affair'. For Godefroot and Maertens it was a case of déjà vu; in 1974, the then Flandria teammates had both tested positive for a previously undetectable class of stimulant, piperidines, unaware that the Gent professor Michel Debackere had secretly developed a method of tracing the substances in urine.

In 1977, Godefroot and Maertens were on different teams and a different kind of stimulant, Stimul, of the pemoline family. The drug could be used to treat attention-deficit hyperactivity disorder and narcolepsy – and heighten alertness and concentration in athletes, while attenuating feelings of fatigue. Again, the same professor, Michel Debackere, the same top-secret research and this time an even weightier catch of major names within a fortnight of each other in 1977, including the biggest fish of all, Eddy Merckx.

To say that Merckx didn't contest the charge would be inaccurate. At the time he claimed that he had 'never heard of Stimul' and 'no longer believed in dope tests', despite declining the 'B' test to which he was entitled. The idea that he was oblivious to the drug's existence struck Debackere as implausible for a simple reason: three years earlier, the effects of Stimul had been the subject of Merckx's brother Michel's thesis at the end of his degree in medicine at the l'Université Libre de Bruxelles. Not only that but once Merckx had finally admitted his guilt years later, he also suggested that, in his opinion, Debackere had become interested in Stimul and suspicious that Merckx was using it the moment he got wind of Michel's research. 'I'm convinced of this,' Merckx told the journalist Joël Godaert.

To anyone not familiar with how cyclists down the ages had been almost as adept at shirking moral responsibility as pedalling their bikes, it would have come as a surprise to hear the incriminated parties slamming Debackere for his conniving, or bemoaning their misfortune. At the time only Walter Godefroot was honest enough to admit that 'Ninety per cent of riders take Stimul', but even that sounded like a way of discharging the blame. Merckx told Godaert, but only two decades later, that 'the riders who weren't caught that year were lucky' and was adamant that Stimul was 'no magic potion'. Both points probably contained large elements of the truth. Nonetheless, and despite support for the guilty parties from the public and the press, the scandal highlighted the extent to which the riders' ethical paramaters differed from the ones to which they were supposed to adhere, the ones laid down by the list of banned products.

The start of Merckx's career had of course coincided with the very first of those dope controls that he claimed by 1977 had lost all credibility. In reality, the war on drugs in cycling had come a long way since the first official tests at the French national championships in July 1965, and the first at a Tour de France and a World Championship the following year. Given what we have already said about how cyclists would gladly discredit any measure they saw as an encroachment on their freedom or popularity, some of their horror stories about those primitive first tests should be treated with caution, but perhaps not blanket distrust. Although himself caught three times between 1967 and 1972, the 1968 Tour winner Jan Janssen admits today that action to combat doping was necessary to 'stop second-tier riders doing these sensational performances, then the next day finishing half an hour down'. Nonetheless, Janssens maintains, the testing conditions could be alarming. 'One day you had to piss one way, the next day another way; one day with a doctor, one day without,' he says. 'Also, there was a certain doctor on the Tour de France who everyone had concluded was a pervert! He thought it was great fun to see naked bike riders. Oh yes, he'd be kneeling right down in front of you holding the bottle when you gave the urine sample...'

Merckx never complained about this particular 'breach', but he did propose several others to justify his positive test in Savona in 1969. After the uncertified mobile laboratory, the unauthorised B-test, then the possibility of swapped samples, with time Merckx appeared to settle on sabotage as the explanation for what remains the murkiest of his three transgressions. In more than one interview since his retirement, he has blamed but refused to name a particular individual who, Merckx has said, 'bows his head when I see him'. 'I know what happened. I know who spiked my water bottle,' he told the journalist Gianpaolo Ormezzano in 1982. 'There is someone who, when they see me, has to hide in the next doorway or behind the next corner.'

At the time, Janssen and a few others other apart, most of his peers sympathised, just as they do now. Rumours still flourish about former teammates knowing 'the real truth of what occurred in Savona', but those individuals, like his roommate in Italy Martin Van Den Bossche, feign ignorance or refuse to answer when pressed. The same warped solidarity, the *omertà* or law of silence which only now is fracturing in the modern peloton, still reigns among riders whose last race was in the 1970s or even '60s. 'A couple of years ago, I did a fantastic four-way interview with Godefroot, Herman Van Springel, Merckx and Sercu, the generation of 1965, but as soon as I broached the subject of doping, they started coughing and looking at the floor,' says Walter Pauli, the former *De Morgen* cycling writer.

Pauli says that his predecessors in the Belgian media had a similar attitude to doping as Merckx and the riders with whom they shared hotels, dinners and often friendships. Their feelings were encapsulated in a euphemism which became de rigueur in the reporting of positive tests in the Flemish press: the rider had taken some 'forbidden candy'. In fairness, it was hard to take doping seriously when the authorities clearly did not, at least if the sanctions were any gauge. A meagre time penalty of 10 or 15 minutes, a one-month ban or sometimes just disqualification were the judicial equivalent of a slap on the wrist. Whether the sentence was intended to fit the perceived crime or unfair advantages, including financial, that substances like stimulants were supposed to bring – or whether the authorities just felt that they had to do *something*, implement even meagre deterrents, with substance abuse becoming ever more rampant and dangerous – only the men in power could really know. Either way, the tests were too little, too late to uproot a culture of indifference and complicity which far pre-dated Merckx and would persist when his career ended.

It bears repeating: it was hard for riders in Merckx's era to take doping seriously, or even get upset about one rider being more medically 'enhanced' than another, when officialdom did not. It is often erroneously stated that attitudes to doping changed only after Merckx's heyday, when syringes, so-called 'heavy doping', took the place of tablets similar in appearance if not composition to what professional riders had been ingesting since the first Tours de France. Thus, 'forbidden candy' and its purveyors were overtaken by evil needles and shady Svengalis who could alter not only the outcome of races but also upend the hierarchy of the sport. Only then did drugs in cycling become such a moral hot potato, and with good reason. This interpretation, though, is flawed: as discussed in an earlier chapter, Gastone Nencini was injecting hormones and morphine even before Merckx turned professional. It would also be disingenuous to suggest that stimulants 'wouldn't have permitted you to win Paris–Roubaix', as Merckx has said about Stimul. If there was no benefit, who would have subjected himself to the sleepless nights that Merckx claimed were the drug's most potent effect? Merckx took many of his 525 wins by kilometres rather than centimetres, but he of all people knew that the most meagre advantage could be the difference between victory and second place. Even Jacques Anquetil, who never concealed his opposition to dope tests, admitted that 'doping can turn a mule into a thoroughbred race horse'. No, both then and now, the Merckx generation's ambivalence about doping is mainly a result of the fact that they were never truly held to account, never received punishments proportionate to sometimes game-changing misdeeds, and had been steeped in a culture too old and established to revolutionise its view of doping just because it had become actionable.

Where Merckx would be correct is in thinking that almost no one, either then or now, would argue that his superiority was the product of the laboratory. By 1973, he had been subjected to over 500 dope tests and by 1977 had lived and won consistently through 12 seasons and two big breakthroughs in testing technology – Debackere's development of a test for pipedrines in 1974 and pemoline in 1977. In theory, Merckx could have been taking pemoline with impunity for years, but if that was the case, no, it wasn't unreasonable to assume that 90 per cent had been doing the same, at least since pipedrines became detectable in 1974. Over half of the riders (52 per cent) who started the 1977 Tour de France had, after all, tested positive or would at some point in their career, despite the fact that only frequent winners were regularly summoned to give samples. By doing so they had proved that most would take any advantage that they could get – and certainly that using banned substances posed them no great moral dilemma.

The same riders would surely have no qualms whatsoever about products and methods that weren't yet forbidden – unless that is they posed dangers to their health. Merckx told Rik Vanwalleghem in 1993 'the conventional medical supervision you received in cycling scared me off a little' and Ormezzano in 1982 that he 'always had a terrible fear of certain products, a fear greater than the temptation to try them'. Presumably this applied to cortisone. That is, if Merckx was aware, on starting his career, of the ruinous long-term effects that surely outweighed the hormone's pain-numbing advantages. Evidence of cortisone use on the Tour de France was first uncovered in 1960 by the assistant race doctor Robert Boncour, but it wasn't until 1978 that the International Cycling Union added it to their banned list, and not until 1999 that a detection method was finally ratified. Perhaps the real landmark moment, though, also came in 1978 when Bernard Thévenet, none other than the '*tombeur de Merckx*', admitted in *France Vélo* that three years of cortisone abuse had wrecked his health to the point where he was 'no longer capable of getting on a bicycle'. The treatments dispensed by Peugeot doctor François Bellocq had helped Thévenet to win two Tours de France, but also ravaged his adrenal glands. Of course there was no question of Thévenet losing his Tour titles because at the time cortisone use was legal.

Speculation about Merckx and the same substance had appeared years before Thévenet's mea culpa, but was seemingly based on flimsy evidence. One of the known side-effects of prolonged cortisone use is severe bloating and weight gain, and Merckx's expanding waistline (Ormezzano in 1982: 'Eddy Merckx has put on weight. He's in danger of ending up like a football') in his post-retirement years led some to conclude that he had used the drug, despite all Merckx's claims to the contrary. This is precisely what former director Jacques Goddet was getting at in an interview with the *Sport '90* magazine in 1992. 'I remember that Merckx put on a couple of kilos in weight when he retired,' Goddet said. 'Not that cortisone was a banned substance in those days, it's just that the famous always have trouble coping with the first signs of decline. It is a very difficult time for many athletes, and it explains why so many of them look for artificial ways of seeing them through their problems.'

Merckx told Rik Vanwalleghem that the comments betrayed Goddet's long-standing prejudice against him. 'When I won the Tour for the fourth time in a row I can remember the way the Tour organisers celebrated it with a forced sense of merriment. They had had enough of me, they were afraid that I might ruin everything for them. I think it is very small-minded of Goddet to attack me in such a way so many years later.'

If Merckx could claim that personal animosity was driving Goddet, he would certainly say the same about Freddy Maertens. Maertens admitted in an interview with Eric De Falleur of *Vélomédia* in 1987 that he had used cortisone during his career 'but only on medical advice'. He then added, 'From time to time you need that kind of thing, otherwise why would it exist?' This was all a prelude to Maertens claiming that he was 'far from the only one'.

In the past Maertens has also, incidentally, made accusations against two prominent members of Merckx's entourage, Guillaume Michiels and Gust Naessens. Maertens alleges in his autobiography that Belgian drugs police searched Michiels's home in 1984 and found amphetamines. In the same book, he writes that at the World Championships in Montreal in 1974, Merckx's masseur Naessens spiked his water bottle with a substance that brought Maertens's challenge to an abrupt and painful end. 'The culprit admitted it... His name was Gust Naessens; he was the physio for Eddy Merckx at the time and later became my personal soigneur. He can't confirm the story himself any more as he died a couple of years ago, but he did admit to me that he had put something into my bottle that day to enable Merckx to win the rainbow jersey for a third time without any problems.'

When talking about himself, if the robustness of the *omertà* was in any doubt, Maertens is capable of rebuffing even claims of doping that have come from his own mouth. Asked now to confirm what he said in an interview with *La Dernière Heure* a few years ago about having taken amphetamines in 'small races' throughout his career, Maertens purses his ample lips and asserts, 'The press made that up. I never said that. I never took amphetamines.'

There is, it's true, one prominent contemporary of Eddy Merckx who seems delighted when anyone mentions dope tests. In his kitchen in Kaprijke, Roger De Vlaeminck grins as proudly when you remark that he was one of the few active riders in the '60s, '70s and '80s never to have failed a drug test as if you had just told him that a democratic vote of everyone who ever saw The Gypsy and Eddy Merckx on a football field had unanimously confirmed that, yes, he was by far the better player.

'At the Tour of Flanders that I won in 1977, the second and third riders were both positive. But if you don't take anything you can't be caught!' De Vlaeminck says triumphantly.

In his first season as a professional, with the Flandria team, De Vlaeminck claims that he rode the Tour de France 'without even a vitamin'. In that 1969 Tour De Vlaeminck says that he went 'three days without even a bottle' and 'certainly had no team doctor', unlike Merckx who was already under the care of Enrico Peracino with the rest of the Faema team. Things only seriously changed for De Vlaeminck, he says, when he also moved to an Italian team, Dreher, in 1972.

'There we had Doctor [Piero] Modesti, and I used to take the vitamins that he used to give me,' De Vlaeminck says. 'There was also a masseur who said, "You have to take all this." I looked and his hand was full of tablets. "This is for the heart, this is for the lungs…" but I said, "No, keep it all." There was a lot of cortisone at the time, and amphetamines…but not in Italy. In Italy you were always tested. In Belgium there were a lot of amphetamines. At my time, in Italy, no one took anything. They spoke to me about blood transfusions. When I was riding for Francesco Moser [in 1984], they asked whether I wanted to give half a litre of blood to put in the fridge. I said no…'

De Vlaeminck has just dropped a small bombshell. Unfortunately he realises, and realises that we have realised. 'Who asked you about blood transfusions? Moser?'

'I can't say. I didn't see anything.'

'Was it Moser who asked you?'

'I didn't see anything…'

The association of Moser with blood transfusions is actually not news. It is a well-known fact, admitted by Moser, that he used this then legal if highly dangerous and effective method of performance enhancement to break Merckx's Hour record in 1984. The revelation here would be the Italian proposing the same 'treatments' to teammates like De Vlaeminck, at a time when few would have imagined that so-called 'blood-doping' could be any more than a few mavericks' crazy experiment.

The truth of course is that blood transfusions were already being used to devastating effect in endurance sports in the early and mid-1970s, when Merckx was in his pomp. In the late '60s, one of cycling's great pharmaceutical pioneers, Jacques Anquetil, reportedly took to visiting what the journalist Roger Bastide said was a 'luxury clinic' every winter for an 'exchange transfusion'. This consisted of replacing a large quantity of blood with an equal amount of compatible donor blood, supposedly to remove accumulated toxins. If in theory this technique had no significant effect on performance, the same could not be said of the transfusions used by Finnish distance runners in major athletics championships from the beginning of the 1970s, which *increased* the volume of red blood cells in the body and hence its ability to pump oxygen to the muscles.

The most famous exponent was the 1972 5,000- and 10,000-metre Olympic champion Lasse Viren, who admitted in a press conference in Münich that he had used transfusions. Seven weeks later, Merckx broke the Hour record having 'categorically refused' a blood transfusion according to the journalist Joël Godaert. Godaert did not specify the source of his information or whose offer Merckx had refused.

That blood transfusions were already part of the doping panoply was confirmed again in 1976, when Joop Zoetemelk confessed that he had benefited from the technique the previous year, presumably while leaching Merckx and Thévenet's wheels en route to fourth place in Paris. Zoetemelk's treatment had been advised and overseen by the French doctor, Henri Fucs. Since a bad crash in 1974, Zoetemelk had purportedly suffered from anaemia, and Fucs believed that multiple transfusions during the 1975 Tour would be the perfect remedy. Zoetemelk was satisfied with the results but still seemed uneasy about the public's reaction, so much so that he declared on arrival at the 1976 Tour that he would not be repeating the experiment.

While the French Cycling Federation, with the blessing of the French Sports Ministry, was including a public warning against the dangers of transfusions in its official magazine in 1977, endorsements of the procedure in other sporting disciplines continued to multiply; hence, in the spring of 1977, at around the time when Merckx was taking the fateful dose of Stimul, the German World Cup-winning footballer Franz Beckenbauer told *Stern* magazine that he underwent exchange transfusions several times a month.

This is all to show that, contrary to what some would have us believe, Merckx was not dominating at a time when the only doping methods on offer were either unsophisticated or ineffective. After the blood, Fucs would soon be giving Zoetemelk nandrolone, which like all other anabolic steroids was only outlawed in 1978 and first tested for the following year...when Zoetemelk was caught at the Tour de France. There is documentary evidence that at least some members of Thévenet's Peugeot team were also being prescribed anabolic steroids, as well as cortisone, in 1976. Steroids, it was known, had been at least used since the Mexico Olympics in 1968. Altogether, these products and methods constitute a chemical arsenal almost identical to what Floyd Landis admitted using in the 2006 Tour de France, where he was disqualified and professional cycling perhaps sunk to its lowest, most sordid ebb.

In the absence of any conclusive proof either for or against Merckx, we therefore find ourselves clutching at straws, or at least relying on best estimates and common sense. The answer also depends on the question: if we want to know whether he ever consumed banned substances, we have three ready-made answers in his three positive tests. If, however, the issue at hand is to decide whether his drug-use was systematic and a serious threat to our view of Merckx as the finest rider of his generation, one question leads to another. Were there any huge spikes in his performances that coincided with the advent of new products or methods? No. Could he have lasted as long at the top if he had continuously plied himself with cortisone? If three years were enough to destroy Thévenet, then probably not. Could he conceivably have fudged some tests like other riders from his era have admitted doing? Conceivably, yes. But around

700 of them? Of course he couldn't. Did he ever say anything to indicate that he was in the medical vanguard like Anquetil? Depends if you count the acupuncture he tried for his sciatica in 1974, or purportedly giving up all conventional medicine to 'go homoeopathic' in the summer of 1977, with 'staggering results' (not that we saw them). Was Merckx so loved, so fawned over by the fans, the authorities and the media that nothing would have come to light, even if he was doping more often and with more potent substances than anyone else? Well, that's just it – not everyone did fawn over him, and among the opponents there were people with enough nous, influence and motivation to expose a flagrant cheat if they knew one.

If it comes as any reassurance, some of the men who rode with and against Merckx share our uncertainties. 'He was way better than anyone else, but we mustn't shut our eyes either: there was doping in the peloton,' says Christian Raymond, Merckx's teammate in 1966 and '67. 'Did he have some product that others didn't have access to? That's the eternal question. You'd have to ask his masseur, Gust Naessens...'

Little chance of that, because as Freddy Maertens has told us, Naessens is dead.

'Now, of course, everyone would look at some of his performances and immediately ask questions, because of all the scandals in cycling over the past few years, but then it didn't even enter our minds,' says Bernard Thévenet. 'You look at what Ocaña did at Orcières-Merlette, out-riding a whole peloton on a mountain stage by nine minutes, and you say to yourself "Wow!" But at the time, neither the press nor the other riders said, "Blimey, what's Ocaña been taking?" It didn't even cross anyone's mind. Everyone said, "Oohlalala, he's strong, that was an amazing ride" but we weren't suspicious like people are now. We asked fewer questions back then. Plus, the products also weren't as effective.'

That, we have established, may be a misconception, but it is certainly true to say that both riders and their doctors had less expertise and experience of using and correctly dosing performance-enhancing drugs than they do today. An investigation authored by the cycling journalist Pierre Chany and published in *Paris Match* in 1978 listed 17 active or recently retired riders who had died of heart attacks between 1974 and 1977. 'They are the victims of amphetamines and cortisone,' said Jean-Pierre de Mondenard, who worked as a doctor on the Tour de France between 1973 and 1975.

If the deaths thankfully slowed in the early 1980s, only to resume under the impulse of the new poison EPO in the late 1980s and early '90s, Merckx's stance continued to perplex and sometimes disappoint. His son Axel became a professional cyclist in 1993 and in 1994 was offered advice by the Italian sports doctor Michele Ferrari. A year later, Ferrari said in an interview with the website Cyclingnews.com in 2004, Eddy Merckx introduced the doctor to Axel's then Motorola teammate Lance Armstrong. Armstrong said under oath in 2005 that he couldn't remember whether it was Merckx who had connected him and Ferrari, but confirmed both that Merckx was his 'close friend' and that Ferrari had become his training adviser. Armstrong had been called to testify before an arbitration panel when the 'prize insurance' company SCA Promotions became concerned, on learning of Armstrong's relationship with Ferrari, that he had used banned drugs to win the Tour de France and trigger resulting bonus payouts from SCA. Ferrari is now banned from working with cyclists in Italy. An appeal judge ruled in 2006 that the statute of limitations on a doping-related sentence against him in 2004 had run out, but also said in his summing up that there was a 'persuasive set of clues' to indicate that Ferrari couldn't be considered 'clearly innocent'.

Merckx's support of Armstrong has remained steadfast in the face of mushrooming allegations against him, most recently from his old US Postal Service teammates. 'If the reality was what they say it was, they should have spoken before, not after,' Merckx said in an interview with his old friend Philippe Brunel in 2011. 'That's called spitting in the soup,' he added.

This final remark reveals both Merckx's unwavering love of his sport as he knew it and the belief that public airings of cycling's dirty laundry equate to nothing but self-harm. It is a familiar and self-serving point of view from a former cyclist. It is also a questionable – or negligible – contribution to a clean-up operation which has accelerated since 2000 partly because more riders are opening up about their former misdeeds, Armstrong's old teammates included. With not only his own reputation but that of cycling down the ages at stake, no one should be surprised now if Merckx neither endorses nor participates in the soul-cleansing.

19
reinvention
and reappraisal

'He's not only the greatest rider of all time but the most
important sportsman of all time, in any discipline.'

<small>Giancarlo Ferretti</small>

Joseph Bruyère thinks that it may have been the first day of March
1978. He remembers because his son had been born on 27 February,
two days earlier. After a winter which Bruyère says now had been
'*fracassant*', shattering, for his team-leader Eddy Merckx, Bruyère
exited the highway before Brussels and drove through Kraainem
thinking that, with Het Volk just three days away, it was time to look
forward. He took his usual route on to the Snippenlaan, past immac-
ulately tended hedges and wrought-iron gates, and turned into the
driveway of the least ostentatious of the dozen properties on the
street – the modern, low-slung, thatched-roofed villa belonging to
the Merckxes. Within a few minutes, Bruyère had unpacked his bike
and he and Merckx were out on the open road, heading east towards
the cobbled *bergs* which at the weekend would determine whether
Merckx could repeat his 1971 and 1973 victories in 'Volk' – or
whether Bruyère could win again like he had in '74 and '75.

They had been riding for around two hours when, at the top of a small hill, Bruyère heard a familiar grunt.

'Joseph!'

Bruyère turned around to see Merckx's head sagging over the multicoloured bands of his C&A jersey's collar.

'Joseph, I've had enough. I feel terrible,' Merckx said.

It is typical of Bruyère to insist now that Merckx hadn't been dropped, and was just acting on a '*coup de tête*'. His head had gone, more than his legs. 'Never for a second did it cross my mind that it was over,' Bruyère stresses. 'It could just have been one of those days. We all have them.'

Nevertheless, Bruyère was soon turning around and riding back to Kraainem with his disconsolate friend. In a way it was a lot like any other day, with Bruyère's legs turning like the giant oars of a Viking longboat, and Merckx's thudding beside him – only the speed was 10 or 15 kilometres an hour slower than usual. 'We didn't talk much,' Bruyère says. 'It was just a case of keeping him company, plus I was anxious to get back and see my son.'

For that reason, when they arrived at Kraainem, Bruyère was quickly back in his car and on his way towards Liège and home. Eddy's own son, five-year-old Axel, was recovering from whooping cough but had passed it on to his eight-year-old sister Sabrina. Eddy would have enough to distract him and enough on his mind.

That night, in fact, Claudine would be the only one in the Merckx family who wasn't ill. In the evening, Eddy had driven to a clinic in Brussels and would remain there for the next two nights. Tests revealed that had colitis, an inflammation of the colon. It had been aggravated if not caused by stress. Merckx may not have already been suffering from clinical depression, but he was heading in that direction.

Needless to say, he missed Het Volk and Milan–San Remo. If Roger De Vlaeminck's victory on the Via Roma wasn't a kick in the teeth, Freddy Maertens's comments before the race had been. 'Eddy's finished,' Maertens said, 'and the only person who doesn't realise it is him. He says that he wants revenge at the Tour de France, but if you ask me he's not even going to start.'

Contrary to what Maertens had said, Merckx was beginning to get the picture. The day after San Remo, before setting off for a race in Sint-Niklaas near Antwerp, he told his soigneur Pierrot De Wit, 'I've got a feeling this is going to be the very last time I race.' Later that afternoon De Wit was there waiting for him at the finish line, which Merckx had crossed in 12th place, 15 seconds behind the winner Frans Van Looy. 'You see, it wasn't bad at all!' De Wit cajoled.

'Believe me, it was the last one,' Merckx told him.

But his moods still fluctuated and in April there were rumours of him having identified the problem – a virus caught at the '77 Worlds in Venezuela – as well as talk of pathetic attempts to train. 'Pathetic' was also the word the Belgian national champion Michel Pollentier used to describe Merckx's present state. 'What does Eddy still want?' asked De Vlaeminck. 'Cycling has given him everything: money and glory. He has nothing to gain from getting back on his bike.'

For another few weeks Merckx would stand by what he said to De Wit one day, then persuade himself otherwise the next. Having pulled out of the Tour of Belgium at the last minute, he rounded up the family and headed to Crans-Montana in the Swiss Alps. The Merckxes were regulars there, and Eddy soon slotted into a routine of daily cross-country skiing *randonnées* with his old mate Alfred 'Bouby' Rombaldi, an ex-slalom racer. A few times, he spoke on the phone to Bruyère. In Merckx's absence, his faithful old footman won Liège–Bastogne–Liège, and Bruyère called Crans-Montana that night to tell Merckx 'that was for you'. 'But generally, you couldn't speak to him about cycling. You had to treat him like a normal man in the street, not the superhuman he had been before,' Bruyère says. 'Everyone on the team knew that he was suffering, and we felt that we had to give something back.'

Merckx was in Geneva at the time of the Tour of Romandy, but only to sign autographs in a C&A shop. The next day, 8 May, he went on his bike to the GP de Wallonie...but only as a spectator. Three days later, Jos Huysmans, who had already retired from riding and was now Merckx's directeur sportif, met Merckx while he was training near Charleroi. 'I still don't feel good,' Merckx told him. They said goodbye with Huysmans none the wiser about whether Merckx was still a racer or not. The same day, the organisers of the Tour of Switzerland announced that they could wait no longer to hear whether Merckx intended to enter their race. They had given C&A's place to another team.

At eight minutes past four on Monday 18 May, Eddy Merckx entered the conference room of a Brussels hotel. He was dressed in a jacket and tie. He took the microphone, faced the large gathering of assembled journalists who had guessed what was coming, and he spoke.

'I have taken the most painful decision of my career,' Merckx said. 'I have decided to stop competing. My doctors have said unequivocally that I can't ride for the moment. As a result, it would be impossible for me to get ready for the Tour de France, my number-one goal of the season. I've had to come back down to earth but the decision I've taken, as cruel as it is, is the only reasonable one that's available.'

It was reported in some places that Merckx cried, but he didn't. The only tears were coming from the audience.

Paul Van Himst knew exactly how his friend Eddy Merckx felt. A year earlier, Van Himst had stared into 'the black hole' of retirement, as he calls it today, having also known what it was like to become a Belgian national icon purely because you were good at a sport. Once dubbed the 'White Pélé' by *L'Equipe*, Van Himst was the greatest Belgian footballer who ever lived. Van Himst and Merckx went back years. To the time, precisely, says Van Himst, 'when I was already playing for Anderlecht but was also selling coffee part-time – one of the shops I sold to belonged to Eddy's parents in Woluwe-Saint-Pierre'.

Van Himst had not seen Merckx on a regular basis during their careers, but right from their chance meeting as teenagers he had only ever known Eddy as the kid racing and winning on his bike. Now though, Merckx had only been retired a matter of weeks, and he already looked to Van Himst like a different person. While their wives, Claudine and Arlette, swapped news of the children, Van Himst looked across the living room at Merckx and saw the struggling 33-year-old man described to him a few days earlier by Guillaume Michiels.

That, after all, was really why they were here: Van Himst had been driving through Auderghem, just up the road from Merckx's house, and seen Michiels washing his car. 'How's Eddy doing?' Van Himst shouted out of the window. Nicknamed 'The Grave' – either because of his stony disposition, or because that was where he was taking his secrets about Merckx – even Michiels couldn't hide his concern. 'He's away on holiday with the family, but he's not good, not good at all…' Michiels said. Van Himst replied that he would give Merckx a call a few days later when he was back.

Now Van Himst glanced across at his friend on the other side of the room and knew instinctively that it wasn't the time for rousing speeches. Like Van Himst had done, Merckx would figure it out himself. In a way it was easier for footballers – in Belgium in the 1960s and '70s many still had second, part-time jobs. But cycling was all Merckx had ever known. Consequently, at age 33, having spent his entire adult life as the best in his field, Merckx had emerged from the cocoon of a glorious past with little or no idea about the present or future.

'Eddy had nothing prepared, nothing to go straight into,' Van Himst confirms now. 'He could have become a representative for Adidas, or taken on some kind of public relations role, but that wasn't something that interested him. The only thing to do while he decided where he would go professionally was get him active and doing sport. We started doing a lot together. In the beginning, Eddy didn't want to cycle. He was done with that. So we played tennis and football, with the Anderlecht veterans' team. Only later did we start cycling again, first on a mountainbike, then on the road bike. I was OK because I'd done a lot of riding after my career, and Eddy took it slow, so we had the same pace more or less. Later on a few of his retired old teammates started joining us. And we kept playing football...'

So can the man voted the best ever to represent Belgium on a football field settle an argument? Was Eddy Merckx a good player?

'Eddy was a great footballer!' Van Himst says with no hesitation. 'He could strike a really good ball and he had great vision. Of course as you can imagine, his movement was a bit stiff, not like a normal football player. His muscles, after all those years of riding a bike, weren't adjusted to it. But he was good.'

Paul Van Himst, like Joseph Bruyère, is known to be a master of understatement, so it is no surprise that neither of them uses the word 'depression' when describing those first few weeks and months of Eddy Merckx's retirement. The diagnostic criteria of that illness are, in any case, as hotly debated as its causes. What most psychologists would agree is that rumination is a significant risk factor, and there wasn't a soul who knew Merckx who didn't also know that he was a worrier. Lack of purpose is also often cited as one germ from which depression can burst forth. 'Depression is the inability to construct a future,' said the influential existentialist psychologist Rollo May – and he could have been talking about Eddy Merckx in the second half of 1978.

Merckx's first Tour de France as a directeur sportif for C&A convinced him that this couldn't be his second career. The autumn was approaching, he still seemed lost, and Claudine was worried. 'His retirement was so different to how I imagined it would be,' she said in an interview in September. 'The climate at home has changed completely. We have stumbled into a vacuum, into a void, the tension and the hellish pace of life, unique to competition, has fallen away totally. I miss that, more than I could ever have feared. It's been hard for me to get used to.'

Merckx called the same period 'horrible'. The more he tried to embrace freedom – the parties and indulgences that a cyclist wasn't allowed – the worse it felt. He said later that he 'knew he was doing some stupid things' and that 'the danger comes when you're not self-aware and you think that's what life is'. What exactly he got up to, however, neither he nor anyone else ever revealed in public.

The limbo lasted months, until a conversation with one of his old mechanics and framebuilders, Ugo De Rosa, from Milan. It was March 1979. 'Why don't you get into this business? Start making bikes?' De Rosa suggested.

At first Merckx just smiled, but the seed had been planted. There was one thing that he loved nearly as much as cycling, and that was bikes. Once at the start of his career he had totally dismantled one just so that he could count the pieces, 'for fun' he said. Now he spent six months studying the art of the master framebuilder, often travelling to Milan to watch De Rosa at work. By the start of 1980, he had bought disused farm buildings formerly owned by his business adviser Freddy Liénard in Meise, just north of Brussels, and made plans to convert them into a factory and a new family home. With De Rosa's help, he then started buying up equipment. On 28 March the factory was officially opened. Among his first employees were former team-mates Jos Huysmans and Edouard Janssens and his old directeur sportif Bob Lelangue.

Thirty years later, the Eddy Merckx bike brand is firmly established among the most prestigious in the world, with an annual turnover of around six million euros. However, Merckx relinquished a majority stake in the company to the investment group Sobradis in 2008.

Money was certainly never his motivation, for all that he was believed to have passed the equivalent of one million euros in earnings around 1974. 'He wouldn't know or care how much money he has in his account,' says a friend, the journalist Hugo Coorevits, echoing something that Claudine has often said in interviews. She, incidentally, was 'fifty per cent of Eddy's career' by Coorevits's reckoning. 'Claudine was everything, the PR person, the manager, the accountant, the mother – she was everything. Now they have created ten positions to do what she did,' he says.

Sometimes, however, Merckx has had to rely on people other than his wife, and sometimes he has regretted it. Thus, the first major scandal of his retirement arose just nine months after his bike company opened for business, when he was charged with committing tax fraud. It had nothing to do with the factory, was apparently his adviser Liénard's fault, and the full details never emerged. The sum involved was too small to warrant an arrest but, in one way or another, with legal fees and so forth, Merckx said that it cost him 'earnings equivalent to several racing seasons'. That and considerable embarrassment;

at a bicycle trade fair where Merckx was exhibiting months later, the Belgian Prime Minister Wilfried Martens refused to shake his hand.

There would be other minor controversies, some relating to cycling, others not. In 1988, the Flemish television network BRT aired a documentary about the Second World War which connected Merckx's birthplace, Meensel-Kiezegem, the Merckx family name and the touchy issue of collaboration with the Nazis. Merckx was incensed, later protesting that the only collaborators in his family were cousins of his father, and pointing out that he had been given the middle name Louis in memory of a maternal uncle who had been captured by the Nazis and never returned. Memories of the war were so painful, he said, that it was a taboo subject in the Merckx household when he was growing up.

On the whole, though, there was little appetite for muck-raking. Criterium audiences had plummeted within a year or two of Merckx retiring, as the press and public slowly realised that there would be no Merckx redux or even pale equivalent any time soon. What popularity cycling had started to lose was gobbled up by football, with Belgian clubs Anderlecht and Club Brugge suddenly among the best in Europe and the national side reaching the final of the European Championships in 1980. With a few years' hindsight, Merckx's era in Belgian cycling began to take on the glow of exactly what it had been – an unrepeatable golden age. Instead of thriving, the men who for years had looked or made out as though only Merckx blocked their path to a cycling Eldorado also plateaued or floundered. De Vlaeminck carried on winning Classics – but only really for a couple more years. Freddy Maertens had all manner of problems, from financial to personal, and says today that 'only the best wife in the world saved me'. He won another World Championship in 1981 but not too much else. Johan De Muynck finished fourth in the 1980 Tour de France and got slaughtered for it. De Muynck, who of course Merckx had nearly salvaged when De Vlaeminck went AWOL in the 1976 Giro, had once looked at Merckx and seen a 'recluse' trapped by his own popularity and lust for success, and his teammates held captive with him. De Muynck was not envious. Now, though, with Merckx gone, he and others found themselves in their own form of confinement, with Merckx's ghost their cruel jailor.

So, no, against this backdrop, it came more naturally to celebrate Merckx than to scrutinise or forget him, with the odd exception. In 2004, the extra kilograms that he had gained since the end of his career seemed to disappear overnight, and Merckx had to deny claims that the reason was a form of cancer or cosmetic surgery. The real explanation, he said, was an operation on a long-standing and hereditary stomach problem that had caused a hernia.

'The Belgian press wasn't interested in his private life, and even if they knew they wouldn't write anything negative,' says Walter Pauli, once of *De Morgen*, now with the Belgian news magazine *Knack*. 'We have so-called tabloid press but by British standards it's very mainstream. *Het Laaste Nieuws* is a "tabloid", but when Merckx was a rider the journalists from that paper would eat out of his hand and lick his shoes clean.

'As a human being...Merckx is a human being. He is not a saint,' Pauli goes on. 'He was treated like one from the age of 21 – and after that you almost have to be superhuman to be human, extraordinary to be ordinary. You have to be bigger than bigger than big to be beyond that kind of adulation. Other guys from his generation, like Patrick Sercu and Walter Godefroot, are smarter, have more experience in life. If you lose, you have an experience. Merckx also has the experience of losses, but for the others it was also a kind of reality. For Merckx, it wasn't reality – it meant that something was wrong if he lost a race. It wasn't normal. The rest of us win some, we lose some. But with Merckx there was always an excuse, always a reason. It never just was. In 1968, Herman Van Springel beat him in the Tour of Lombardy, and Merckx said to him, "Herman, today you were the best." Van Springel started remonstrating with him, "No, no, it's impossible. You were the best, Eddy." You see even when Merckx has these moments of clarity, there's always someone to reassure him that he's the greatest.'

If the trend has continued since his retirement it is also, undeniably, because some of Merckx's most attractive and long-hidden qualities, particularly his warmth and humour, have risen slowly to the surface, above his natural shyness and suspicion. Gianpaolo Ormezzano, who has covered more Olympic Games as a journalist than anyone on the planet, and met more sportsmen than most, says that his enduring image of Merckx is of a laughing fit on the podium of Paris–Roubaix, and not his victory that day or any other.

'He saw me running and said, "Hey, *Senatore,* you're running well. You've lost weight!" I told him that it was because of these herbal diet pills I'd been taking, but that unfortunately they were also giving me diarrhoea. "Well, they're working. You've lost weight," he said. I said, yeah, I had shifted a few kilos – but only because of all the running I was doing to and from the toilet. He couldn't stop giggling. He almost toppled off the podium.'

Attributes that once Merckx manifested only in flashes now shine more brightly, so much so that Godefroot says, 'he can seem like a different person'. That was no doubt how he appeared to Luis Ocaña, once his bitterest enemy, when before Ocaña's death Merckx helped him find Belgian distributors for his Armagnac. The former French rider Raymond Riotte says that he had relatively little contact with Merckx during his career, but that Merckx still helped out Riotte's friend with bikes for his amateur team a few years ago. When the friend didn't settle his debt, Riotte was mortified, but Merckx told him it was no big deal. 'He was always a gentleman, even as a rider. He would always return any favours,' Riotte says.

Mainly now, the riders he once infuriated rhapsodise about what they gained, not what they lost, from having him as an opponent. The cycling press at the time often made unfavourable comparisons with his predecessors, but no pundit worth his salt could today argue that Merckx's palmarès doesn't dwarf that of any other rider. Lance Armstrong won seven Tours de France, two more than Merckx, but these were his only major tours. The score in one-day Classics (including Gent–Wevelgem and Flèche Wallonne) and world championship road races is Armstrong three, Merckx 30. Merckx indeed won twice as many Classics and road race world championships as Armstrong and the five-time Tour winners Jacques Anquetil, Bernard Hinault and Miguel Indurain combined. Purely in terms of panache, bravery and tactical inventiveness, Merckx also far outshone any of his fellow nonpareils apart, perhaps, from Fausto Coppi. 'Cycling in Merckx's era had a touch of the old and a touch of the modern about it, but what he was doing seemed to belong outside any time frame,' says the former Italian national coach Alfredo Martini. For Barry Hoban, quite simply, 'Merckx reinvented cycling.'

Presumably for these reasons, Merckx was voted the best sportsman in the world three times in the early 1970s, and finished second only to Michael Jordan in one poll to elect the greatest athlete of the millennium.

'He's not only the greatest rider of all time but the most important sportsman of all time, in any discipline,' argues Giancarlo Ferretti. 'In football there was Pelé but there was also Maradona. In tennis there was Borg but there was also McEnroe. There hasn't been anything remotely like Merckx in cycling.'

This is also, Ferretti's former teammate Gimondi says, why headlines like the *Corriere della Sera*'s 'Merckx first, Gimondi beats the rest of the world' after the 1971 World Championships in Mendrisio were the source of pride, not indignation.

'Today, I look back and I'm glad that my generation and I had Merckx,' Gimondi says. 'I'd have won more without him there, earned more, but life isn't just about money. The respect, the rivalry, the memories…they're all more valuable. Even three million euros more doesn't have the same impact on your life as that stuff, some of the battles I had with Eddy.

'We were friends, but it was a beastly rivalry,' he goes on. 'I never actually got depressed but it was like being beaten with a stick, time after time. He could be cruel, Eddy. People in my family would tell you – he never let me win a race. Never. His engine capacity was superior to ours, he could change pace a lot more easily than I could – he could go from a hundred and twenty heartbeats per minute to two hundred in the blink of an eye. He was faster. There was nothing you could do. And on top of it all, there was this great determination, this application, this rigour. He didn't just have God-given talent. It was that plus his temperament, his character, his determination. Everything he did, he did with amazing rigour. Where did the hunger come from? Some people have cycling in their heart. It's in your DNA. You can be born here or there, in this family or that family, but that's the bottom line. The passion burns inside.'

Gimondi's bitter rival, Gianni Motta, regrets only that, 'When Merckx was reaching his peak, I was on the way down because of my blasted left leg. I would love to have fought against Eddy at my best.

He was determined, nasty on the bike, clever and strong. He'd been built to ride a bike.'

Even the one surviving rider who according to the Belgian journalist and broadcaster Mark Uytterhoeven 'never accepted Merckx's superiority', Roger De Vlaeminck, today acknowledges that his was an unwinnable crusade. In 1986, Merckx began a ten-year stint as the coach of the Belgian national team at the World Championships in Colorado Springs, and De Vlaeminck and Merckx found themselves renewing hostilities on what was supposed to be a friendly pre-Worlds trundle with VIPs. At one point, Uytterhoeven found himself riding next to and chatting with De Vlaeminck when all of a sudden The Gypsy broke off mid-sentence to ask whether they couldn't carry on the conversation a bit later. 'Look, there's Merckx, five positions ahead of me. I can't have that,' he called over his shoulder to Uytterhoeven as he sped off up the road.

Today, though, De Vlaeminck admits that Merckx was 'just more talented than me' and a 'fabulous athlete'. So fabulous, in fact, that De Vlaeminck chose 'Eddy' as the name of his son born in 2000.

Such is De Vlaeminck's esteem for Merckx, you will no longer even hear him bragging on behalf of his hero Rik Van Looy that Van Looy won every Classic, including Paris–Tours, which eluded Merckx. Merckx and Van Looy themselves still have a complicated relationship, alternating periods of rapprochement with murmurs of the old rancour. Merckx was touched when Van Looy attended his mother's funeral in 2009 (Merckx's father, Jules, had died in 1983), and they occasionally bump into and eat together at official functions. Merckx, though, seems the one more inclined to forgive and forget.

Merckx's son, of course, ended up becoming a successful professional cyclist in his own right. In his teens, Axel had seemed destined for the football career that his father would have pursued, he said, if he hadn't been a cyclist. One day, though, when he was injured, Axel decided that he would rather try cycling. The legend goes that he scrawled, 'I want to give up football' in lipstick on a mirror in his parents' bedroom. The reality was slightly different – he left a letter in the bathroom – but it amounted to the same thing. In a decade-and-a-half spent riding for some of the world's leading teams, and unfortunately coinciding with the most scandal-laden chapter in cycling history, he won 15 races and an Olympic bronze medal in 2004 in Athens. His best result in the Tour de France was a 10th place finish overall in 1998. Théo Mathy, the old TV journalist and family friend, put these achievements nicely in perspective: 'When he started racing, kids would fight tooth and nail to beat him in a sprint for eighth place. Frankly, I never thought he'd become a professional. To make it, he must have had an amazing head on his shoulders. What's amazing is that he accepted the situation. He never knew whether he was getting offers because of who he was or who his father was.'

As of 1996, when King Albert II made his father one of around 300 titled barons in Belgium, Axel, his mother and sister also became part of a noble lineage. Already a 'Cavaliere' of the Italian Republic, in December 2011 Eddy Merckx received the even higher honour of '*Commandeur de la Légion d'honneur*' from French president Nicolas Sarkozy at the Palais de l'Élysée in Paris. On receiving his medal, the man who once detested lounges and awards ceremonies smiled boyishly, his mother might have said even 'commercially'. Who knows, perhaps Eddy Merckx would have made a decent green grocer after all.

epilogue

'Come on, can we go? Let's go. Can we?'

Eddy Merckx looks and sounds restless. His fingers are wrapped tightly around his handlebars and carbon dioxide is spewing from his nostrils into the chilly November air. Either side of him, Jos Huysmans, Jos De Schoenmaecker, Roger Rosiers, Herman Van Springel and their bikes stand in perfect alignment, blocking the right-hand lane of the road, but their heads are turned to face each other and their gloved hands act mainly as props to add humour or emphasis to noisy banter. Two or three minutes ago, Merckx was in the line and in the thick of the jokes, but now he positions himself a few paces ahead of them on his own – Roger De Vlaeminck would probably say like the lone striker ahead of a four-man midfield.

'Can we go yet? Let's go…'

De Vlaeminck, by the way, is also here, instantly recognisable in a different, dark-blue jersey from the rest. Like a *libero* he lurks slightly behind and apart, and he also looks noticeably younger and leaner than the others, even if it's them who were up at dawn to ride 40 kilometres, and De Vlaeminck who has just unpacked his bike from his car. A few minutes ago, another big, silver saloon like his pulled into the town square in Erps Kwerps, where 1960s and '70s

Belgian cycling royalty is assembled. Walter Godefroot got out, and now moves up the line shaking hands. In September, at his house in Nazareth near Gent, Godefroot explained that he was recovering from a heart operation. When his friends ask now why he's dressed in a suit, and not lycra, Godefroot points to his throat. 'I've got a bit of a cold. The doctor says best not, after the operation...'

Merckx listens as patiently as he can then turns. 'OK, come on, we go...'

As he leads one gathering on the road, another small one of Godefroot, a couple of photographers and journalists step out of the cold and into a brasserie overlooking the square. Godefroot takes the seat next to the fireplace, while everyone else huddles their hands around cups of coffee. Fifteen minutes later, a voice announces that 'they' – as in the riders – are back and the group again decants outside just in time to see Merckx and Van Springel swinging into the square. The rolling reunion is expected to stop but instead only slows to take instructions from the camera crew filming out of the back of an estate car. No, apparently, they have ridden the lap too fast again, for the second time, and will have to repeat the circuit again for a third.

Today is all about Herman Van Springel and the book documenting his career by the television presenter and journalist Mark Uytterhoeven. In many ways, Van Springel's memoirs are interchangeable with those of all of the former riders here today – except of course Merckx's. He would figure in each of them as he has here, a hopeful face and an unwritten script like all the others in a class photograph which years later would be rescued from attics and pinned on walls, but then only because of *him*. The title of Van Springel's biography, *Herman Van Springel 68*, dates not only his best season but also the moment when life and Merckx began their cruel discrimination.

A man so mild of manner that his every word and action seems like an apology, Van Springel wouldn't dream of bearing a grudge. Merckx signed him for Molteni in 1971, partly because it was better to have a rider as talented as Van Springel riding with rather than against you, only to then leave him out of the 1972 Tour de France team. That, at least, is assuming Merckx was in charge of or at least had significant influence over selection, which Van Springel did assume, and Merckx denied. The mystery of why Merckx often seemed so loath to take responsibility for fractious decisions was solved when they grew close again in retirement, and a convivial *bonhomme* emerged from the rigid shell of the former cyclist. It turned out that Merckx was and always had been a people pleaser. You try that, though, when you're also busy being a cannibal.

Having finished their ride, while Merckx, De Vlaeminck and the others convene and reminisce in the other room, Van Springel tries not to dwell on what might have been. This can't be easy for a man who lost the 1968 Tour de France in a time trial on the final day – 'my last chance. I knew Merckx was coming' – but Van Springel has at least had forty years' practice. 'It was an amazing generation in Belgium, and we should be happy that we could at least put up some resistance and win a few incredible races ourselves...' he says.

Still, Van Spingel will admit under duress, it wasn't easy to live with a man so fixated on constantly feeding his winning addiction, yet seemingly so insensitive to the fact that others, just on the odd occasion, might need the same sort of affirmation. Van Springel now laughs when you ask him about the 1972 GP Mendrisio, but only with time has the memory lost its bitter edge.

'We were riding off the front in a group of eight, with all the best Italians and Eddy, who of course was my teammate,' he remembers. 'I attacked, got away and with two kilometres left was sure I was going to win. That was until I looked back and saw Eddy coming on his own. Before I knew it, he was past me and had won the race – yet *another* race. I can remember us getting into the elevator together back at the hotel, just me and him, and me just turning to him and saying, "Eddy, could you not have given me just this one?" He said, "But, Herman, the fans, the organisers…everyone wants me to win". When I heard that I let out a big sigh. "Yeah, but Eddy," I said, "everyone *always* wants *you* to win…"'

'*Avec plaisir.*'

The first words that Eddy Merckx has spoken to me, or at least in my vicinity, since our serendipitous meeting in May midway through an interview with Felice Gimondi, are these.

Merckx has of course declined to collaborate with my project. That is his right, just as it was his right to attempt to win every race that he entered. With time, I have also come to be grateful for his decision, not only because his input might compromise my objectivity, but more because there is an unknowable quality that is central to Merckx, more than to other, apparently less accessible stars. If a biographer who did get to know him, the Frenchman Philippe Brunel, tells me, 'When I see Merckx, I wish it could be just as another human being and not Eddy Merckx, because he's a wonderful person to spend time with,' I realise that even Merckx himself has become crushed, submerged beneath his aura. The flesh-and-blood Eddy Merckx may just have died, been eaten with all the other mortals, the moment that Merckx became Merckx. There came a day, different for everyone, when the palmarès was overtaken by a mystique, and from which there was and never will be any going back.

Nevertheless, this is the closest I will get, the last and only opportunity. Merckx doesn't know my face, won't remember my name and therefore won't suspect my motives. As we know, he also has trouble saying 'No'. As it turns out, after one interview with a TV crew, intercepted between a lounge in the front of the restaurant and the bar where his old colleagues are now drinking to Van Springel, he says, '*Avec plaisir*'.

So we turn back into the lounge, find a table, and sit down. Merckx wears a blue, open-neck shirt under a brown suede jacket and black trousers. His hands are folded in his lap and his expression is neutral. The first question is about him 'ruining' Van Springel's career, and is supposed to be light-hearted, but Merckx also light-heartedly interrupts it by protesting that 'ruin' is too strong a word. If anyone has reason to curse him and his domination, he'll say in a minute, it's Felice Gimondi, who had won the Tour de France, the Giro d'Italia, Paris–Roubaix and Paris–Bruxelles, all before Merckx became Merckx.

He speaks quickly, Eddy Merckx. His eyebrows are almost permanently raised, not in surprise but arched almost like brackets around everything he says, or around everything he is; almost as if to say, 'I'm telling you this, but you have to remember that I'm Eddy Merckx, and not even I know what that means...' That, at least, is my impression. It could be just a mannerism.

In 1970, the journalist Odélie Grand likened the experience of interviewing Eddy Merckx to a 'black-out'. She had the distinct feeling that Merckx's gaze '[erased] you from the picture'. From where I'm sitting now, it's himself that Merckx at least manages to hide if not efface. His replies are detailed but also instantaneous and shorn of any kind of emphasis, emotion or dramatic intonation. His eyes flit like a metronome back and forth between me and the same empty space on the tile floor.

We talk for ten minutes, all he has before the next journalist and the next round of questions he has heard endless times before. Why did you always want to win? 'It's not a question of wanting to win. The strongest wins. It's the law of sport'; Why were you the best? 'Talent and hard work'. When did you become Merckx? 'I think at the Giro '68 everyone realised that I would win the Tour de France the next year...' Why were you so ruthless? 'You give gifts at Christmas and birthdays, not at bike races...'

The answers will appear in print or on film but their essence, like Merckx's, will never be as vividly reflected as on the road where his legacy really resides, a road strewn with the shattered dreams of the men whom, after he's shaken my hand and said 'you're welcome', he'll rejoin in the bar for a glass of champagne. They say they don't mind, that the greatest cyclist ever added lustre to their careers, but who knows what they'll be thinking in a few minutes' time, when someone proposes a toast to Herman Van Springel and it's their turn to clink glasses, look into the eyes and consider the effect on their lives of Baron Edouard Louis Joseph Merckx.

Behind the smile, he, we know, will be thinking '*Avec plaisir.*'

acknowledgements

Much like many of Eddy Merckx's victories, this book has been a collaborative effort, facilitated and infinitely improved by a team, nay an entire peloton of loyal domestiques.

In the Lomme Driessens role, but definitely not his mould, Andrew Goodfellow and Liz Marvin at Ebury Press should receive my eternal thanks for their faith in the project and their patience, as should Justine Taylor for her editing. My literary agent, the inimitable David 'The Deal' Luxton, may be no Jean van Buggenhout, but is just as adept at dealing with a sometimes fragile and difficult client. I am also sincerely grateful to him.

Dozens of fellow journalists in the UK and abroad, the cherished colleagues of a decade covering cycle races, have contributed to this book, be it with help arranging interviews or simply advice. In Belgium, I would especially like to thank Jan Pieter de Vlieger and Bert Heyvaert, both mates and lieutenants de luxe, as well as Walter Pauli, Hugo Coorevits, Marc Ghyselinck, Joeri de Knop, Walter Pauli, Eric De Falleur, Philippe Van Holle and Sven Spoormakers. Charlotte Elton's humour and translations have also been hugely appreciated.

In Italy, Ciro Scognamiglio, Luigi Perna and Pier Augusto Stagi have proven to be formidable *gregari*, and Herbie Sykes a kind supplier of books and press cuttings. Pierre Carrey, in France, was extremely generous in providing research materials. Be it for help directly relating to this book, or over the last ten years culminating in this project, I would also like to say thank you to dear fellow hacks or photographers overseas Andy Hood, Leon De Kort, Gregor

Brown-Burgundy, Pier Maulini, Gary Boulanger and Bonnie Ford in particular – providers of quotes, beds for the odd night and emergency supplies of Haribo sweets.

If I am still writing about cycling, it is in large part thanks to (or the fault of) friends and former colleagues at *Procycling*, Pete Cossins, Ellis Bacon, Paul Godfrey, James Poole and especially Jeremy Whittle. Now instead of workmates I have…Richard Moore, a one-man reservoir of piss-taking, irritation and occasionally great friendship, ego-massaging and advice. Rich, seriously, thanks.

I would also like to thank my dear mum and dad, to whom this book is dedicated, and my sister and brother-in-law Maria and Rob Sellers for their unstinting support and generosity/hospitality. My darling girlfriend, Kate Clarence, has been a paragon of serenity, grace and love throughout the hectic months I have devoted to this book, as she always is. Kate, thank you.

My gratitude should go, finally, to the people who agreed to be interviewed. Take a bow, Vittorio Adorni, Felice Gimondi, Freddy Maertens, Claude Lair, Rini Wagtmans, Giancarlo Ferretti, Philippe Crépel, Barry Hoban, Raymond Poulidor, Shelley Verses, Bernard Thévenet, Johny Schleck, Dino Zandegù, Joseph Bruyère, Marino Vigna, Gianpaolo Ormezzano, Alfredo Martini, Raymond Riotte, Davide Boifava, Chris Boardman, Christian Raymond, Italo Zilioli, Roger De Vlaeminck, Walter Godefroot, Martin Van Den Bossche, Walter Pauli, Patrick Sercu, Jan Janssen, Franco Bitossi, Hugo Coorevits, Philippe Brunel, Gaston Plaud, Herman Van Springel, Gianni Motta, Mark Uytterhoeven, Paul Van Himst, Gianbattista Baronchelli, Hennie Kuiper, David Lloyd, Michel Audran, Helge Riepenhof, Giancarlo Lavezzaro, Rik Van Looy (for two minutes) and finally, Eddy Merckx.

index

EM indicates Eddy Merckx.